Public Employee Trade Unionism in the United Kingdom: The Legal Framework

COMPARATIVE STUDIES IN PUBLIC EMPLOYMENT LABOR RELATIONS

Public Employee Trade Unionism in the United Kingdom: The Legal Framework

B. A. HEPPLE
CLARE COLLEGE, CAMBRIDGE UNIVERSITY

PAUL O'HIGGINS
CHRIST'S COLLEGE, CAMBRIDGE UNIVERSITY

ANN ARBOR

INSTITUTE OF LABOR AND INDUSTRIAL RELATIONS

THE UNIVERSITY OF MICHIGAN—WAYNE STATE UNIVERSITY

1971

This monograph is one of a series prepared under the direction of Professors Russell A. Smith and Charles M. Rehmus of The University of Michigan, and is a part of their comparative international study of labor relations in public employment. Financial support of this research project has been derived from a number of sources. Basic grants came from the comparative law research funds of The University of Michigan Law School; the Institute of Labor and Industrial Relations, The University of Michigan—Wayne State University, the comparative economics research funds of The University of Michigan Economics Department; and the research programs of the New York State Public Employment Relations Board and the United States Department of Labor.

Public Employee Trade Unionism in the United Kingdom:
The Legal Framework

Library of Congress Catalog Card Number: 70-634397

International Standard Book Number:
0-87736-011-1 (cloth edition)
0-87736-012-X (paper edition)

Printed in the United States of America
Second printing, 1972

Preface

To describe the legal framework within which public employee trade unions function in Great Britain is a virtually impossible task, since the legal framework is rather like a spider's web in which great holes have been torn by insects successfully forcing their way through it. The analogy is misleading for of course the holes in the web of legal rules surrounding public employee trade unions are not the result of damage caused by bodies escaping from the web. They are the historical result of the way in which legal rules on the one hand, and practices, habits, customs, conventions, call them what you will, have fused together to provide a framework of "rules," some legal, some not, which go to make up the British "system" of industrial relations. We have sought to limit ourselves in a way which concentrates the main focus of the reader's attention on the legal rules and their operation, without straying so far afield that we are describing the whole system. On the other hand, to describe the legal rules alone would be to describe a flawed web, when in truth the web is not flawed, but merely not woven of whole thread. We have chosen, therefore, to describe the whole thread, that curious amalgam of law and practice which in truth provides the framework.

This book will, we hope, be read in conjunction with the parallel studies in this series by Professor Harold Levinson and Dr. Ray Loveridge. Ours is an anatomical study, theirs physiological.

B. A. HEPPLE
PAUL O'HIGGINS

Cambridge
September 1970

Contents

Public Employee Trade Unionism in the United Kingdom: The Legal Framework

ABBREVIATIONS

ASCL   H. W. R. Wade (ed.), *Annual Survey of Common-
              wealth Law for 1965, 1966, 1967, 1968,* and *1969*
              (Oxford, 1966–70). Contains chapters on Labour
              Law by B. A. Hepple and P. O'Higgins.

Citrine   *Citrine's Trade Union Law* (3rd ed., by M. A. Hick-
              ling, London, 1967).

Donovan   *Royal Commission on Trade Unions and Employers'*
Commission   *Associations, 1965–1968; Report (Chairman: The
              Rt. Hon. Lord Donovan)* (H.M. Stationery Office,
              1968. Cmnd. 3623).

Grunfeld   C. Grunfeld, *Modern Trade Union Law* (London,
              1966).

I.R. Bill   Industrial Relations Bill (Bill 164, 19th April 1970).

Public   Trades Union Congress, *Report of a Conference of
Sector   Affiliated Unions to discuss the conclusions and
              recommendations of the Donovan Commission on
              Trade Unions and Employers' Associations, Congress
              House, London, March 21st, 1969. Public Sector*
              (London, 1969).

RCME   Royal Commission on Trade Unions and Employers'
              Associations (1965–1968). Minutes of Evidence
              (H.M. Stationery Office).

RCWE   Royal Commission on Trade Unions and Employers'
              Associations (1965–1968). Written Memoranda of
              Evidence.

Wedderburn   K. W. Wedderburn and P. L. Davies, *Employment
and Davies   Grievances and Disputes Procedures in Britain*
              (Berkeley and Los Angeles, 1969).

Introduction

THE aim of this monograph is to describe the legal framework of relations between trade unions and the government as employer and to assess its impact upon that relationship. The term "legal" is used to describe those rules and norms which can, in the event of violation, be enforced by some compulsory mechanism provided by the state. But since, in Kahn-Freund's words, "there is no major country in the world in which the law has played a less significant role in the shaping of these relations than in Great Britain,"[1] we must, in order to explain the nature and significance of the legal rules, describe and explain other rules and practices which are fortified by purely social sanctions. These latter mechanisms will be described by the term "voluntary," and a major theme of the monograph will be the relationship between the "legal" and "voluntary" rules and practices.

The initial difficulty one meets with in discussing this subject is that there is no clear demarcation in British law between public and private employees, just as the sharp distinction which exists in some European continental systems of law between "public law" and "private law" has no counterpart in Britain. This does not mean that there are no special legal rules governing certain categories of public employees, but in practice the legal position of both may be remarkably similar.

The major focus will be on those groups of employees whose wages and salaries are mainly financed out of taxes, and in respect of whom the major locus of managerial decision-making rests in the hands of government.

For our purposes the term "public employee" covers something like four and a half million workers[2] belonging to the following categories:

(1) *Civil servants.* For these the working definition generally adopted is "those servants of the Crown, other than the holders

1. In A. Flanders and H. A. Clegg, *The System of Industrial Relations in Great Britain* (Oxford, 1954), p. 60.
2. If the nationalised industries were to be included the figure would be approximately six and three quarter million. In fact owing to the Government's influence over the pay of workers in the nationalised sector it is now usual to regard such workers as being within the public sector. See *Public Sector,* p. 13.

of political or judicial offices, who are employed in a civil capacity, and whose remuneration is paid wholly and directly out of monies voted by Parliament."[3] This therefore excludes from our consideration military servants of the Crown, the armed forces, the judiciary and holders of political posts in the government, i.e. those who are nominated by the Prime Minister and who lose their offices following the defeat of the government at an election. Civil servants are divided into two broad classes, the nonindustrial civil servants who carry out the executive functions of government, and the industrial civil service, industrial employees of the government (excluding nationalised industries), e.g. civilian defence employees, stationery office employees, government shipbuilding employees, and other employees in government industrial establishments.

(2) *Post Office employees.* Until the Post Office Act 1969 the Post Office was a Department of State and its staff were civil servants. Now the Post Office has become a public corporation.

(3) *National Health Service employees.* Their formal employer may be: (i) regional hospital boards in the case of hospital and specialist services (day to day instructions by local management committees and costs borne by Treasury); (ii) local executive councils (direct employers of small clerical and administrative staffs concerned with the general practitioner and other services); (iii) local authorities, who provide public health, domiciliary nursing, ambulance and other preventive services (but excluding general practitioners and other nonsalaried persons in the health services).

(4) *The police*: not "servants" but appointed by and subject to dismissal by local police authority (the Metropolitan Police Commissioner in case of London metropolitan police) and subject to the central administrative control of the Home Secretary.

(5) *Fire Service employees*: employed by local authorities (this was a National Service during war) but subject to administrative control of the Secretary of State.

(6) *Teachers*: local education authorities subject to administrative control of the Department of Education.

(7) *Other employees of local authorities*: note in particular those

3. G. A. Campbell, *The Civil Service in Britain* (2nd ed., London, 1955), p. 11.

cases where the local authority shares responsibility with other authorities (e.g. justices, clerks, waterworks, approved schools).

The position of the employees of the nationalised public corporations will be referred to from time to time for purposes of comparison. One should also note that the Government and Parliament exercise a significant influence over the labour relations policies of the nationalised industries, so that features to be found in the civil service, e.g. special pension rights, are also found in the case of employees of the nationalised industries.

Part One
The Background

·I·

The British System of Industrial Relations Law[1]

1. LABOUR LAW

THE United Kingdom[2] possesses a system of labour relations law which is strikingly different from that which exists elsewhere in Europe; indeed it differs very markedly from that which exists elsewhere in the "Common Law World." Its main characteristics may be summarised as follows:[3]

(1) There is no code of labour law; the rules of the system are found in acts of Parliament, rules made by ministers and government departments, rules made by the courts (in some cases by special tribunals which decide particular questions of labour law), and in rules made by the parties themselves. There are no special courts having exclusive jurisdiction over labour relations. Instead most questions of labour law are decided, should they come before a judicial tribunal, by the ordinary courts, although on certain questions specialised tribunals may exist for special

1. For the British system of industrial relations the following may be consulted: B. C. Roberts, *Industrial Relations—Contemporary Problems and Perspectives* (London, 1968); and H. A. Clegg, *The System of Industrial Relations in Great Britain* (London, 1970). In many ways a most useful account may be found in the *Report of the Royal Commission on Trade Unions and Employers' Associations, 1965-1968: Report* (H. M. Stationery Office, London, 1968, Cmnd. 3623). N.B. H. M. Levinson and R. Loveridge's books in this series.
2. Although most of what is said in this monograph will be true for the whole United Kingdom of Great Britain and Northern Ireland we are primarily concerned with the position in England and Wales. Because the United Kingdom includes three distinct legal systems, the Scottish, the Northern Irish, and the English, there are important differences of detail between them. What we say therefore must be understood as applying essentially to England and Wales; it may also apply elsewhere in the United Kingdom, but not always.
3. Cf. Wedderburn and Davies, Pt. I. Enumerated in the text are the characteristics most relevant to the position of public employees. For a general account of the other characteristics of the British system of labour law see P. O'Higgins, "Collective Bargaining in Britain" in T. Mayer-Maly (ed.), *Kollektivverträge in Europa* (Munich and Salzburg, 1970).

9

questions. Thus questions of entitlement to compensation in the case of workers dismissed for redundancy under the Redundancy Payments Act 1965 are decided by Industrial Tribunals, although there is a right of appeal on questions of law from the Industrial Tribunals to the High Court.

(2) When compared with other systems, especially in Europe, there are very few legal rules relating to two main central areas, collective bargaining and strikes and lock-outs. That is not to say there is no law, but by comparison with other systems there is relatively little law. This fact is sometimes referred to as "the abstention of the law in British labour relations." There is no general absence of labour relations law in the United Kingdom. On many 'questions British labour law is immensely detailed, complicated, and sophisticated, but in these two areas there is a relative absence of legal rules. This is because the law does not impose any general duty to bargain, does not regulate the capacity of the parties to the bargaining process, does not prescribe the subjects about which bargaining may occur, does not lay down any automatic rules for the legal application of the terms of collective bargains to workers and employers, and does not seek to prescribe in any detail what the precise limits are to the injurious action workers and employers may inflict upon one another in the course of the bargaining process. The law does not play a central role in collective bargaining. Its function is limited to encouraging parties to engage in bargaining, and when the bargain has been struck the law encourages compliance with the standards established therein. The law does not permit "lawful strikes" and forbid "unlawful strikes"; it merely sets limits to the methods that may be used by workers and employers to inflict damage on one another.

Although no explicit formulation of its policy objectives is ever embodied nowadays by Parliament in its legislation, the legal rules established by Parliament in this area are based upon the following principles: (1) collective bargaining rather than legal regulation is the best method of resolving disputes and establishing standards in labour relations; (2) in order to have effective collective bargaining one must have trade unions which are given sufficient legal protection to carry out their functions effectively,[4] and (3) there must be freedom for workers and trade unions to take strike action.[5]

These principles have particular reference to the private sector of employment, but it is worth noting that as we shall see in Chapter VIII that there is very little special law applicable to public employees which restricts their freedom to take strike action, although there may be internal disciplinary rules, backed up by special sanctions which discourage public employee strikes. One is tempted to say that the problem of strikes in the public service was dealt with indirectly, rather than by direct prohibition, by providing procedures, such as appeals against dismissal, which all too often in the past did not exist in private industry and were a frequent cause of work stoppages.

(3) A further characteristic, although it is in fact implicit in what we have said already, is the absence of collective labour law in Britain. There is no such thing in Britain as a lawful or an unlawful strike. There are only individual strikers who have committed a crime or a tort or who have broken their contracts of employment. The legal liability of every striker must be assessed in terms of his individual legal responsibility for his own acts, qualified of course by the law of civil and criminal conspiracy. Similarly collective agreements do not have any automatic application to individual workers or employers. Ordinarily the collective agreement is enforceable in law in relation to an individual worker or employer only when that bargain has come to be incorporated in his contract of employment. In other words, many questions which would be a matter of collective labour law in other systems in Britain are dependent upon the rights and obligations of individual workers and employers.

(4) The individual contract of employment occupies a central position in British labour law. Very many questions are resolved by asking, "What are the terms of the contract of employment of this particular worker with this particular employer?" It is noteworthy that even when there is statutory extension of the terms of a collective bargain, such extension often operates,

4. The Trade Union Act 1871 and Trade Disputes Acts 1906–65 give trade unions such protection.
5. This was conferred by the Conspiracy and Protection of Property Act 1875, and by the Trade Disputes Acts 1906-65.

as under the Terms and Conditions of Employment Act 1959, by means of an award of a special tribunal which makes the terms of the collective agreement *implied terms* of the individual contracts of employment of workers employed by a particular employer.

(5) There is a general lack of minimum standards for conditions of labour applicable across the board to all employees. True, there are often statutes protecting particular groups of workers, e.g. women and children, who stand in need of special protection, but the law does not guarantee all workers minimum pay, holidays, conditions of work, hours, sick pay, etc. Why is this? The answer is that collective bargaining is the preferred method of establishing minimum standards, although this has its defects as collective bargaining does not automatically regulate the conditions of employment of workers directly. Thus many workers are left unprotected where there is no collective bargaining or where the collective bargain for some reason cannot be or has not been incorporated into individual contracts of employment.

Professor Kahn-Freund has explained[6] this curious phenomenon by saying that in Britain organised labour had already obtained for itself acceptable minimum standards by means of collective bargaining long before it was significant enough politically to demand legislative intervention to lay down minimum standards. In other words collective bargaining was well established before the organised working class obtained the franchise. This of course did not help the unorganised, but in the past trade unions have not tended to demand legislation to protect nonunionists. The atmosphere is now changing however, and there is a general tendency for trade unionists to demand minimum standards that shall apply to all across the board. Already in the sixties there were indications that this trend was gaining momentum. In 1963 there was the Contracts of Employment Act which guaranteed to all workers a minimum period of notice of dismissal and guaranteed them a minimum income for the period of notice. In 1965 the Redundancy Payments Act guaranteed compensation to all workers, the quantum being dependent upon their length of service, who were dismissed because of redundancy. In 1968 the Race Relations Act guaranteed all workers against

6. *Labour Law–Old Traditions and New Developments* (Toronto, 1968).

discrimination in admission to a job, in promotion within the enterprise, and as regards dismissal on the grounds of race, national, or ethnic origin. Already some trade unions have begun to demand a national minimum wage.

(6) Traditionally the contract of employment, although it was central to the worker's rights, gave him very little protection in practice. Workers had, and indeed still have, very little legal security in their job. Insofar as in practice in private industry they enjoy security, it is largely the outcome of effective collective bargaining by trade unions.

(7) In the United Kingdom little practical significance is attached to the distinction which is important in many systems between conflicts of "right" and conflicts of "interest." Indeed in a recent work Professor Wedderburn has said, "In truth what we in Britain may have to offer to this topic is the need to place as little emphasis as possible in industrial relations on this distinction."[7]

2. TRADE UNIONS

The existence of trade unions has come to be accepted as essential in a democratic society today. Trade unions are not only protected from the original common law rules which made them unlawful conspiracies before 1871, by the Trade Union Act of that year, they are also protected from liability for actions giving rise to civil liability (other than breach of contract[8]) by section 4 of the Trade Disputes Act 1906. The reason for this wide protection, which is not confined to industrial conflict, is interesting, for its reflects the value which the community places upon the continued existence of trade unions. The problem facing Parliament in 1906 following the decision of the House of Lords in the Taff Vale case,[9] in which it was held that

7. In B. Aaron (ed.), *Dispute Settlement Procedures in Five Western European Countries* (Los Angeles, 1969), p. 90.

8. The Trade Union Act 1871, s.4, forbids the enforcement by means of a claim for damages, or by any other means of direct enforcement, of any agreement between two trade unions. Owing to the oddities of the British legal definition of a "trade union" this has the effect of inhibiting the enforcement of certain collective agreements between a workers' organisation and an employers' association, assuming such an agreement in any event to be a contract.

9. *Taff Vale Railway Co.* v. *Amalgamated Society of Railway Servants* [1901] A.C. 426.

a trade union could be made civilly liable for acts committed by its members, was that if employers could sue trade unions for loss caused in this way, employers could by bringing claims for substantial damages destroy trade unions. Because of the uncertainty as to how the judges might extend or apply the law relating to liability for the acts of members of the union who committed torts contrary to union instructions it was felt insufficient to say that a union should be liable only for the wrongs of its agents. Even to confine the protection so that the unions were liable only for the acts of their authorised agents was felt to be insufficient because it would leave open all the assets of the union to be attacked by claims for damages. This was undesirable because while some of the funds of the union could be seen as fighting funds, a large part of the unions' assets, then as now, were composed of contributions—aid by members in expectation of being entitled to benefits, such as sick pay, unemployment pay, widow's pension, etc. In other words trade unions were and still are mutual insurance institutions which protect their members against the ordinary hazards of life. To allow the benefit funds of a union to be attacked by claims arising out of torts would be to leave union members without the benefits towards which they might have been contributing for years. It was largely because Parliament was unable to think of any other practicable method of protecting the benefit funds of unions that section 4 of the Trade Disputes Act 1906 laid down a blanket prohibition of claims for damages for tortious acts being brought against trade unions.[10]

The essential role of trade unions in society consists not only in the part they have to play in collective bargaining[11] but also in the field of social security law. Trade unions have an important part to play in the welfare state. So long as social security benefits payable under the state scheme are basically paid at a flat rate, irrespective of the previous earnings of the worker,[12] then so long will the benefits payable by trade

10. For a fuller account of this episode see P. O'Higgins, "The Legal Definition of a 'Trade Dispute,'" 22 (1971) *Northern Ireland Legal Quarterly*.
11. A small wage-related supplement to the basic flat-rate benefit was introduced by the National Insurance Act 1959.
12. Cf. *Evans* v. *National Union of Printing, Bookbinding and Paper*

unions be an important addition. The interest of trade unions in social security law is recognised by the fact that a trade union is entitled in its own right to dispute the grant or refusal of social security benefit by a local appeal tribunal under section 70 of the National Insurance Act 1965 and section 46 of the National Insurance (Industrial Injuries) Act 1965, notwithstanding that the individual worker involved does not wish himself to complain about the decision of the National Insurance authorities.

In very many fields, education, financial assistance, the provision of legal advice and representation, pensions, recreational facilities, etc., trade unions are means of compensation for the chaos and deficiencies of the British welfare state.

The state has necessarily accepted the value of the part played by trade unions in society. This acceptance shows itself in many ways. If the Government is considering any legislative reforms which are likely to affect trade unions or their members, then before the Government's intentions are made public in any precise forms a memorandum will be sent to the trade unions concerned[13] and their opinion and comment invited. This applies not only to cases where the Government is considering reforms in the law relating to trade unions, or strikes, or such questions as apply directly to trade unions, but also to cases where members of the trade unions concerned may have their working conditions affected by the changes proposed. In the field of local government, if the government were considering altering the structure of local government, this would clearly affect the jobs of members of the National and Local Government Officers Association (and perhaps of other unions as well). In such a case NALGO (and other relevant unions) would be consulted in advance. This is not done, as a cynic might think, in order to disarm potential opposition, but also because trade unions are accepted as responsible bodies whose opinions on these questions ought to be given careful consideration before the Government finally settles upon the legislative programme to be proposed to Parliament. Similarly in preparing subordinate

---

Workers [1938] 4 All E.R. 51, at 54, per Lord Goddard, L.C.J., ". . . the great benefit of a trade union is that you can have collective bargaining between employers and employed."

13. Cf. J. F. Garner, *Administrative Law* (2nd ed., London, 1967), p. 47.

legislation Government departments will consult trade unions and other bodies likely to be affected.[14]

Trade unions are represented on innumerable governmental committees, usually of an advisory character,[15] and this may enable them to influence governmental or parliamentary action. Trade unions may make direct representations to Government departments advocating reforms of public importance. Thus in 1942 the Inland Revenue Staff Federation and the Association of H. M. Inspectors of Taxes proposed the introduction of PAYE.[16] The Government was at first lukewarm but eventually adopted the suggestion.[17]

For their part trade unions are aware that governmental activity may affect their interests, and therefore many trade unions do not content themselves merely with being the passive recipient of Government proposals but themselves seek to play a more active role in the determination of governmental policy. This is done by all the means open to any person or body wishing to influence the Government and the legislature, by petitioning Parliament, by addressing letters to M.P.s or Government departments, etc.[18] Above all, trade unions seek to influence governmental and parliamentary activity by taking a full part in political life.

In the United Kingdom trade unions are not organised on religious lines as in some other countries. There are no Catholic or Christian Democratic trade unions nor are trade unions organised on overtly political lines. There are no Conservative or Communist trade unions. By and large trade unions are open

14. See J. F. Garner, "Consultation in Subordinate Legislation," (1964) *Public Law* 105–24, esp. 115–17.

15. For a critical account see V. L. Allen, *Trade Unions and the Government* (London, 1960), chaps. I, II.

16. I.e. Pay As You Earn, a system of tax collection whereby the employer deducts tax due from wages before he pays them, and then pays over to the state the money so deducted.

17. James Callaghan, *Whitleyism: A Study of Joint Consultation in the Civil Service* (London, 1953), p. 6.

18. One qualification should be added that where the Whitley system has established a system of collective bargaining for the civil service and an agreement has been negotiated there is a "feeling that, when a bargain has been struck through Whitley machinery, the staff side should not seek to improve unsatisfactory features through parliamentary agitation": Callaghan, op.cit., pp. 34–35.

to all shades of religious or political opinion. This is possible because the main aims of trade unions are economic: the advancement of the economic welfare of their members. However, trade unions have long believed that a Government of the left is more likely to show an understanding of the economic needs of trade union members than a Government of the right. Hence from the last few decades of the nineteenth century trade unions and trade union leaders have played an important part in the establishment and continued existence of the Labour Party. Despite the exceptional and early participation of some trade union leaders in the activities of the First International when it was based in London under the leadership of Karl Marx, most trade union leaders have eschewed doctrine of any kind and have played a conservative role in the Labour Party, not as a party which would bring about a social revolution but as a party which would mitigate the severity of the capitalist system in the workingman's favour. The earliest working-class M.P.s were members of trade unions. The unions were willing to pay their wages while they sat in Parliament, to which they were elected under the umbrella of the Liberal Party. Later trade unions continued to sponsor in this way the election of their members to sit as Labour M.P.s.

In *Amalgamated Society of Railway Servants* v. *Osborne*[19] the House of Lords decided that it was unlawful for a trade union to levy contributions from its members for the purpose of securing parliamentary representation. This decision was undone by the Trade Union Act 1913, which permits a trade union to spend its funds on political objectives provided its own rules permit. Where money is to be spent by the union on paying an M.P. or helping him to secure election, or if the union wishes to spend money on other party political objectives, then there must be a ballot of members approving the setting up of a distinct political fund out of which all such expenditure must come. No member may be forced to contribute to the political fund; such a member is entitled to contract out of paying the political levy.[20]

Since that time many trade unions have actively taken steps

19. [1910] A.C. 87.
20. Grunfeld, pp. 251 et seq.

17

to encourage their officials or other members to secure election to Parliament, usually as Labour M.P.s, including trade unions catering for public employees. Thus in the Parliament of 1951-55, a typical Parliament, there was one member from each of the following unions: Inland Revenue Staff Federation, National Association of Local Government Officers, National Association of Fire Officers; two M.P.s each came from the National Union of Public Employees and the Union of Post Office Workers; and there were four M.P.s from the National Union of Teachers.[21]

The relationship between M.P.s and outside bodies from whom they receive financial payments is a delicate and important issue which has not been faced up to in Britain today.[22] In 1942 W. J. Brown, general secretary of the Civil Service Clerical Association, was elected to Parliament. The Association then made him their "parliamentary secretary" and made an agreement with Mr. Brown under which (1) he was to be entitled to engage in his political activities with complete freedom; (2) he was to deal with all questions arising in the work of the Association which required parliamentary or political action, and (3) he was not entitled to represent the political view of the Association in his political or parliamentary activities. The Association and Mr. Brown fell out over Mr. Brown's adoption of views opposed to the policies of the Association. The Association then decided to terminate the agreement under which Mr. Brown received a financial reward. Notwithstanding the fact that Mr. Brown believed that the agreement limited his freedom of action as an M.P.,[23] the House of Commons did not disapprove of the agreement explicitly and contented itself with making the general point that any contract limiting an M.P.'s freedom of action would be contrary to the interest both of Parliament and the public. It is clear from this kind of arrangement, whatever its explicit terms, that the trade union making payments to an M.P. believes it gains some advantage. The advantage may be only that the trade union has easier means of access to civil servants and ministers when it wishes to put forward its views to such authorities on any question of concern to the union.

21. J. D. Stewart, *British Pressure Groups* (Oxford, 1958), Appendix B.
22. *Report from the Select Committee on Members' Interests Declaration* (H.C. 57, 1969). This report avoided any recommendation for a register of lobbyists, etc.
23. Stewart, op.cit., pp. 189–94.

It is quite clear that if some of the relationships which exist in the United Kingdom between Members of Parliament and outside bodies, under which the M.P. receives a financial reward from the outside body (in addition to his ordinary salary as a Member of Parliament), existed anywhere else, a cynical interpretation would certainly be placed upon their nature.[24] That some such relationships are worth special attention is incontestable. One such relationship of interest in the sphere of public employee organisations is the strange case of Mr. Callaghan and the Police Federation. The Police Federation employed Mr. Callaghan for some years at a salary of £1,500 a year as their "parliamentary adviser." When in 1964 the Labour Party, of which Mr. Callaghan[25] was a leading member, was returned to office Mr. Callaghan resigned his post with the Police Federation upon his appointment as Chancellor of the Exchequer in Mr. Wilson's government.[26] A Mr. Eldon Griffiths, a Conservative M.P., succeeded Mr. Callaghan, although it is understood Mr. Callaghan still had the option of returning to the employment of the Police Federation upon his vacating his ministerial office should he desire.[27] Some time after his first ministerial post Mr. Callaghan was moved to the Home Office, where as Home Secretary he was the minister with overall responsibility for many police questions, including conditions of service, pay, etc. Mr. Callaghan as Home Secretary had to weigh up the interest of members of the Police Federation in improved pay, etc., against the public interest.[28]

24. F. Noel-Baker has aptly called the law and practice regarding such relationships the "grey zone" in his article " 'The Grey Zone'—The Problem of the Business Affiliations of Members of Parliament," *Parliamentary Affairs* (1961–62), pp. 87–93.

25. It may be added that Mr. Callaghan had originally been assistant secretary of the Inland Revenue Staff Federation when first elected to Parliament.

26. For this case see *The Times,* 5 September 1970.

27. The chairman of the Police Federation commenting on the likelihood of Mr. Callaghan's return to their employment somewhat uncharitably said: "I don't think he will come, he is bound to receive more lucrative offers elsewhere" (*The Times,* 5 September 1970). In fact Mr. Callaghan has now dcided not to return to the service of the Police Federation after all (*The Times,* 7 September 1970).

28. Mr. Callaghan did not always do this to the satisfaction of the Police Federation and he came to be unpopular with many members of the police force.

What is clear from all this is that public employee trade unions do not hang back in seeking to advance the interests of their members. By encouraging the election of members to Parliament, and by paying a salary to an existing M.P. to act as "parliamentary adviser," it is hoped to aid the interests of the union in some way.

For its part the state accepts the utility of trade unions not only in the private sector but in the public sector as well.[29] According to the Treasury handbook, *Staff Relations in the Civil Service,*

> A civil servant is free to be a member of any association or trade union which will admit him under its rules of membership. Civil servants are, moreover, encouraged [e.g. in the *Handbook for the New Civil Servant,* issued by the Treasury to new recruits] to belong to associations, for the existence of fully representative associations not only promotes good staff relations but is essential to effective negotiations on conditions of service. [p. 5]

A similar attitude is adopted in local government, and in the nationalised industries there are statutory obligations to take steps for joint consultation with trade unions. These obligations clearly indicate acceptance of the value of trade unions amongst the employees of the public corporations.

29. See *Handbook for the New Civil Servant,* p. 37: "You are not only allowed but encouraged to belong to a staff association. Besides being a good thing for the individual civil servant to belong to an association, which can support him in his reasonable claims and put his point of view before the authorities on all kinds of questions affecting his conditions of service, it is also a good thing for Departments and for the Civil Service as a whole that civil servants should be strongly organised in representative bodies. It is only common sense to meet the wishes of the civil servant about his conditions of service as far as possible, for a contented staff will work much more efficiently than a staff which feels that its interests are being completely ignored by the 'management.' But it is hopeless to try to find out the wishes of a scattered, unorganised body of individual civil servants each of whom may express a different view. When they get together in representative associations, their collective wish can be democratically determined and passed on to the 'management' with real force and agreement behind it; the 'management' know where they stand, and can act accordingly. So join an association and do your bit to see that it is a 'live' and representative one."

·II·

The Traditions of
Public Employment and
the Public Service

1. DEVELOPMENT OF CIVIL AND LOCAL GOVERNMENT SERVICE

a. History of the Civil Service[1]

IN the eighteenth century appointment to a post in the civil service was by patronage. This changed only gradually in the course of the nineteenth century. During the first half of the nineteenth century it also became established that civil servants should hold permanent positions unaffected by changes in the political complexion of Governments in power. This change, according to Holdsworth,[2] is illustrated by two sets of statutes. The first deals with pensions. After some provision for particular categories of civil servant the first general statute making a general provision for grant of a pension with Treasury consent was passed in 1810. As early as 1821 a system was proposed for civil servants to make some contribution out of their own pocket to a superannuation fund, but from 1801 the principle had been established that civil servants should have a pension which reflected in its amount the length of their service. The second set of statutes and rules dealt with the disqualification of civil servants from sitting in Parliament, now governed by the House of Commons Disqualification Act 1957.[3]

The system of patronage gradually gave way to a system of appointment based upon the qualifications of the candidate, but the process was a lengthy one. The first proposal for recruitment by open competitive examination was made by the historian and administrative reformer George Macaulay in 1833, in a speech on the Charter Act of the East India Company which contained

1. G. W. Griffiths, *The Civil Service, 1854–1954* (London, 1954).
2. W. S. Holdsworth, *A History of English Law,* vol. XIV (ed. A. L. Goodhardt and H. G. Hanbury, London, 1964), p. 132.
3. The members of police forces are also disqualified.

a clause that entrants for the Company's college, Haileybury, should be chosen in this way.[4] The model of the East India Company was one of many examples of the way in which an administrative practice adopted in the light of the needs of governing a colonial country contributed to reform at home.[5] The suggestion was adopted in the Northcote-Trevelyan Report (1854),[6] but was not fully adopted until 1870.

The existence of a permanent civil service appointed on the basis of their qualifications has had important consequences.

It is the existence of this trained professional civil service which has rendered possible the system of cabinet government, under which the heads of the great departments of the executive government change with each change of ministry. It supplies the knowledge of the problems of the departments of the executive which is necessary to guide Parliament as to the course which reforming legislation should take. It ensures a continuity of policy in the routine business of the government.

b. Local Government

The modern system of local government dates from the Municipal Corporations Act 1835. By the end of the nineteenth century there were established a large number of elected multipurpose authorities subject to central control to an ever-increasing extent but still administering very many important services, e.g. education, and now employing something like one and a quarter million employees.

c. Nationalisation[8]

Nationalisation in its modern form dates from the postwar Labour Government, when, as a result of a rising demand for more public control of industry, the state took over control of a number of industries to be run as public services and not for profit. Hopes were aroused of a new deal for workers

4. Holdsworth, op.cit., pp. 134–35.
5. Even the term "civil service" was first used in relation to certain employees of the East India Company. See Wyn Griffith, op.cit., p. 7.
6. Reprinted in full in *Public Administration,* vol. 21 (1954).
7. Holdsworth, op.cit., p. 137.
8. See R. Kelf-Cohen, *Twenty Years of Nationalisation: The British Experience* (London, 1969).

in such industries, but these hopes were to be disappointed to some extent in that they were subject to heavy burdens of paying interest on the sums needed to compensate the former owners, and the idea of workers' control, or even of workers' representation on the boards, was rejected.[9] Despite disappointed hopes considerable advances were obtained in improved conditions of work for the employees of such industries.

d. Ministers and Civil Servants

That there is no spoils system in Britain is a statement often made. It is true in the sense that the officials in civil and local government do not lose their posts with a change of Government. But it is misleading if anyone were to conclude that the British Prime Minister does not have at his disposal a large number of posts to reward friends and others.[10] It has been estimated that he has in his gift something like 50,000 posts,[11] but these it should be noted are rarely in the executive arm of government, but range from bishoprics to chairs of Roman law in the ancient universities, membership of the board of nationalised industries, etc. But even here once appointed, except for last minute appointments by retiring Prime Ministers, these appointments are honoured by later governments and are not forfeited on a change of government, save for a small number of cases.

In the British system of government it is the political minister who is the impermanent figure; his civil servants remain unchanged by vicissitudes of the political world. This has certain constitutional consequences. In theory, whatever be the fact, the decisions are the decisions of the minister. He takes responsibility for what is done in his department, and only very rarely will the veil of anonymity be lifted from a civil servant. This is an aspect of the doctrine of ministerial responsibility. The minister must answer in Parliament any question relating to the conduct of the affairs of his department. His is the responsibility: he cannot place the blame for an error on a civil servant, unless

9. At the very same time the Labour Government was resisting workers' representation at home it was insisting upon it in its occupation zone in Germany in respect of German iron and steel companies. Cf. A. Kelin, *Codetermination and the Law Governing Works Councils* (Bonn, n.d.).
10. Peter G. Richards, *Patronage in British Government* (London, 1963).
11. *The Spectator* (London), June 5, 1970.

in exceptional cases, as where the civil servant disobeys a ministerial instruction. In exchange for anonymity the civil servant is supposed to give his minister the best possible advice, advice not tainted with political bias, to which lack of bias the rules relating to the political activities of civil servants discussed below may contribute.

2. CONDITIONS OF SERVICE

a. Civil Service

If we bear in mind the poor conditions under which many unorganised workers were employed with little security and with no prospects of a pension, we can see how from an early date employment in the civil service had many advantages. Even today some employers in private industry refuse to negotiate with trade unions, and as the law stands such refusal is perfectly lawful. In contrast with this, even before the First World War a favourable view was taken of civil service associations.

In general terms the legal rules governing the relationship between a civil servant and the Crown are to be found in the regulations and instructions issued formerly by the Treasury and now by the Civil Service Department, the government department responsible for the running of the civil service. These rules are collectively known as Estacode. Estacode was first published in 1944, and it is now in its third (1958) edition. It is constantly kept up to date by supplements as new regulations are issued. There are also statutes, e.g. the Aliens Employment Act 1955, which regulate the admission of aliens to the civil service. In addition there are the rules of the common law.

Security of tenure is traditionally one of the most characteristic features of employment in the civil service, yet it has sometimes been a matter of doubt whether a civil servant has a contract of employment.[12] The balance of authority[13] is now, however, clearly in favour of the view that there is a contract, and

---

12. See L. Blair, "The Civil Servant—A Status Relationship?" 21 (1958) *Modern Law Review* 265 et seq. See generally G. L. Williams, *Crown Proceedings* (London, 1948).

13. *Brandy* v. *Owners of S.S. Raphael* [1911] A.C. 413; *Sutton* v. *A.-G.* [1923] 39 T.L.R. 294; *Reilly* v. *The King* [1934] A.C. 176, and *Kodeswaran* v. *A.-G. of Ceylon* [1970] 2 W.L.R. 456.

earlier cases,[14] which had denied the right of a civil servant to recover arrears of pay, must now be taken to have been wrong.[15] The contract is subject to an implied term that the civil servant is dismissible at any time at the will of the Crown, with or without notice as the Crown wills.[16] In consequence no compensation can be recovered by a civil servant for wrongful dismissal. Where the Crown has expressly promised not to dismiss at will, despite doubts which have been strongly expressed,[17] it is likely that in that exceptional case the civil servant could recover damages for breach of contract.[18] However, there have been cases[19] where the court has held that, where the Whitley Council has agreed a procedure for dismissal, such a limitation on the Crown's right to dismiss at will was unenforceable.[20] In practice however, whatever be the strict legal position, and in all ordinary cases, the civil servant is dismissible at will. The actual position is that a civil servant has greater security of tenure than an employee in private industry but that the Crown has a reserve of authority it may rely upon to rid itself of a civil servant it wishes to dismiss. But again, such civil servant has a right of appeal, in practice although not in law.

Another respect in which civil servants may be less well protected by the law than other employees is as regards the application to them of protective labour legislation. Thus the Contracts of Employment Act 1963, which guarantees to all workers written details of their basic conditions of employment, a guaranteed income while they are under notice of dismissal, and a minimum period of notice, has no application to civil servants. The reason why the Contracts of Employment Act does not apply to civil servants is because there is a rule of interpretation that no act of Parliament applies to the Crown unless the

14. E.g. *Lucas* v. *Lucas* [1943] p. 68.
15. *Kodeswaran* v. *A.-G. of Ceylon* [1970] 2 W.L.R. 456.
16. *Shenton* v. *Smith* [1895] A.C. 229, and *Gould* v. *Stuart* [1896] A.C. 575.
17. *Riordan* v. *War Office* [1961] 1 W.L.R. 210.
18. *Reilly* v. *The King* [1934] A.C. 176, at pp. 179–80.
19. *Rodwell* v. *Thomas* [1944] K.B. 596.
20. See D. W. Logan, "A Civil Servant and His Pay," 61 (1945) *Law Quarterly Review* 240; and I. L. M. Richardson, "Incidents of the Crown-Servant Relationship," 33 (1955) *Canadian Bar Review* 424-59.

act itself expressly so provides, or it is a necessary implication from the words and purpose of the act that Parliament intended that the Crown was bound.[21] The 1963 act does not expressly or by necessary implication bind the Crown, and therefore the Crown is not bound to give its employees the minimum standards laid down in the act. Where an act giving protection to employees does not bind the Crown, then all persons who are employed by entities treated as the Crown are not legally entitled to such protection. The term "Crown" covers not only the sovereign personally, but also the central Government departments and any other person or body who in law is regarded as acting on behalf of the Crown. In consequence it has been suggested that employees of Regional Hospital Boards may not be protected by legislation not binding on the Crown.[22] However, it has also been held that the commercial nationalised public corporations are not acting on behalf of the Crown and consequently are not entitled to immunity from statutes which are not binding on the Crown.[23]

As regards superannuation most public employees, using the term in its broadest sense, have rights to superannuation which are often markedly an improvement upon the ordinary pension under the National Insurance Act 1965.[24] The justification for this is not easy to see, because it establishes a social inequality which may not serve any public purpose, unless it be to attract to the public service people who are attracted by the idea of a higher pension. One argument is that the ultimate rewards to the best are higher in private employment, but that the certainty of a good pension may attract some able people to the public service. Humanly of course, when the system of

21. *Bombay Province* v. *Bombay Municipal Corporation* [1947] A.C. 88.

22. D. Foulkes, "Are Hospital Officers Crown Servants?" 114 (1964) *New Law Journal* 703–34, and "Crown Servants in the National Health Service" 115 (1965) *New Law Journal* 689–91, 703–04. Mr. Foulkes' discussion is based on the decision in *Pfizer Corporation* v. *Ministry of Health* [1965] 1 All E.R. 387. Letters from the authors to the Department of Health and Social Security, whether the Department took the view that health service employees were "Crown servants" (and hence not covered by the Contracts of Employment Act 1963), were acknowledged but no answer given to the question: a nice example of the way in which Government departments prefer to leave fundamental questions unresolved.

23. Cf. *Tamlin* v. *Hannaford* [1949] 1 K.B. 18.

24. G. Rhodes, *Public Sector Pensions* (London, 1965).

flat rate pensions is inadequate, one cannot disapprove that some get better pensions. The payment of higher pensions to persons in public employment may in the end lead to a general improvement of the pension under the National Insurance Act 1965. In the civil service a distinction is made between "established" staff, who are entitled to superannuation, and nonestablished, often temporary, staff, who are not.

There is no legal right to a pension in the civil service. The statutes have been carefully worded to prevent the establishment of a legal right. "In fact, of course, the civil servant need have no doubts about receiving his superannuation allowance if he satisfies the regulations."[25]

As regards the quantum of the civil servant's pay, we must distinguish between industrial civil servants and nonindustrial civil servants. As regards the former a simple enough practice has been followed since the 1890s when the first "Fair Wages Resolution" was passed by the House of Commons. Addressing the Donovan Commission a spokesman for the Treasury[26] said:

> In the industrial Civil Service we have always adopted as our principle that of the Fair Wages Resolution of the House of Commons on 14th October 1946. This in terms refers to Government contractors; but it has long been accepted ever since the first Fair Wages Resolution was passed in the 1890s that the same principles would apply to Government industrial employees, and the operative part of that resolution is that the contractor—for this purpose the Government—"shall pay rates of wages and observe hours and conditions of labour not less favourable than those established for the trade or industry in the district where the work is carried out by machinery of negotiation or arbitration to which the parties are organisations of employers and trade unions representative respectively of substantial proportions of the trade or industry in the district." Then there is an alternative, that "in the absence of rates of wages, hours or conditions of labour so established, the contractor—that is the Government—shall pay rates of wages and observe hours and conditions of labour

25. L. Blair, "The Civil Servant—Political Reality and Legal Myth," (1958) *Public Law* 32–49, at 41.
26. RCME No. 10 (The Treasury), para. 1595.

which are not less favourable than the general level of wages, hours and conditions observed by other employers whose general circumstances in the trade or industry in which the contractor is engaged are similar." This of course refers to a district, but for the most part industrial rates of pay are national rates, and in fact the criterion is for all practical purposes the national rate of pay. It is this criterion we employ in a number of ways in settling pay for our industrial employees.

As regards nonindustrial civil servants, the MacDonnell Commission (1910) stated, "It is an accepted principle with all parties that the Government should be a 'model' employer."[27] The concept of model employer is not the easiest to apply, as was the opinion of the Tomlin Commission (1931), who pointed out that "different interpretations have been placed on this phrase. We think that a phrase which lends itself to such varied and contradictory interpretations affords no practical guidance for fixing wages or for indicating the responsibilities of the state towards its employees."[28] The Tomlin Commission took the view that

broad general comparisons between classes in the service and outside occupations are possible and should be made. In effecting such comparisons the State should take a long view. Civil Service remuneration should reflect what may be described as the long term trend, both in wage levels and in the economic conditions of the country. We regard it as undesirable that the conditions of service of civil servants when under review should be related too closely to factors of a temporary or passing character.[29]

In 1953 the Priestley Commission laid down the principle of comparability with remuneration for comparable work outside the civil service. A Treasury spokesman qualified this for the Donovan Commission:[30]

This was, following the Priestley Royal Commission from 1953 to 1955, the primary principle; but there always have

27. G. A. Campbell, op.cit., p. 51.
28. Ibid.
29. Ibid.
30. RCME No. 10 (The Treasury), para. 1595.

been other considerations; an obvious one is the manpower situation, but also considerations such as that when you are recruiting you may have to look across the board to what qualifications are required. You may also have to look at internal relativities between various grades—there are very many grades, there are 2,500 grades in the Civil Service. One has to look particularly at what we call vertical relativities —in other words, the hierarchy. This necessarily involves what we call pay research, although there you can sometimes get a nonsense result.

Following the Priestley Commission the Civil Service Pay Research Unit was set up in 1956, as an impartial body. The director is appointed by the Prime Minister and it is controlled by a steering committee composed of members of both sides of the National Whitley Council.

For each survey, the Unit investigates a representative sample of jobs in the Civil Service and seeks to find information about pay and associated conditions of service in comparable jobs outside the Civil Service, mainly in commerce and industry. Information from outside is given to the Unit on a confidential basis, and its report is confined to factual information making no recommendation. On receiving the Unit's report, it is for the Civil Service Department and the relevant staff associations to negotiate a settlement. At present nearly all of the three main classes in the non-industrial Civil Service are surveyed by the Unit every three years.[31]

The pay in the higher civil service is determined separately by the Government on the advice of the Standing Advisory Committee on the Pay of the Higher Civil Service.

A further committee to investigate the civil service, the Fulton Committee, reported in 1968.[32] It recommended that central management of the civil service should be transferred from the Treasury to a new Civil Service Department which has now been set up; that a simplified structure should be established; and

31. *First Report of the Civil Service Department* (H.M. Stationery Office, 1970), p. 57.
32. *Report of the Committee on the Civil Service 1966–68* (1968, Cmnd. 3683).

that more ruthless personnel management should be adopted and those not suitable or efficient should be encouraged to leave. It also recommended that the convention of anonymity be modified. The staff side of the National Whitley Council in general welcomed these proposals, which were accepted by the Government.[33]

A special feature of the work of a civil servant is the obligation of secrecy, with respect to information obtained in the course of his work.[34] Since 1948 there has been in force a system of "security measures" under which a civil servant may be removed from his employment or transferred to other work if he is believed to be a Communist or a Communist sympathizer. The civil servant concerned has a right to make representations— and he may not know the full nature of the case against him—to the Three Advisers, an advisory body consisting of two retired civil servants and a retired trade union officer.[35]

There are also restrictions on the political activities of certain civil servants. The position has been summarised as follows:[36]

> No Civil Servant may become a Member of Parliament without first resigning his appointment; though "industrial" Civil Servants may stand for election and are only required to resign if, in fact, they are elected. Second, senior Civil Servants in the administrative and professional grades and many of the executive and clerical grades are not permitted to take any part in national politics whatever. This includes not merely standing as a candidate for Parliament but taking part in any activities of national political parties and writing for the press or appearing on public platforms on party-political questions. This category comprises some 11% of the whole of the Civil Service. Its members may, however, with permission, take part in local government and local politics. Third, there is another category totalling some 26% of the Civil Service who may take part in all political activities except standing as candidates for Parliament, provided they first have

33. *Developments on Fulton—Report by the National Whitley Council's Joint Committee on the Fulton Report* (1969).
34. Official Secrets Act, 1911, s.2(1). See generally D. G. T. Williams, *Not in the Public Interest* (London, 1964).
35. See *Civil Service Clerical Association Compendium,* 15.21.
36. G. de N. Clark, contribution to Theme II of the 6th Congress of the International Society for Labour Law and Social Security, Stockholm, 1966.

the permission of their department and that they accept a code of discretion laid down by the Treasury.

The remainder of the Civil Service, including the bulk of the clerical and so-called minor and manipulative grades and all industrial Civil Servants, are free to engage in political activities except while on duty or on official premises.

Although this restriction of the political activities of senior civil servants may be justified on the grounds of the need to preserve the impartiality, or at least the appearance of the impartiality, of civil servants, clearly some civil servants no longer consider it desirable. In his presidential address to the Inland Revenue Staff Federation, Mr. Joseph Bibby said that it was indefensible that so many people were denied the right to full and active membership of the community.[37]

Having considered some of the special aspects of the conditions of service let us consider other public employees.

b. Local Government Service

Although a Scheme of Service was agreed upon between the trade unions and the associations of local authorities in 1946, there is still not a uniform set of conditions of service in operation. On the other hand local authority employees have considerable security of tenure. Although such appointments would normally be at pleasure, as in the case of the Crown, the Local Government Act 1933, section 121(1), expressly validates a term providing for reasonable notice in contracts of employment. Most of the restrictions which limit the freedom of action and opinion of civil servants have no application to local government officers.

3. THE MATURITY OF THE PUBLIC EMPLOYMENT COLLECTIVE BARGAINING SYSTEM

The demands of production during the first World War and the hope of a better world, with a reformed governmental structure, contributed to the establishment of the modern system of Whitleyism in the civil service.[38] In 1917 a report was published

37. *The Times,* 20 May 1970.
38. See generally L. D. White, *Whitley Councils in the British Civil Service* (Chicago, 1933), E. N. Gladden, *Civil Service Staff Relationships* (London, 1943) and B. V. Humphreys, *Clerical Unions in the Civil Service* (London, 1958).

by the Ministry of Reconstruction committee on relations between workers and employers under the chairmanship of the Speaker of the House of Commons, the Rt. Hon. J. H. Whitley, M.P. The report was concerned with the improvement of relations between parties in industry and it recommended the establishment of a system of Joint (National) Industrial Councils, District Councils, and Works Councils. A second report in 1919 recommended that public authorities should consider how far such machinery could be adopted in central and local government.

We have formed the opinion that the expression "employers and workmen" in our reference covers State and Municipal authorities and persons employed by them. Accordingly we recommend that such authorities and their work people should take into consideration the proposals made in this and in our first report, with a view to determining how far such proposals can suitably be adopted in their case.[39]

The Government not over-reluctantly accepted this suggestion with regard to the industrial civil servants, and Whitley Councils were established for industrial workers under the Crown.[40] Some local authorities followed suit but the nonindustrial civil service was not catered for. Under pressure from civil service associations an interdepartmental committee was set up to consider the problem, and on 7 March 1919 the *Report of the Sub-Committee of the Interdepartmental Committee on the Application of the Whitley Report to Civil Service Establishments*[41] was published, recommending the application of a modified Whitley scheme to the civil service. Under the ordinary Whitley proposals joint councils were to be set up which would regulate relations within industry. The report provided for joint committees within the civil service which were to be purely consultative and advisory. The report attached great weight to the special position of the state as employer and pinpointed the essential differences between public and private employment:

39. Ministry of Reconstruction: Committee on Relations between Employers and Employees: *Second Report on Joint Standing Industrial Councils* (Cd. 9002, 1918), para. 24.
40. L. D. White, *Whitley Councils in the British Civil Service* (Chicago, 1933), p. 5.
41. Cmd. 9, 1919.

(1) The fact that the State is the ultimate employer of government servants through the heads of Departments who consequently have not the freedom of decision enjoyed by the private employer.

(2) The absence of the check imposed by considerations of profit and loss and its replacement by Treasury control which, so far as questions of remuneration are concerned, is now subject to an appeal to the Conciliation and Arbitration Board for Government employees [a wartime institution].

(3) The fact that an employee in a Government office is not merely a private individual in public employment but is in a very real sense a servant of the public and as such has assumed obligations which, to some extent, necessarily limit his ordinary rights as a private citizen. (Para.7)

The report further noted the heads of department, who are the closest there is in the civil service to a real employer, had "no personal incentive to oppose demands of employees." The civil service had to be carried on in the public interest, and the duty of the minister to be answerable and responsible to Parliament for running the civil service in the public interest had to be maintained. These considerations led to the recommendation of purely consultative joint bodies for the civil service, and further to the strict limitation of the topics which could be discussed on these joint bodies to "matters which directly affect the conditions of service of the staff and working of Departments." General principles were laid down for the composition and structure of these joint bodies: (1) numbers on each side did not have to be even because the bodies were purely consultative; (2) representation need not be constant; (3) staff associations should be represented by active civil servants rather than by full-time organisers of associations; (4) there should be a written constitution for each joint body; (5) only statements issued by authority of the joint body should be disclosed outside the body, and (6) expense should be shared by Treasury and staff association.

The recommendations were not wholly welcome to civil servants because they had not been consulted, and indeed the Constitution proposed gave less power to Whitley Councils for the civil service than was the case for Whitley Councils generally.[42] After joint consultation and negotiation a new constitution for Whitley Councils in the civil service was agreed upon, whose language— "The decisions of the Council shall be arrived at by agreement between the two sides, shall be signed by the Chairman and the Vice-Chairman, shall be reported to the Cabinet, and shall thereupon become operative"—implied that the new councils were to be more than merely consultative bodies.

Today there is a National Whitley Council for the civil service, Departmental Whitley Councils, and there may also be Regional or Branch Whitley Councils concerned with questions which are purely local. Departmental Whitley Councils deal with questions which are domestic to a particular department. The National Council deals with matters affecting the conditions of service of all nonindustrial civil servants.

At first there was a tendency to ensure that the official or management side of Whitley Councils outnumbered the staff side, but in practice this is rarely the case now on a Whitley Council. Numbers on each side are either equal or on occasion the staff side may outnumber the official side. This is possible because there is no voting. Decisions are arrived at by agreement; if there is no agreement then the official side view holds the day. The staff side particularly functions as a body, and indeed the national staff side functions as a body meeting regularly on its own. Meetings of the National Council are extremely rare, even departmental committees do not meet frequently, and the bulk of the joint discussions takes place in committees of the National or Departmental Whitley Councils. Facilities are provided to enable members of the Councils and their committees to have time off work, etc., for their work as members of such bodies.

Theoretical difficulties arose because the official side consists of civil servants themselves not of employers and hence official side members might have to discuss questions of pay which might affect themselves. For this reason, without any formal alteration of the Constitution of Whitley Councils, it is not usual for the pay and grading of senior posts to be discussed by Whitley Councils. Since 1957 the Standing Advisory Committee

42. White, op.cit., pp. 6–8.

appointed by the Prime Minister has a general oversight over the remuneration of higher civil servants.

Whitley Councils were also established for employees of local authorities and for other public employees, e.g. those in the National Health Service. In the local government area such bodies are not usually entitled to Whitley Councils. Decisions in local government joint councils usually require that a majority on both sides present be in favour of a proposal before it is carried. In local government joint councils the local authorities represented on the management side are the employers, although subject to varying degrees of control and influence by the central government.

One cannot but be impressed by the immense amount of work performed by joint bodies in central and local government service, as well as in the nationalised corporations. Agreements are often extremely formal and are meticulously printed and circulated to all persons concerned.

Part Two
The Structure of Bargaining in Public Employment

·III·

Organisation for Bargaining on the Employee Side

1. THE LEGAL STATUS OF PUBLIC EMPLOYEE ORGANISATIONS

a. The Legal Tensions: Professional Associations, Trade Unions, and Public Employment

ONE of the major postwar shifts in the orientation of white-collar organisations in general, and of public employee white-collar bodies in particular, has been the movement away from narrow concern with professional standards and training towards militant union objectives. The law in the United Kingdom has subtly and indirectly complicated this development. This stems from the definitions of "trade union," "trade dispute," and "workmen" which appear in U.K. labour legislation and which leave the legal status of many public employee organisations and their disputes with employers and with one another in remarkable obscurity.

It must be remembered that the three main statutes which make up collective labour law in the U.K.—the Trade Union Act 1871, the Conspiracy and Protection of Property Act 1875, and the Trade Disputes Act 1906 (as supplemented by later statutes)—were all products of an industrial movement dominated by manual workers in private employment. Organisations of public employees emerged *after* the manual workers' unions had won their charter of legality in the form of acts of Parliament which relieved them from the main disabilities to which they had been subjected by earlier anticombination laws and by the judges. Before the general strike of 1926 public service organisations were not concerned with legal attacks on trade unionism. So the *Taff Vale* case (1901), in which the House of Lords held that a trade union registered under the 1871 act could conflict, did not affect the still small public employee organisations before its effect was reversed by the Trade Disputes Act 1906. And the *Osborne* case (1910), in which trade union political

39

funds were made illegal, was modified by legislation before public service organisations had reached the stage of wishing to undertake political affiliation. It is not surprising, therefore, that these three basic statutes, all of which grant "negative" protections against the common law illegalities which threatened the activities of trade unions, did not, in terms, include public employees and their organisations. It has been left to judicial interpretation to determine whether or not the legal definitions should be applied to these later arrivals in the industrial relations system. Added to this historical factor has been a psychological one, namely the resistance of the professional and lower middle classes themselves to the traditional aims and means of trade unionism.

The most important consequences of an organisation falling within the definition of a "trade union" in the act of 1871 (as amended in 1876 and 1913) are: (1) it is not an illegal combination, simply because its objects are in restraint of trade at common law, either for criminal purposes[1] (although this may be merely declaratory of the common law) or for civil purposes;[2] (2) many of its agreements are legally unenforceable by virtue of an express statutory provision;[3] (3) it is immune from actions against it in tort;[4] (4) the application of its funds for political purposes is restricted;[5] and (5) it may take advantage of the provisions of the 1871 act for voluntary registration.[6]

b. Registration of Public Employee Unions

Registration is a formal act which must be performed by the Registrar of Friendly Societies, on the application of at least seven authorised union members,[7] provided a number of formal requirements are satisfied,[8] and in addition the union must have certain compulsory rules (regarding, *inter alia,* the purposes for which funds may be used, members' qualifications for benefit,

1. Trade Union Act 1871, s.2.
2. Ibid., s.3. On the consequences of this see below.
3. Ibid., s.4. See below.
4. Trade Disputes Act 1906, s.4(1).
5. Trade Union Act 1913, s.3.
6. Trade Union Act 1871, s.6.
7. Ibid. The Trade Union Regulations 1876, reg. 3, empower the Registrar to require evidence of authorisation.
8. These requirements are set out in Trade Union Act 1871, ss.13–16 and sch. 1; Trade Union Act 1913, s.2; the Trade Union (Amalgamations) Act 1964, and in the Trade Union Regulations 1876. For a full discussion see Citrine, pp. 146–62; 231–39.

fines and forfeitures, the appointment and removal of officers and trustees, and the audit and inspection of accounts).[9] The Registrar may not register a union if he does not consider it to be a "trade union" for statutory purposes, or if any of its objects are unlawful,[10] or if its name is identical with or so nearly resembles the name of an existing trade union, registered or unregistered, as to be likely to deceive members of the public.[11] An appeal from the Registrar's refusal to register a union may be made to the High Court (or, in Scotland, Court of Session), within a two month period, which may be extended. But it is to be noted that the Registrar cannot reject *part* of a union's rule book; his legal duty is simply to see that the prescribed conditions are satisfied. In practice he makes suggestions for improvements which are usually acted upon.

The advantages of registration are not very significant. A registered union enjoys certain tax and administrative benefits which an unregistered union does not; a registered union can sue and be sued in its own name (subject to the immunity enjoyed by all unions, whether registered or not, against actions founded in tort), whereas litigation by or against an unregistered body is procedurally impracticable in England, Wales, and Northern Ireland.[12] Registration is also conclusive evidence that it is a trade union,[13] but even an unregistered union may obtain a certificate from the Registrar of Friendly Societies that it is a trade union in law and this is similarly conclusive.[14] The main benefit from registration is probably the psychological one of affording members and the public some outward token that it is a properly and well-conducted union.

9. Trade Union Act 1871, s.14, sch. 1; Trade Union Act 1876, s.14 (dissolution); Trade Union Act 1913, s.3 (political rules of political objects are adopted). The latter provision also applies to unregistered unions.

10. Trade Union Act 1871, s.6 (i.e. unlawful for any reason other than being a restraint of trade).

11. Ibid., s.13(3); and see the Trade Union (Amalgamations) Act 1964, s.6, and Trade Union Regulations 1964, reg. 9, regarding changes of name.

12. For a full discussion see Citrine, pp. 146 et seq. In Scotland a procedural device permits unincorporated bodies to sue and be sued in their own name. Scottish members of U.K. unions are thus more amenable to legal process than their English and Northern Irish counterparts.

13. Trade Union Act 1913, s.2(1).

14. Ibid., s.2(3) (5). There is an appeal to the High Court (in Scotland, Court of Session) against the Registrar's decision. Certificates may be withdrawn in defined circumstances (e.g. wilful and continued violation of the T.U. Acts, or if the principal objects are no longer statutory ones): Trade Union Act 1876, s.8; Trade Union Act 1913, s.2(2).

The vast majority of organisations of public employees have *not* sought registration. Of 118 organisations listed in the DEP's Directory of Trade Unions, as at June 1969, as being solely or mainly concerned with employees of national government, the educational services, medical and dental services, and local government, only 14 were *registered* as trade unions. A list of these organisations will be found in Table 1.

Table 1.

Employees' Organizations, Solely or Mainly Active in Public Services, Registered Under the Trade Union Acts 1871–1964 (as at June 1969)[1]

1. *National Government*[2]
Civil Service Clerical Association now called Civil & Public Services Assn.
Civil Service Union
Society of Technical Civil Servants[3]
Customs & Excise Federation
Customs & Excise Preventive Staff Assn.
Inland Revenue Staff Fed.
Min. of Labour Staff Assn.
County Court Officers Assn.
Prison Officers Assn.
  Number of unregistered organisations: 31

2. *Educational Services*
Assn. of Teachers in Technical Institutions
  Number of unregistered organisations: 38

3. *Medical and Dental Services*
Medical Practitioners' Union
Confederation of Health Service Employees
Health Visitors' Assn.
  Number of unregistered organisations: 13

4. *Local Government Service*
National and Local Govt. Officers' Assn.
Fire Brigades Union
Nat. Union of Public Employees
Greater London Council Staff Assn.
  Number of unregistered organisations: 19

Source: Ministry of Labour, Directory of Employers' Associations, Trade Unions, Joint Organisations etc. (1960, with amendments to June 1969)

1. Postal services are not included here. Some 7 of the 19 unions in those services are registered.
2. Nonindustrial civil service only. Many of the general workers' and industrial unions which are active in both the private sector and in government and local authority undertakings are registered.
3. This Society has decided to merge with the Institution of Professional Civil Servants (unregistered).

The registered unions, solely or mainly active in the public services, represent less than half the total union membership in those services. This is in marked contrast to the position in the economy as a whole, in which there were some 345 registered unions representing over 87 percent of all union members. The proportions for the public services are given in Table 2.

Table 2.

Proportion of Total Trade Union Membership in the Public Services Represented by Registered Unions (as at the end of 1967)[1]

	%
National government services	53.2
Educational services[2]	0
Medical & dental services[3]	32.5
Local Government services	45.8

Sources: (For total union membership) *Employment & Productivity Gazette,* November 1968, p. 911.
(For registered unions) Report of the Chief Registrar of Friendly Societies for the Year 1967. Part 4. Trade Unions (1968).

1. The classifications used here are the Registrar-General's *Standard Occupational Classifications.* As indicated in the next two notes, these do not tally exactly with the classifications used in the Ministry of Labour's *Directory* on which Table 1 above is based.

2. The ATTI (see above, Table 1) *sub. nom.* "Educational services" appears to have been classified under "local government services" by the Chief Registrar of Friendly Societies.

3. These are not separately listed by the Chief Registrar but form the major part of the Standard Classification for "all other professional and scientific services." The percentage is expressed in terms of the number of union members in that classification.

The significantly lower proportions of registered unions in the public services (particularly in education and in medical and dental services) may be due to several factors. As we shall see later, several of these organisations are not trade unions in law and so cannot be registered. Those which are trade unions may feel that they are unlikely to commit torts and so do not require the evidential security afforded by registration or certification. By setting up their provident funds as separate societies they can obviate the tax disadvantages suffered by unregistered unions (this is the case, for example, with the National Union of Teachers).[15] Most important of all, several public em-

15. RCME (30/12/65) Q. 1476 et seq. (Chief Registrar of Friendly Societies).

ployee organisations have found it to be to their advantage to maintain an ambiguous position by avoiding the formal step of applying for registration as a trade union. An example in this regard is the National Union of Teachers (whose legal status we shall examine presently) which has been able until very recently to maintain the image of a professional association ("it considers itself," said the Chief Registrar of Friendly Societies of this Union in 1965, "to be . . . like the British Medical Association"[16]) while at the same time engaging in collective bargaining. Had the NUT applied for registration it would not only have lost an image which it apparently valued, but it would also have *conceded* the illegality of its practice of supporting parliamentary candidates and MPs (of all three main political parties), without approved political fund rules.[17]

This very ambiguity has led to resentment on the part of certain unions in the private sector. The Draughtsmens' & Allied Technicians Union (DATA) has complained that the apparent immunity of the NUT "creates a feeling that the law is not applied equally to all unions."[18] Similarly the National Association of State Enrolled Nurses (not a trade union) has disclosed that it experiences difficulties in its relations with trade unions of health service employees because of its nonregistration. It asked the Donovan Commission (without success) to propose in its Report that professional bodies which engage in collective bargaining as a subsidiary object should be entitled to register as trade unions.[19]

These difficulties stem no doubt from the present definition of "trade union," but registration is the badge of trade union status, and so long as it remains a voluntary matter it is possible for organisations which engage in collective bargaining to avoid any definitive inquiry into their legal status. As Mr. George Woodcock said to the Chief Registrar of Friendly Societies:

16. Ibid., paras. 1414–19.
17. Registration would be conclusive evidence of its obligation to have such rules; on the other hand, nonregistration does not imply that the body is not in law a trade union so as to exempt it from the political fund rules if it pursues political objects as defined in the Trade Union Act 1913.
18. RCME (17/5/66) para. 202, p. 1548 (DATA).
19. RCWE (1966) by Nat. Assn. of State Enrolled Nurses, p. 3.

"Neither you nor the NUT know whether they are a trade union or not."[20]

At the present time registration has no legal effect whatsoever on the questions of free association, recognition and bargaining, or (apart from the evidential advantage) the statutory immunity of trade unions from tort actions. However, the Donovan Commission[21] proposed that in future all unions should be given corporate status (so resolving many of the moot problems which have arisen about the legal capacity of both registered and unregistered unions)[22] and be obliged to register, and a majority of the Commission wanted the immunity of the first limb of section 3 of the Trade Disputes Act 1906 (which says that no action may be maintained against "any person" who induces another to break his contract of employment in the course or furtherance of a trade dispute) to be confined to registered unions and those acting on their behalf.[23] The aim of the latter suggestion was to expose unofficial strikers to civil liabilities. As the minority pointed out, this would mean that even those who gave strike notice[24] might be sued for damages or an injunction on grounds of civil conspiracy. The result would be to curtail seriously the existing liberties of nonunionists and even of union members who lack official authority to take or exhort strike action. This would jeopardise particularly shop stewards who stand outside the formal constitutional structure of most British unions.[25] It would illegalise action taken in the course of recognition disputes where employees have not yet managed to gather sufficient strength to form and register a trade union. It would, above all else, introduce a fundamental shift in British labour law by limiting immunity to the functionaries of state-registered corporations. An

20. RCME (30/12/65) Q. 1481. He added that if the NUT applied for TUC membership (as a "bona fide trade union") it would be "immediately accepted." This in fact occurred in 1970.

21. Cmnd. 3623, 1968, paras. 788–805.

22. For a full discussion of the legal complexities, see Citrine, pp. 173–75.

23. The Commission did not explain what this mean), but according to Lord Tangley (in his Note of Reservation, p. 287) it me ins "those acting in an authorised capacity."

24. This assumes that strike notice offers meaningful protection: see Chap. VIII.

25. See McCarthy, *The Role of Shop Stewards in British Industrial Relations*. R.C. Research Paper No. 1 (HMSO, 1967), pp. 5 et seq.

important side effect of this would be to deprive the officers and members of bodies which are not "trade unions" in law of the equal protection of the law which they at present enjoy with all other persons. Paradoxically, one of the results of the majority Donovan proposal, if implemented, would be to induce professional associations, which are at present in an ambiguous legal position, to crystallise their trade union objectives and to seek registration.

The Conservative Government[26] is likely to introduce legislation which goes even further than Donovan proposed, by using compulsory registration as a vehicle for regulating internal union affairs. Only registered unions, which would have corporate status, would have a new *legal* right to trade union recognition by employers; only *registered* unions would have the right to initiate statutory machinery for the arbitration or conciliation of disputes;[27] and only they would enjoy immunity from actions in tort and then only in the circumstances of a "lawful" trade dispute which is not in breach of an agreement.

c. The Definition of "Trade Union"

These present, and possible future, distinctions between a body which is in law a "trade union" and one which is not (including the possibility of registration) make it essential for us to discuss the legal definition of a "trade union" (which involves, as well, the definition of "workman") and, in the light of this, to examine the legal status of certain bodies active in the field of public employment.

The present composite definition of a trade union (to be found in the acts of 1871, 1876 and 1913) is

any combination, whether temporary or permanent, the principal objects of which are under its constitution statutory

26. See its pre-election policies set out in *Fair Deal at Work* (CPC, 1968), pp. 19, 21–22. While in office Labour made proposals which did not go as far as those made by Donovan: see *In Place of Strife,* Cmnd. 3888, paras. 101–13, and Industrial Relations Bill 1970.

27. At present any "organisation of employees" can invoke the provisions of the Terms and Conditions of Employment Act 1959, s.8, and any party to a "trade dispute" (as defined) may report it to the Secretary of State who may refer it for arbitration to the Industrial Court under the Industrial Courts Act 1919. Under the now repealed Order 1376 of 1951 only a "trade union" (as defined in the 1871–1913 acts) could report an issue or dispute.

objects [namely] the regulation of relations between workmen and masters, or between workmen and workmen, or between masters and masters, or the imposing of restrictive conditions on the conduct of any trade or business, and also the provision of benefits to members.

An organisation of persons working for government may not fall within this definition for one or more reasons: (1) they may not seek to *regulate* relations or to *impose* restrictive conditions as their *principal* objects; (2) even if these are principal objects, the relations may not be between *workmen* and masters or *workmen* and *workmen*, or the conditions may not be imposed on the conduct of *any trade or business*.

(1) *Principal objects.* In the first category would fall those organisations which engage in collective bargaining but which are *principally* concerned with the general promotion of professional efficiency and training. The Registrar of Friendly Societies has regarded organisations such as the National Union of Teachers[28] (whose principal objects as set out in its written constitution are "to raise the status of the teaching profession" and to advise educational authorities) and the National Association of State Enrolled Nurses (which has two statutory, i.e. trade union, objects in its written constitution but, additionally, seeks "to foster a spirit of professional relationship") as not being trade unions. It is a matter of controversy whether the Registrar, and the courts, should confine their investigations to the *written* constitutions of such organisations or should, additionally, consider their actual practice.[29] The Registrar seems to be prepared to consider factors such as the ways in which the organisation has expended its funds and whether it is affiliated to the TUC.[30] It is not necessary to pursue this legal controversy here. It is sufficient to observe that most professional and higher-grade

28. RCME (30/12/65) Q. 1414. This was in 1960–61 on a complaint made to the Registrar that the NUT was not observing the political fund rules.
29. Citrine, p. 397, considers the arguments in detail.
30. RCME (30/12/65) Q. 1416. The Donovan Commission (Cmnd. 3623), para. 766, proposed a new definition which would have obliged the Registrar to look at the principal *activities* of the organization. It is beyond doubt that the activities of the NUT bring it within the statutory definition (note in particular its strike policy and its application for TUC affiliation in 1970). However, the Labour Government's Industrial Relations Bill 1970 did not implement the Donovan proposal.

Table 3.

Principal Written Objects of Selected Organizations

Assn. of First Division Civil Servants	"To promote the efficiency of the civil service, and to represent and further the interests of members, as regards their careers, conditions of service and matters of common concern."
Assn. of Grade I Officers, Ministry of Labour	"To safeguard and advance the interests of its members and to promote the efficiency of the service."
Assn. of H.M. Inspectors of Taxes	"To watch over and consider all matters, legislative and departmental, affecting the Service, with a view to safeguarding and promoting the interests of H. M. Inspectors of Taxes."
Assn. of Local Government Finance Officers	"To do all such things as from time to time may be necessary to elevate the status and pursue the advancement of the interests of the profession."
Assn. of Teachers of Domestic Science	"To safeguard the professional status of teachers of domestic science . . . [and] to provide a means of communicating resolutions and suggestions to [educational] authorities."
Health Visitors Assn.[1]	"To safeguard the interests and improve the status of Health Visitors."
National Assn. of Schoolmasters[1]	"To endeavor to secure separate consideration of the claims of schoolmasters . . . [and] to afford H. M. Government and other organisations . . . the advice and experience of the Associated Schoolmasters."
Nat. Assn. of Inspectors of Schools	"To provide a means whereby professional interests may be safeguarded."
Nat. Assn. of Head Teachers	"To provide a ready means of communication, of ascertaining and giving expression to their opinions and of taking action, when necessary, on behalf of Head Teachers throughout the country . . . [and] to uphold the high standard of professional conduct among teachers."
Nat. Union of Teachers[1]	"To afford [educational authorities] the advice and experience of the associated teachers . . . [and] to raise the status of teachers."
Royal College of Nursing and National Council of Nurses in the U. K. (royal charter)	"To promote and advance nursing as a profession."
British Medical Assn. (incorporated)	"To promote the medical and allied sciences, and to maintain the honour and interests of the medical profession."

1. Affiliated to TUC (whose constitution limits membership to "bona fide trade unions")

48

organisations, which in practice engage in collective bargaining, are in an ambiguous legal position. Table 3 contains examples of what appear to be the principal objects (as set out in their *written* constitutions) of some of these bodies whose legal status is uncertain; the list is not meant to be exhaustive.

None of these bodies possesses the power under its constitution to compel its members to strike or otherwise to "impose restrictive conditions"; accordingly, their legal status depends entirely upon the question whether or not their *principal* objects are to regulate relations—and, in this context, there is legal controversy about the meaning of "regulate." We need not go into this controversy here, except to observe that some organisations deliberately shelter behind vaguely worded object clauses in order to leave room to doubt whether they actually seek to *control* conditions of employment (which, according to one view, is what "regulate" implies[31]).

A further complication is that several organisations of employees in the health and educational services have obtained incorporation under the Companies Acts, invariably as companies limited by guarantee.[32] Some of these have obtained a licence from the Board of Trade to dispense with the word "Limited" as the last word of their name (an obligation otherwise attaching to companies),[33] and so it is not possible to draw up a complete list of these bodies simply by reference to the list of employees' organisations in the DEP's *Directory*.[34] Nevertheless, Table 4 lists some of the bodies which are incorporated as companies. The importance of incorporation under the Companies Acts is

31. For a full discussion, see Citrine, p. 401.

32. This means that each member undertakes to contribute to the assets of the company in certain circumstances such amount as may be required not exceeding a specified amount. The memoranda of association of most of these companies also contain a clause to the effect that the income and property of the company shall be applied solely to the promotion of its objects and that none of it shall be paid or transferred to members.

33. This is permitted by s.19 of the Companies Act 1948, if the Board is satisfied that the company is formed to promote "commerce, art, science religion, charity or any other useful object and intends to apply its . . . income in promoting its objects and to prohibit the payment of any dividend to its members."

34. The Registrar of Companies keeps no index or register which would enable these employees' organisations to be identified. He has reported that (in 1965) there were 118 *employers'* associations on his register: RCWE /153/ 1965 (Registrar of Companies). On the latter problem see M. A. Hickling, "Trade Unions in Disguise," (1964) 27 MLR 625.

Table 4.

Organisations of Educational and Health Service Employees Incorporated under the Companies Act

	Negotiating body (if any) on which represented on staff side
Assn. of Headmistresses (Incorporated)	None
Inc. Assn. of Asst. Masters in Secondary Schools	None
Inc. Assn. of Head Masters	None
Inc. British Assn. for Physical Training	None
British Dental Assn.	Dental WC*
British Medical Assn.	Medical WC
Institute of Hospital Administrators	Admin & Clerical WC
Society of Male Nurses Ltd.	None
Junior Hospital Doctors Assn. Ltd.	None
Assn. of Dispensing Opticians Ltd.	Optical WC
British Dietetic Assn.	Prof. & Tech. WC
British Orthoptic Society	Prof. & Tech. WC
Institute of Almoners	Prof. & Tech. WC
Co-operative Union Ltd.	Pharmaceutical WC
Company Chemists Ltd.	Pharmaceutical WC

*WC = Whitley Council

that these bodies have in effect declared a decision not to be regarded as trade unions in law, although they engage in direct consultation with management and, in many cases, are members of joint negotiating bodies. This decision is implicit in the fact of incorporation because section 5(3) of the Trade Union Act 1871 provides that the Companies Acts "shall not apply to any trade union, and the registration of any trade union under any of the said [Companies] Acts shall be void."[35] If any of these organisations are trade unions in law their incorporation is void and their legal status is that of unregistered unions. In view of this the Registrar of Companies until 1965 required a proposed company with written objects analogous to those of a trade union to insert in its objects clause a statement to the following effect: "Provided always that the objects of

35. This applies as well to registration under the Friendly Societies Acts and Industrial and Provident Societies Acts.

the company shall not extend to any of the purposes mentioned in [the Trade Union Acts]." The legal effect of this statement is that any attempt at "regulation" or "restriction" (which is implicit in agreements of joint negotiating bodies) by the officers of the association is *ultra vires* and void. This raises the possibility of legal action by any member of the association to restrain the association from participating in collective bargaining. This has not turned out to be a serious danger in practice, but, according to Clegg and Chester,[36] it has been enough to persuade certain incorporated associations in the health services to hold back from formal negotiations, and led professional staff bodies to adopt the device of setting up a separate professional staffs association (unincorporated) to serve as the staff side of the Joint Negotiating Committee for Hospital Staffs and to affiliate themselves to it.

Somewhat anomalously those bodies which are incorporated by charter (such as the Royal College of Nurses and the Royal College of Midwives, which are represented on the Nurses and Midwives Whitley Council) are not similarly debarred by their constitutions or the Trade Union Acts from engaging in statutory trade union objects, nor are they subject to regulation under the provisions of the Companies Acts.[37] Like companies, these chartered corporations enjoy the advantages (not shared by other bodies with "trade union" objects) that the legal liability of their members is limited, they have legal continuity despite changes in membership and do not need trustees because they have the right to own property in the corporate name.

(2) *Who are "workmen"?* Uncertainty about the legal status of professional associations because of the "principal objects" definition is not peculiar to organisations active in the field of public employment, but the interpretation of the terms "workmen" and "trade or business" in the legal definition of a "trade union" does introduce special problems for organisations of those engaged in the public services.

36. H. A. Clegg & T. E. Chester, *Wage Policy and the Health Service* (Oxford, Blackwell 1957), p. 11.
37. The Companies Act 1948, s.435, which applies certain provisions of that act to all bodies corporate, does not cover nonprofit-making bodies (s.435(2)(b)).

There is no statutory definition of "workmen" in the Trade Union Act 1871, and it is probable that in ordinary usage in 1871 and 1876 the word meant a manual worker.[38] In 1906, when the legislature had to define a trade dispute for purposes of immunity from tort actions, the term "workmen" was defined for those purposes as "all persons employed in trade or industry."[39] The Chief Registrar has taken the view that this restrictive definition should not be applied to the interpretation of "workmen" in the 1871 definition of a "trade union." As early as 1896 the Devonport Government Labourers' Union was registered as a trade union, and since the enactment of the 1906 definition, organisations of local government, educational and medical employees, and Crown servants have been registered. (See Table 1 above for the list at June 1969.) This practice has never been challenged. The position of organisations of Crown servants is particularly interesting because, as we have seen, it is far from clear that Crown servants are "employees," i.e. under a contract of service. This means that the Registrar has been prepared to give a very wide interpretation to the word "workmen." The Donovan Commission proposed a new definition of trade union confining the term to combinations of "employees." Its definition of "employee" (based on that in the Industrial Courts Act 1919, section 8) is restricted to those who have a "contract with an employer" (or at least once had a contract which has since been terminated). The effect of this would be to cast serious doubt on the legal status of organisations of Crown servants, a particularly serious ambiguity if the other Donovan proposals about certain statutory immunities being confined to registered *trade unions* were to be implemented.[40]

In the case of local government employees, there are important (but not binding) judicial opinions from the highest appellate tribunal (the House of Lords) that administrative, professional, and technical officials of a municipal corporation may be "workmen,"[41] and, indeed, that the term is hospitable enough to

38. The Employers and Workmen Act 1875, s.10, limited the definition of "workman" for purposes of that act to those engaged in manual labour.
39. Trade Disputes Act 1906, s.5(3). This is discussed in Chap. VIII below.
40. Cmnd. 3623, paras. 767, 821. This difficulty was resolved in the ex-Labour Government's Industrial Relations Bill 1970, cl.1, by making express reference to those in Crown service.
41. *NALGO* v. *Bolton Corporation* [1943] A.C. 166, 175 (Viscount

include all wage and salary earners. But this is not free from doubt.

The Donovan Commission proposed that the definition of "trade union" should be narrowed by removing the "imposing of restrictive conditions on the conduct of any trade or business."[42] The purpose of this is to remove from the ambit of "trade union" law those trade associations which have nothing to do with labour relations. The phrase "trade or business" also creates doubts about the status of some associations of public employees which do not engage in collective bargaining. For example, if an association of hospital doctors did not seek to *regulate* labour relations, it could, at present, only be regarded as a trade union if its principal object was imposing restrictive conditions on the conduct of "any trade or business." The view has been taken by the Chief Registrar of Friendly Societies (in 1918 in dealing with the Kent Medical Guild application for registration[43]) that a medical practitioner could not be engaged in a "trade" but that his practice was a "business." He defined "business" as "anything which occupies the time and attention of a man for the purposes of profit."[44] This would clearly not include the hospital doctor (as opposed to the part-time consultant who may engage in limited private practice). Since the

Simon), 184–85 (Lord Wright), 192 (Lord Porter) over the doubts of Lord Thankerton, 182. Viscount Simon, 176, expressly noted that there can be a "trade" union to which the higher grades of officers of a municipal corporation may belong, and Lord Wright, 185, said "Professions have their trade unions." The actual decision was concerned with the definition of "workmen" in the definition of a "trade dispute," for the purposes of wartime Order 1305 of 1940. The definition was the same as that in the Industrial Courts Act 1919, s.8 (on which, as we have seen, the Donovan proposals for a new definition are based). It omitted the phrase "employed in trade or industry" which appears in the Trade Disputes Act 1906, s.5(3), a fact which at least Lord Atkin, 181, thought to be significant. In later cases concerned with this definition, the following were held to be "workmen": schoolteachers (*Re Birkenhead Corp.* [1952] Ch. 359); laboratory technicians employed by a university (*R* v. *Industrial Disputes Tribunal, ex p. Queen Mary College* [1957] 2 Q.B. 483). See generally Citrine, pp. 608–13, and the discussion of "trade disputes" in Chap. VIII, below.

42. Cmnd. 3623, para. 766. This was followed in the (lapsed) Industrial Relations Bill 1970.

43. Report of the Chief Registrar of Friendly Societies for 1918, p. 26. For a critique, see Citrine, pp. 404–06. At present, the Medical Practitioners' Union is registered as a trade union.

· 44. They also involve consideration of the cases on the meaning of "trade or industry" for purposes of the Trade Disputes Act 1906.

imposing of restrictive conditions is simply a residuary object, however, and public employee organisations do in practice seek to regulate labour relations, these difficulties have not, so far, had to be faced. It is hoped that the Donovan reforms would resolve them.

d. Summary

We conclude, then, that the organisations of public employees stand in a much more ambiguous legal position than is the case with organisations concerned principally with workers in private industry. In part this is attributable to the tension between the professional and trade union objects of many organisations; in part it is due to the historical circumstances in which trade unions emerged from the shadows of common law illegality. This ambiguity has had both advantages and disadvantages for the public employee organisations. Among the advantages have been the opportunities presented for avoiding the requirements of the Trade Union Acts in regard to political objects, for seeking the benefits of incorporation either under the Companies Acts or by way of charter, and for maintaining the image of a professional body while enjoying the benefits of collective bargaining. Among the disadvantages have been a certain amount of hostility from private sector unions, and inhibitions on bargaining introduced by that hostility and by the possibilities of legal action to restrain them from bargaining. In the future these disadvantages are likely to increase, in particular if current proposals for compulsory registration of trade unions are implemented, proposals for the removal of certain statutory immunities from all but registered trade unions and the Conservative Party plan for linking the right to recognition with registration.

2. THE RIGHT TO ASSOCIATE

There is no legally guaranteed "right" to belong to an employees' organisations in either the public or private sector. This is so although the U.K. has ratified two ILO Conventions, Nos. 87 and 98 (dealing with freedom of association and the right to organise and bargain collectively), as well as the European Social Charter and the Council of Europe Convention for the Protection of Human Rights and Fundamental Freedoms, which recognise these rights.

However, certain types of antiunion discrimination may shortly become illegal if proposals of the Donovan Commission[45] are implemented. The first proposal is to make it a term of all contracts of employment, with certain exceptions, that the employer shall not obstruct the employee from belonging to an independent trade union, i.e. one which is not under the domination or control of an employer. This will not, however, preclude the employer from limiting the employee's choice to or as between independent trade unions that he recognises. Nor will it prohibit discrimination against trade unionists in *engagement* for employment, i.e. before the worker has a contract of employment. The limitation of this legal right to those "under a contract of employment," with certain exceptions, means that the position of Crown servants is left in doubt, and those who are self-employed (a growing phenomenon particularly in the construction industry) are definitely excluded, as are the police.

The second proposal, which would apply to Crown employment but not to the police or forms of self-employment, is to grant a legal remedy in respect of unfair dismissal, including dismissal for membership of an independent trade union or for refusing to join a nonindependent trade union, for trade union activity which, if in working time, has the consent of the employer or is in accordance with agreed arrangements, or for making a complaint or taking part in any other legal action, in good faith, against the employer. This proposal would also not apply to teachers in Scotland, for whom similar provisions already exist under the Education (Scotland) Act 1962, section 85.

Neither of these projected reforms is likely to be of much practical importance to unions in the public services, because freedom from acts of antiunion discrimination was achieved, without the aid of legislation, in the civil service before 1900, and in most sectors of local government by 1945. This section begins with an analysis of the reasons for this extra-legal achievement, and this is followed by a description of the exceptional case of the police.

"Freedom of association" may also be regarded as including

---

45. Cmnd. 3623, paras. 245, 545–65. These were put into legislative form in the ex-Labour Government's Industrial Relations Bill 1970.

the individual's free choice of union; in the second part of this section we consider the institutional limitations on this freedom. Finally, we shall give a brief account of the extent of interference by the courts and Parliament in the internal affairs of employee organisations in the public services.

a. The Extra-Legal Achievement of Freedom of Association

There are two reasons for the fact that the public employee organisations have found it unnecessary to press for legislation against antiunion discrimination.

The first reason is that the public employee organisations emerged *after* the trade unions had won their charter of legality. In the period 1870 to 1890 the nascent civil service unions encountered administrative hostility rather than legal disability. There was, however, a belief, "held on no foundation whatever but held religiously by the staff, which formed secret committees, and by the officials, who vigorously punished agitators,"[46] that combination was forbidden in the civil service. It was not until 1898 that this belief was finally laid to rest by the Secretary of the Treasury, who informed the House of Commons: "Officials of [the postal] department are at liberty to combine in any way they think proper. They may, except during official hours, meet when and where they like. . . . All the privileges which trade unions enjoy . . . are thus accorded to the unions of postal officials."[47] The recognition of this "liberty" throughout the public services was, therefore, the outcome of the earlier victory of the general trade union movement. Moreover, before the general strike of 1926, public service unions were not concerned with legal attacks on trade unionism.

There was, however, one period in which some of the civil service unions conducted a fight against a legal restriction on their freedom of association. This was between 1927 and 1946. Until 1927 there was no prohibition against affiliation of civil service unions with the Trades Union Congress and the Labour Party. Over a thirty-year period the associations of the lower grades of civil servants had come to align themselves with the

46. G. H. Stuart-Bunning (a founder of the Union of Post Office Workers) as quoted by L. D. White, *Whitley Councils in the British Civil Service* (Chicago, 1933), p. 292.
47. Hansard (4th ser.) vol. LIII, col. 1136 (18 February 1898).

wider labour movement. The Baldwin (Conservative) Government used the general strike of 1926 as an opportunity to curb this development. The civil service had not gone on strike in 1926 but many service unions had given financial aid to the strikers. Although there was no truth in the Attorney-General's claim that "organisations of civil servants . . . were, through their officials, actively engaged in fomenting a rebellion against the state,"[48] the service unions did not deny that they had supported the strikers. They justified this on the ground that they were bound to support fellow trade unionists in their attempt to protect outside wages, since those wages were the standard by which service pay was measured.

Fierce union opposition was unable to prevent the enactment of the Trade Disputes and Trade Unions Act 1927. Section 5 of this measure provided:

> Amongst the regulations as to the conditions of service in His Majesty's civil establishments there shall be included regulations prohibiting established civil servants from being members, delegates or representatives of any organisation of which the primary object is to influence or affect the remuneration and conditions of employment of its members, unless the organisation is an organisation of which the membership is confined to persons employed by or under the Crown and is an organisation which complies with such provisions as may be contained in the regulations for securing that it is in all respects independent of, and not affiliated to, any such organisation as aforesaid the membership of which is not confined to persons employed by or under the Crown or any federation, comprising such organisations, that its objects do not include political objects, and that it is not associated directly or indirectly with any political party or organisation.

The penalty for disobedience, after a warning, was disqualification from membership of the civil service. The Attorney-General could apply for an injunction to prevent the use of union funds in contravention of this measure.

To the disappointment of the unions, the Labour Government

48. Hansard (5th ser.) vol. CCV, col. 1332 (7 May 1927). See too Sir John Simon, *Three Speeches on the General Strike* (London, 1926), p. 15.

which came to power in 1929 did not repeal the act, apparently on the grounds that it was necessary in order to maintain the nonpolitical character of the service. It should be remembered, however, that the effect of section 5 was not only that the service unions had to sever their links with the Labour Party and TUC, but also that they could not associate with other professional bodies and international civil service organisations.

It was left to the Labour Government, elected at the end of the Second World War, to repeal the act in 1946.[49] Only the Union of Post Office Workers then chose to reaffiliate to the Labour Party, but fourteen civil service associations representing 634,036 members are now affiliated to the TUC. (Four of these are postal unions.)

It may be said, then, that apart from the period in which the Trade Disputes and Trade Unions Act 1927 was in force, the civil service unions had not been subjected to legal restrictions. This made it unnecessary for them to demand any specific legal status which had not already been won by the general trade union movement. Paradoxically, the 1927 act had one curious side effect which set the seal of legality on the service unions. The regulations made by the Treasury in terms of section 5 required the unions concerned to obtain a certificate from the Registrar of Friendly Societies to the effect that they had complied with the regulations. Unlike the provisions of the Trade Union Act 1871, under which union registration was (and is) purely voluntary, the Treasury regulations made certification of the union a *precondition* of union membership.

The second, and more important, reason why the public service unions have not sought any legal guarantee of freedom of association is the fact that since 1906 there has been an official policy of *encouraging* trade union membership among service employees. This started in a small way with the advent of the Liberal Government in 1906. The Liberal Postmaster-General, Mr. Sidney Buxton, declared that "the stronger and more representative the associations [of postal employees] became, the less would be the friction, and the more easy it would be to arrive at a conclusion satisfactory to both sides."[50] This

49. Trade Disputes and Trade Unions Act 1946.
50. Hansard (4th ser.) vol. CLIX, col. 396.

gave a great boost to union organisation. No less than seventeen new associations were formed in 1906, and by the outbreak of the First World War there were seventy-three in the civil service.

The MacDonnell Commission in 1914 reflected the official view when it reported that

> We do not doubt that generally such associations serve a useful and worthy purpose in promoting cooperation amongst many individuals serving under similar conditions; and we are glad to find that the heads of public departments generally "recognise" such Associations in the sense of receiving from them directly representations on matters affecting their interests.[51]

Then occurred two unique events which ensured the present strength and character of public employee unions. The first was the economic and social crisis produced by the First World War. Within the service this produced a united effort which reduced official hostility to the lower grades; externally it produced a general acceptance by the upper and middle classes of the inevitability of industrial unionism and at the same time a fear of postwar radical political unionism. We have seen that one consequence of this last fear was the act of 1927; a consequence of the other changes wrought by the war was the acceptance of the full implications of civil service unionism. The second event was the Government's decision in 1919 to apply the Whitley scheme, originally invented for industry, to national and local government. This decision, discussed in an earlier chapter, was taken in the immediate postwar euphoria of reconstruction and hope for a better social order. There was an unreal sense of national prosperity in which Treasury control was temporarily at a minimum. By 1921 the psychological atmosphere had changed and the desperate financial and economic situation became apparent. Yet Whitleyism had been established in the civil service, and with it came the crucial official decision to encourage union organisation in the unorganised grades, throughout the civil service. The official policy then, as now, was that "the existence of fully representative associations not only promotes good staff rela-

51. P.P. 1914, xvi, p. 98.

tions but is essential to effective negotiations on conditions of service."[52]

This policy is today followed throughout the public service. Moreover, government seeks to act as a model employer in this regard. Since 1946 the Fair Wages Resolution of the House of Commons has recommended government departments to include in their commercial contracts with suppliers a standard clause that "the contractor shall recognise the freedom of his work-people to be members of trade unions." Most local authorities and nationalised industries include a similar clause in their contracts for works, supplies, and services.[53] The most important sanction for violation of the clause is the threat of termination of contract and the removal of the offender's name from the list of officially approved contractors.

Favourable official attitudes to union activities are reflected in the growth of the checkoff system, which is wide spread in central and local government. A study in 1966 showed that 32.2 per cent of trade union members in central and local government and 46.8 per cent in public corporations were on checkoff.[54] These percentages included members of the key public service unions. Indeed, the largest proportion of checkoff membership is to be found in unions which have all or most of their interests in public employment. Since 1966 this tendency has grown, especially in local government. From the point of view of this paper it is worth noting that no specific legal authority, apart from the express or implied agreement of the union member concerned, was required for this development of the checkoff system.[55]

Management facilitates union activities in other ways as well.

52. *Handbook for the New Civil Servant* (CSD).
53. In the period 1927–46, however, local authorities were expressly forbidden by the Trade Disputes and Trade Unions Act 1927, s.6(2), from inserting such clauses in any contracts. Today all local authorities are *obliged* by act of Parliament to include such a clause in their housing contracts: Housing (Scotland) Act 1950, s.181; Housing Act 1957, s.92.
54. A. I. Marsh and J. W. Staples, *Check-off Agreements in Britain*, Royal Commission on Trade Unions and Employers' Associations. Research Paper No. 8 (1968).
55. There was for some time doubt whether workers whose work is predominantly *manual* could agree to check-offs because of the provisions of the Truck Act 1831, but the case of *Hewlett* v. *Allen* [1894] A.C. 383 is generally understood to have saved check-off arrangements from illegality.

It is an established practice for special leave and time off on full pay to be granted for attendance at Whitley Council meetings and other negotiations. However, most government departmets have local rules that union activities (e.g. collection of subscriptions) and meetings should be conducted outside office hours and, in some cases, off the working premises. Breach of these "rules" may, in some instances, be regarded as a disciplinary matter.

b. The Police

The only group of civilian public employees whose freedom of association is expressly restricted by law is the police. The Police Act 1964, section 47, (re-enacting with minor amendments the provisions of the Police Act 1919) makes it unlawful for a member of a police force to belong to "any trade union, or any association, having for its objects . . . to control or influence the pay, pensions, or conditions of service of any police force." (Any question whether a body is a "trade union" for this purpose has to be determined by the Chief Registrar of Friendly Societies.) In exceptional circumstances, a chief officer of police may permit a person who belonged to a trade union before joining the police to remain a member of that union.[56]

The background to this provision is the attempt which was made from 1913 onwards to form a National Union of Police and Prison Officers.[57] In 1918 this union was able to persuade almost every London constable and sergeant to join a brief strike. It was then crushed by the Government, but its success lay not only in the immediate improvement of the pay and conditions of Metropolitan police, but also in the setting up of a Committee of Inquiry under Lord Desborough. From the report of this Committee came proposals for Police Federations—one for England and Wales, and another for Scotland—to represent policemen.

The Federations were created by the Police Act 1919, which at the same time made it illegal for police officers to belong to a trade union. The National Union of Police and Prison

56. Police Act 1964, s.47(1).
57. Accounts will be found in A. Judge, *The First Fifty Years* (London, 1968); G. W. Reynolds and A. Judge, *The Night the Police Went on Strike* (London, 1968).

Officers called an abortive strike in 1919 in an attempt to prevent this, with tragic consequences for some of the 2,000 strikers, who were promptly dismissed by their police forces.[58] The Federation was branded as "the goose club"—to indicate that it would always move in close step with the authorities. The organisational pattern then adopted has remained in force ever since, with separate but equal representation for each of the three junior ranks of police—constables, sergeants, and inspectors. Since 1919 every police force has had to have a branch board of the Federation.

The Federations cannot be classed as "trade unions" either in fact or in law. Their objects are limited to matters concerning the "welfare and efficiency" of policemen, and questions affecting discipline and the promotion of individuals are expressly excluded from their scope.[59] They cannot take joint action with the labour movement because of a legal obligation to be "entirely independent of, and unassociated with, any body or person outside the police service."[60] Between the two world wars, the English Federation's historians write, "its impotence in the face of a forced lowering of conditions convinced most policemen of its inherent weakness as a company union and disheartened its national leaders."[61] However, in the period since the Second World War the position has changed radically. Legal restrictions on the work of the Federations have been eased, and at the same time they have become more militant and representative of policemen.

The shortage of policemen immediately after 1945 led to the appointment of a departmental committee under Lord Oaksey to investigate police pay and conditions.[62] This committee made important proposals for improving bargaining over pay and conditions, with ultimate recourse to arbitration. These proposals, implemented in 1953 and put on a new legal basis in 1964, will be discussed in Chapter V. The development of Whitley-type negotiating machinery has been one of the contributory causes of the growing strength and prestige of the Federations.

---

58. See Reynolds and Judge, op.cit., pp. 186 et seq.
59. Police Act 1964, s.44.
60. Ibid., s.44(2).
61. Reynolds and Judge, op.cit., p. 235.
62. Cmnd. 7831. Report of the Committee on Police Conditions of Service.

Another important factor has been the amendment of legal regulations to permit the Federations to raise voluntary contributions, instead of relying exclusively on police funds to carry out their activities as they did previously. These voluntary subscriptions are now made by over 95 per cent of the Federations' membership and enable them to engage outside administrative and professional assistance, to publish a journal, and to carry on other quasi-trade union activities.

In recent years there has been increasing discontent, particularly among lower ranks of policemen, at what they regard as "official neglect" of their problems, at the introduction of new organisational schemes, at their growing conflict with civil liberty and minority groups, and dissatisfaction with pay reviews. Yet apart from rumblings on the constables' committees, there has been no serious proposal for free trade unionism from within the ranks of the Federations. Successive governments have justified the restrictions on free association on the grounds that it is necessary to keep the police out of politics and to maintain their "impartiality" in trade disputes.

c. Free Choice of Union

So far "freedom of association" has been considered solely in the sense of freedom from antiunion discrimination. In practice, however, public employees do not enjoy unbridled freedom to join *any* union of their choice. It is true that there is no express *legal* barrier to their joining any of the large number of unions active in the sphere of public employment, or from forming new breakaways. The institutional limitations on freedom of choice are *indirect*.

i. THE CLOSED SHOP

We use this term, in the sense defined by McCarthy in the leading study,[63] to describe the situation "in which employees come to realise that a particular job is only to be obtained and retained if they become and remain members of one of a specified number of trade unions." In some cases the worker may have to belong to a particular union before he can get the job he seeks (the "pre-entry" shop); in others he may be obliged to join it soon after securing the job (the "post-entry"

63. W. E. J. McCarthy, *The Closed Shop in Britain* (Oxford, 1964), p. 3.

shop, which is fairly similar to what would be called the "union" shop in the U.S.).

Both types are of relatively minor importance to employees in the public services. McCarthy found, in 1964, that in industry as a whole some 16 per cent of employees were affected by closed shops, and that about two out of every five trade union members worked in a closed shop. In general, demands for a closed shop tended to arise as the level of organisation rose. The most significant exceptions to this rule existed among groups including nonindustrial civil servants, sections of the industrial civil service, and teachers and other nonmanual groups employed by local authorities.[64] In all these groups there was over 90 per cent unionisation, and in many there was 100 per cent voluntary membership. In the case of manual workers in the civil service and local government there were sometimes semiclosed shops (i.e. strong pressures to join but without the ultimate sanction of loss of job). But even here the pressures were not as strong as in commercial employment. McCarthy attributes this to several interrelated factors including the low labour turnover, the absence of a strike tradition and the satisfaction with recourse to arbitration, the absence of fears of an alternative labour force, favourable attitudes to union activities, and very real official opposition to the introduction of the closed shop. The reasons for this opposition, according to McCarthy, are:

> First, there is the conviction that the principles of Whitleyism presuppose "voluntary trade unionism." . . . Secondly, and more vaguely, one has the feeling talking to official side representatives, that they are particularly sensitive to the effect of public opinion. The Government, they suggest, would be subject to much hostile criticism if it were seen to be supporting coercion of the kind the closed shop is said to represent. This concern for adverse publicity shades over into the third reason advanced by officials; the consequences of recognising a right to the closed shop in fields like the civil service where there is only one employer. Finally there is the very practical objection that the high percentage of "established"

64. Ibid., p. 36, and pp. 36, 110 on the position in Admiralty yards.

civil servants would make the implementation of a formal closed shop policy almost impossible.[65]

It is factors such as these rather than any legal prohibition which account for the relative unimportance of the closed shop in the public services.

The only period in which there has been any direct legal prohibition was between 1927 and 1946, when section 6(1) of the Trade Disputes and Trade Unions Act 1927 made it unlawful for a local or other public authority "to make it a condition of the employment or continuance of employment of any person that he shall be or shall not be a member of a trade union or to impose any condition making employees who are or are not members liable to any disability or disadvantage compared to other members." Since this was repealed, NALGO, the largest association of local government employees, has encouraged the "post-entry" (or "union") shop principle *but with free choice of union.*[66]

Apart from this specific and now obsolete enactment there is very little in the general law which inhibits the unions from pursuing 100 per cent membership objectives. From 1924 onwards the courts have not been prepared to use the vague common law tort of "conspiracy" against those organising closed shops. In 1964, however, the House of Lords invented a new tort (*threatening* to break one's own contract of employment) in order to mulct in damages three union officers who had persuaded the publicly owned British Overseas Airways Corporation to honour a "100 per cent membership" agreement by dismissing an employee who had quarrelled with and resigned from his union.[67] But the immediate effect of this decision was reversed by legislation (which the Conservative Party has promised to repeal), but some of its wider implications could, in the future, afford the courts

65. Ibid., pp. 167–68. The closed shop is more common in local public passenger transport services. In London Transport the closed shop was introduced in 1946 in order to eliminate a breakaway organisation—the National Passenger Workers' Union—in favour of the TGWU: see RCME (16 November 1965) Q. 00, p. 10–917 and written memo. App. 4.
66. A. Spoor, *White Collar Union*, p. 492.
67. *Rookes* v. *Barnard* [1964] A.C. 1129; Wedderburn, *Worker and the Law*, pp. 261–75.

a basis on which to act against certain attempts to enforce closed shop arrangements.

Another judicial development has been the gradual invention of a power to strike down "arbitrary and capricious" trade union rules, more especially when the union operates a closed shop. The clearest statement of such a power is to be found in cases concerning the power to expel a member where this would result in his loss of livelihood,[68] but there have even been suggestions that it could be used to curb unfair admission practices.[69] The precise extent of this power is uncertain. It is a moot point, for example, whether a union, particularly one operating a closed shop, can provide in its rules for a power to expel a member unheard. The courts prefer to deal with such problems by strained constructions of union rules which permit them to discover an implied right to a hearing,[70] and have never had to decide the point directly. Nor is the exact legal basis of this power certain. Some commentators regard it simply as an extension of the restraint of trade doctrines developed by the common law courts in the sixteenth and seventeenth centuries according to which no man could be prohibited from working in a lawful trade, since the law abhors idleness, "the mother of all evil."[71] The difficulty with this view is that section 3 of the Trade Union Act 1871 protects the lawfulness of the agreements and rules of "trade unions" whose objects are in restraint of trade (e.g. closed shop objects). Recent judicial pronouncements seem to suggest, however, that the "right to work" gives rise to an independent cause of action (or at least allows the court to *declare* that the rights of a party have been infringed). This would allow the effect of section 3 of the 1871 act to be avoided, and may foreshadow increasing judicial intervention against closed shops.

The Donovan Commission rejected prohibition of the closed

---

68. *Edwards* v. *SOGAT, The Times,* July 30, 1970 (C.A.).

69. *Nagle* v. *Feilden* [1966] 2 Q.B. 633 (in which the Court of Appeal was prepared to admit the possibility of a declaration that the exclusion of a woman trainer, on grounds of sex, by the Jockey Club, which holds a monopoly of horse racing on the flat, was unlawful as in restraint of trade). This has been severely criticised by some commentators.

70. E.g. *Lawlor* v. *Union of Post Office Workers* [1965] Ch. 712; *Leary* v. *NUVB.* [1970] 2 All E.R. 713.

71. *Case of the Tailors of Ipswich* (1615) 11 Co. Rep. 53a.

shop, but proposed certain statutory safeguards for the individual.[72] These were accepted by the former Labour Government,[73] but the Conservative Party is on record as expressing "fundamental opposition" to the pre-entry shop while being prepared to tolerate union shops subject to stringent safeguards.[74] Judging by the closed shop policies adopted in 1970 by two important organisations—the Association of Teachers in Technical Institutions and the Inland Revenue Staff Association—this may be expected to become a live issue for public employees in the near future.

ii. GOVERNMENT OPPOSITION TO BREAKAWAY UNIONS

A second limitation is the strong antagonism of government to breakaways. This is reflected in recognition policy (discussed in the next section) and in legislation concerning compulsory arbitration and the enforcement of collective agreements in which *locus standi* is invariably conferred on those unions which represent a "substantial proportion" of workers in a trade or industry. From behind this vague formula, government is able to influence the growth of established organisations. An example of this, on the fringes of the public service, is the recognition problem faced by the relatively small Association of Scientific Workers in the Argicultural Research Council and the Medical Research Council. Both Councils allowed the Association to make representations on behalf of individual members but not to negotiate. This led to interunion competition for recruits with the Institution of Professional Civil Servants, and meant that the Association was unable to attract the members it would have had had it been recognised for negotiation.[75]

iii. THE TUC AND INTERUNION COMPETITION

A third limitation on free choice of union is that exercised by the Trades Union Congress. The Bridlington Agreement (so called because it was concluded at an annual conference of the TUC held at Bridlington in 1939, amending and consolidating an earlier agreement of 1924) applies to all unions affiliated

72. Cmnd. 3623, paras. 602–14.
73. Cmnd. 3888, paras. 115–17, but *not* implemented in the I.R. Bill 1970.
74. *Fair Deal at Work*, pp. 24–27.
75. Association of Scientific Workers, Written Evidence to Donovan Commission, paras. 13, 14, and G. S. Bain, *Trade Union Growth and Recognition*. Royal Commission on Trade Unions and Employers' Associations. Research Paper No. 6, pp. 70–71.

to the TUC. It regulates interunion competition between TUC affiliates and provides for the transfer of members from one affiliated union to another. If an affiliate complains of a breach of the agreement, this is referred to a Disputes Committee which bases its deliberations on certain principles. Among these are the following: (1) an application form for membership of a union should contain an inquiry whether the applicant is or has been a member of another union and his financial relationship to that union; (2) an inquiry should be addressed to the former union before he is accepted into membership; (3) no applicant should be accepted who is in dispute with his former union or under disciplinary action or penalty or in arrears; (4) members should not be accepted from unions engaged in a trade dispute; (5) a union should not begin to organise workers of any grade at an establishment or undertaking where another union already has in membership the majority of such workers and negotiates on their behalf, at any rate unless prior arrangements with that union have been made.

The curious feature of this agreement is that the awards of the Disputes Committee are not *legally* binding, the only ultimate sanctions being suspension or disaffiliation from the TUC. From the individual trade union member's point of view the award is not of automatic legal effect. His union may decide to expel him in order to comply with the terms of the award. The expulsion will be lawful only if the union rule book contains an express rule which provides that the union may expel a member if so required by the TUC Disputes Committee.[76] Our analysis of the rule books of public service TUC affiliates has not revealed any which have adopted a model expulsion rule suggested by the TUC to enable affiliated unions to carry out awards of the Disputes Committee without facing the risk of legal action.

Table 5 contains a list of all the interunion disputes involving trade union membership in the public services reported to the TUC Disputes Committee in the ten-year period 1960-69. In each case the name of the complainant union is given first.

76. *Spring* v. *National Amalgamated Stevedores & Dockers' Society* [1956] 1 W.L.R. 585; *Connell* v. *National Union of Distributive Workers, The Times*, 28 January 1928.

Table 5.

Interunion Disputes Involving Public Services Trade Union Membership Reported to TUC Disputes Committee, 1960–69

Year	Parties	Award
1960	None	
1961	TGWU *v.* NUPE (Ancillary grades, Bristol Homoepathic Hospital)	NUPE to exclude members and advise resumption of TGWU membership
1961	COHSE *v.* NUPE (Claybury Hospital staff)	NUPE to exclude members; advised to make future settlement
1962	None	
1963	NUGMW *v.* COSE (Interpretation of interunion agreement)	Advised to redraft and reach settlement
1964	LCC Staff Association *v.* NALGO (LCC staff)	No technical breach by NALGO, but settlement advised because of NALGO sudden change of practice
1965	COHSE *v.* NUPE (Staff at Fairmile Hospital, Wallingford)	NUPE to exclude members
1966	USDAW *v.* NUPE (98 market constables and labourers, Liverpool Corporation)	No breach of principles, but NUPE to meet outstanding financial obligations of transferred members
1967	NALGO *v.* NUPE (6 staff workers, Cumberland Education Authority)	NUPE to exclude members and advise them to rejoin NALGO
1968	None	
1969	NALGO *v.* ASTMS (Technical staffs, University of Salford)	Settled by agreement, in effect allowing NALGO to continue to recruit
	NUWWE *v.* NALGO (Inspector grades, Colne Valley Water Authority)	Settled by mutual agreement
	ASW *v.* NUWWE (Sheffield Corporation Waterworks Department)	NUWWE to exclude three members

Abbreviations:
ASTMS: Association of Scientific, Technical & Managerial Staffs
ASW: Amalgamated Society of Woodworkers
COHSE: Confederation of Health Service Employees
LCC: London County Council
NALGO: National Association of Local Government Officers
NUGMW: National Union of General & Municipal Workers
NUPE: National Union of Public Employees
NUWWE: National Union of Waterworks Employees
TGWU: Transport & General Workers' Union
USDAW: Union of Shop, Distributive & Allied Trades Workers
Sources: TUC Reports of Annual Congresses, 1960–69.

Several observations may be made about the use of this machinery: (1) It was used on only ten occasions in the decade under review, and in some years not at all, in respect of trade union membership in the public services. (2) Its use was confined to hospital and local government employees, apart from the university technicians' dispute. (3) One union, the NUPE (the second largest public employee union affiliated to the TUC), was the respondent in five of the ten reported cases. (4) Two of the ten cases were settled by mutual agreement before conclusion of the hearing, and in three others the award involved advice to negotiate a settlement. (5) In the five cases in which a breach of the Bridlington principles was established, the trade union members were not allowed to transfer their membership to another TUC affiliate. (6) In each of these five cases the established union's right to retain its members was considered to be superior to the individual's liberty to change his affiliation. (7) The 1966 USDAW-NUPE dispute indicates that a union which has representation on an established joint negotiating body for the service in question will be allowed to recruit members in preference to one which does not.

It should be remembered that the TUC Disputes Committee becomes involved only where settlement has proved impossible. Transfers of members regularly occur on a friendly basis between several public employee organisations.

d. Legal Regulation of Internal Union Affairs

A final aspect of freedom of association which needs to be considered is the extent to which Parliament and the courts have attempted to control the eligibility, expulsion, and other internal rules of trade unions in the public employment sphere. Apart from the exceptional case of the Police Federation (discussed earlier), the striking feature of the trade union situation in the U. K., in comparison with most other countries, is the extremely limited degree of external control in these matters.

We have seen that some employee organisations in the public services may not be "trade unions" in law at all and so are free from the limited controls imposed by the Trade Union Acts; those which are trade unions and voluntarily seek and obtain registration must have rules about a number of matters, but the precise *content* of those rules is left to the union concerned; and in theory an unregistered union need not have a written constitution at all. Statutory regulation is confined to control over the expenditure of funds on political objects and the protection from discrimination of noncontributors to the union's political fund (but not against political discrimination as such); to entrenchment of the right of a member to an effective vote on the amalgamation of his union with another organisation; to a special right given to a member of a registered union to assign certain small sums payable to him at his death without making a will; and to duties cast upon registered unions to make annual returns to the Registrar (these are open to inspection), to allow a member (or other person "having an interest in the funds") to inspect the books and membership list, and to make available to anyone, on payment of one shilling or less, a copy of its rules.

Control by the courts depends on the institution of proceedings by a *member* of the union. This is because, in legal theory, the basis for judicial intervention is that the union's rule book operates as a contract to which each member is a party.[77] The effect of this is that a nonmember, such as an applicant for membership, cannot bring a successful action against a union alleging a breach of its rule book; nor, it seems, are the courts likely to grant a declaration that the unreasonableness of a particular admission rule makes it unlawful as being contrary to judge-made public policy. One other possible judicial tack—declaring an admission rule unlawful as in restraint of trade—has been precluded in the case of trade unions (but not professional associations which enjoy a monopoly position[78]) by section 3 of the Trade Union Act 1871. Thus there is nothing in the judge-made law to prevent the National Association of Schoolmasters from limiting its membership to men, despite judicial

---

77. It is uncertain whether this contract is with the *union* or with the other members: *Bonsor* v. *Musicians' Union* [1956] A.C. 104; and comment by Lloyd (1956) 19 M.C.R. 121, Thomas [1956] C.L.J. 67 and Wedderburn (1957) 20 M.L.R. 105.
78. *Nagle* v. *Feilden* [1966] 2 Q.B. 633.

strictures on sex discrimination as "arbitrary and capricious";[79] but professional bodies such as the Royal College of Nursing and the British Medical Association might be prevented from restricting membership in a way which the courts thought restrictive of free trade. The only statutory limitation on arbitrary discrimination by organisations of employees (including professional associations) is to be found in the Race Relations Act 1968, section 4, which makes unlawful any unfavourable treatment on grounds of colour, race, or ethnic or national origin. This obligation is enforced by the Race Relations Board, an independent public agency on which several trade unionists serve. To date (since the act came into operation on 26 November 1968) there have been no complaints of racial discrimination by public employee organisations.[80]

A member may complain to the courts that the rules of the union are unlawful, or that lawful rules are not being adhered to, or that the union has not observed due process (the so-called rules of "natural justice") when expelling him or taking other disciplinary action. The modern tendency of the courts is not to insist that the member must exhaust domestic union remedies before approaching the courts; if the union's action is regarded as being in law a nullity (e.g. a wrongful expulsion in violation of due process), then the member may immediately seek damages, declarations, and injunctive relief (including reinstatement in membership) from the courts, without the need to pursue union appeals. Apart from wrongful expulsion the courts have been prepared to intervene in matters such as unauthorised expenditure of funds on strike pay and improper raising of subscriptions or imposition of levies.

In theory members' actions are inhibited by two legal rules, but both of these have been substantially cut down by judicial interpretations. A rule of company law which has been applied to unions since 1929—that it is for the majority of members, and not the courts, to put right "procedural irregularities"—has been whittled away by exceptions which allow a member to complain where his personal rights (e.g. to vote) have been invaded,

79. Ibid.
80. See Bob Hepple, *Race, Jobs and the Law in Britain* (2nd ed., Harmondsworth, 1970), p. 105.

or the union is acting *ultra vires* or fraudulently. A more important obstacle to the member's action is section 4 of the Trade Union Act 1871. This says that nothing in that act shall enable any court "to enforce directly or allow recovery of damages for breach of" a number of specified agreements which relate, in particular, to the withdrawal of labour, the payment of subscriptions and penalties, the payment benefits to members, or the discharge of fines imposed by a court. Because of the way in which this section is worded ("Nothing in this Act shall . . .") it is clear that it applies only to those trade unions whose objects may be regarded as being unlawful in restraint of trade at common law; possibly (although this is controversial) it also applies where a *lawful* union is sued in its registered name. Most of the trade unions active in the private sector have objects which fall foul of the "restraint of trade" doctrine or are registered. In the case of employee organisations mainly active in the public services, however, the position is far more complex and ambiguous. We have examined the rules of a considerable number of these organisations. As pointed out in an earlier section, it is doubtful how many of them are trade unions in law at all. Of those which clearly are, we found only three whose rules are unequivocally in restraint of trade: the Fire Brigades Union (closed shop objects), and the National Association of Local Government Officers and the Confederation of Health Service Employees (both of which may order withdrawal of labour). But we note that several organisations (e.g. the Civil and Public Services Association and the National Union of Teachers) have recently adopted strike policies and that others are now pressing closed shop policies. These new policies may, through the "restraint of trade" doctrine, render their agreements subject to section 4.

We have not found any examples of litigation involving the rules of public service organisations where section 4 has been raised; but the extreme ambiguity about the legal enforceability of the rules of the majority of these organisations means that the scope for judicial intervention is vague and uncertain. The bark of section 4 is, however, worse than its bite, for even where it applies, the courts have limited its effect to "*direct* enforcement" of the named agreements. They have granted applications for injunctions to *restrain* unlawful action, and they have permitted declarations and injunctions to allow members to remain in membership despite the statutory prohibition on enforceability. This particular legal tangle would be removed if a proposal by the majority of the Donovan Commission, to repeal the whole of section 4, were implemented.[81]

The Donovan Commission was satisfied that "there is no widespread abuse of union power"—an observation which we would think applicable to unions mainly active in the public sector as much as those in private employment—but proposed certain additional safeguards for union members. It recommended, and the former Labour Government accepted, the need for the creation of a new independent review body to hear complaints by individuals in cases of alleged "substantial injustice." In their original form the proposals were that this body would hear complaints only after the Registrar's attempts to reach an amicable settlement had failed, and that all unions would have to employ professional auditors. The Conservative Party's proposals go altogether much further and if implemented would mark a controversial and fundamental shift away from the traditions of union autonomy on which trade union law rests. The Conservatives propose stringent control over the *content* of rule books as a condition of registration (which is to be made compulsory); breach of rules will involve a hearing before proposed new industrial courts, which will also be able to hear appeals against "disciplinary or coercive action" against individuals, and to order compensation and deregistration. The political objective behind these proposals is stated to be the control of unofficial and unconstitutional action by trade union members. In sum, the Conservatives hope to utilise as fully as possible the unions' potential as "managers of discontent."

The *quid pro quo* for reforms such as these may be the extension of legal guarantees of free association and possibly even an entrenched Bill of Rights which includes freedom of association among its provisions. Paradoxically, this may lead to some restriction on the liberties in industrial action enjoyed by trade unions. One may assert this in the light of the attitude taken by the Supreme Court of the Republic of Ireland to

81. Cmnd. 3623, paras. 810-15. It is the policy of the Conservative Party to follow this proposal.

the "freedom of association" article in the Irish Constitution of 1937. In *Educational Co. of Ireland Ltd.* v. *Fitzpatrick (1961)*[82] it was held that this freedom implied a corresponding freedom not to associate. Accordingly, it could not be a lawful object for trade unionists to take action aimed at inducing nonunion workers to join a union. In consequence the provisions of the Trade Disputes Act 1906 were declared void as repugnant to the Constitution insofar as they protected trade union action to this end. Moreover, the Judicial Committee of the Privy Council (consisting of British Law Lords, and whose opinion was delivered by Lord Donovan, the most eminent Labour Law judge) has recently held that the "freedom of association" guaranteed by the Constitution of Trinidad and Tobago does not protect the right to free collective bargaining and the right to strike.[83] This latter decision is particularly important, because it shows that British judges, faced by written guarantees of free association, are inclined to place a restricted interpretation on these guarantees. In particular, the prevailing judicial approach is to treat the right to join trade unions, elect representatives, and affiliate to other bodies as being entirely separate and distinct from the right to collective bargaining and to strike. It is true that "yellow dog" contracts would be rendered unlawful by a constitutional guarantee of free association, but these contracts are, in any event, unknown in the public services in the United Kingdom and there is no active discrimination against union members. Accordingly, public service unions may feel that they would have little to gain, and possibly something to fear, in legal guarantees of the rights they already enjoy on the foundation of union strength.

3. THE RECOGNITION OF UNIONS

a. Introduction

Recognition problems are generally of three kinds: (1) where an employer refuses to recognise any union; (2) where he bargains with some but excludes others; and (3) where he recognises a union but refuses to bargain genuinely with it. The first of these problems does not arise in the public services in the U. K. The second and third do occur from time to

82. [1961] I.R. 345.
83. *Collymore* v. *A.G. of Trinidad and Tobago* [1969] 2 All E.R. 1207.

time, but the outstanding feature of the solutions which have been found to these two problems is that they are almost entirely nonlegal.

In general recognition is a voluntary act within the discretion of the employing authority. Problems of multiunionism have been resolved by affording recognition to only *one* union for a particular craft, grade, or class (although examples of joint recognition of two or more unions for a particular grade can be found);[84] by alliances of several unions for recognition purposes;[85] and by the encouragement of union amalgamations. The result of recognition is that the union concerned is brought into direct consultation with the employing authority for the category of employees in respect of which recognition has been granted, and it is enabled to go to arbitration where this is available. Direct consultation is utilised where a matter is of relevance to a particular grade or class only, and to deal with individual employee grievances. But the decision whether a particular claim should be dealt with this way rather than through the joint negotiating machinery rests on convenience and practice, and not on any guiding principle.

Where the employing authority covers more than one department, a distinction is drawn between national and departmental recognition. For example, in the nonindustrial civil service, national recognition rests on numerical strength (the precise percentages, if any exist, are never announced) within a particular general service grade. Departmental recognition rests on numerical strength in that grade in a particular department. In practice the departmentally recognised unions for general service grades do not differ much from the nationally recognised organisations for those grades, but it is always possible that a nationally recognised organisation will not have sufficient numerical strength in a particular department to achieve recognition in that department. Withdrawal of recognition is usually resorted to only if a rival

84. For example, in the nonindustrial civil service there is joint national recognition of more than one union in respect of each of the following grades: museum technicians I & II; stores supervisory grades; radio technicians; higher clerical officers; photoprinters, draughtsmen (architectural and engineering); fire service officers.

85. For example, the Civil Service Alliance (4 associations) has separate and sole recognition for clerical assistants, duplicators, machine operators, personal secretaries, and typists.

organisation claims a change in membership and this is verified (sometimes by an inspection of membership records).

Recognition for purposes of direct consultation is in theory totally distinct from membership of the joint negotiating (Whitley) body for the particular section of the public services in question. Associations were recognised before the Whitley system was introduced, and the pledge was given that recognised associations would continue to enjoy access to direct consultation on matters affecting their members alone. In practice, however, membership of a Whitley Council is nearly always enjoyed by recognised associations. But exceptions do arise from time to time. For example, the Association of First Division Civil Servants was for years nationally recognised but did not enjoy membership of the staff side of the National Civil Service Whitley Council. Moreover, the staff side of a National Whitley Council may include some associations which enjoy departmental but not national recognition, and departmental Whitley Council staff sides have sometimes included unrecognised associations. The distinction between recognition and membership of a joint negotiating body (the latter alone implying full bargaining status) is to be explained by the manner in which representation on staff sides is settled. The basic approach to this question remains today as it was when recommended in the Report on the Application of the Whitley Report to Administrative Departments in the Civil Service (1919):[86]

> In order to be effective the staff side [of a Whitley Council] must be broadly representative of the Civil Service as a whole, and as far as possible the representatives must be drawn from a variety of departments. . . . The proportion of representation must be determined by negotiation between the different Associations and . . . the experience and advice of the Ministry of Labour . . . should be utilised to the fullest extent.

When a Whitley Council is first set up cn the initiative of an employing authority, that authority will, quite naturally, confine its invitations to recognised associations. Subsequently, however, membership of the staff side is granted by the vote of the existing associations on that side.

86. Cmd. 9 (7 March 1919) para. 21.

In the nonindustrial civil service there appear to have been no serious disputes about representation since the demise some years ago of several small breakaways. In the industrial civil service it has been said that the system is "administratively very convenient"[87] but that it "depends for its complete success upon the effective use at all levels of the provision for co-opting organisations which may not have permanent seats on the various councils . . . whenever business is handled in which they have a legitimate interest." These relatively favourable experiences with a purely voluntary system must be accounted the major reason for the very few instances of a legally defined duty to recognise and negotiate, and for the fact that when it has been imposed the legal duty has been in the form of a vaguely worded ministerial or management discretion which acts as no more than a shadowy legal framework for the support of the voluntary system.

The only part of the public services in which there exists a legal duty to bargain is in respect of the remuneration of teachers. In this section we shall analyse that duty and draw certain parallels with the legal duties imposed on the public corporations. We shall then examine current proposals for extending the legal duty to other sections of public (and private) employment. Finally, we shall describe the indirect use which has been made of the law in order to encourage recognition and bargaining in the public services.

Before proceeding, however, it is necessary to point out that the general absence of a legal duty to grant recognition, and the special form which the duty takes in the case of teachers, means that there is a fundamental difference between the means used in the U.K. in order to secure recognition and those which are found in the U.S. The absence of statutory machinery for securing recognition in the U.K. means that there is no parallel with the problems which exist in the U.S. of determining an "appropriate bargaining unit" for purposes of collective bargaining. The problem of determining the limits of a "trade" or "industry" or "section" does occur, infrequently, in connection with the *extension* of collectively bargained terms to unorganised parts of a trade or industry by statutory means, discussed later.

87. Ministry of Defence (Navy Dept.). Written evidence to Donovan Commission (1966) para. 12.

But the extent of recognition for bargaining purposes is entirely a matter for private negotiation and economic pressure. When discussing strikes and picketing in Chapter VIII, we shall see that, in general, recognition disputes qualify as "trade disputes" (although the position where there is interunion rivalry is not clear), and so those resorting to economic sanctions are protected from most forms of civil and criminal liability. Moreover, agreements which are reached on recognition issues, like other procedural agreements, are not legally enforceable between the employing authorities and the unions. Accordingly, they are not drafted in legal language (indeed, they may often rest upon unwritten practices), and they are highly flexible.

The question of whom public employee organisations represent is central to the recognition issue in the U.S., but it is irrelevant for bargaining purposes in the U.K. An organisation recognised for purposes of direct consultation, or a union belonging to the staff side of a joint negotiating body, "represents" no one in the legal sense, neither its own members nor all employees within the particular department or unit. However, as shall be seen in Chapter V, when dealing with the results of bargaining, the union acts with other bargaining parties as *legislator* for the unit of government concerned, in the sense that the collectively bargained terms may either be translated into statutory regulations by a minister, binding on all employing authorities and employees named in the regulations, or may simply operate as norms which, if appropriate, are expressly or impliedly incorporated into the individual contracts of employment of all persons in that unit. The "representation" issue is legally important in only one context, the *extension* of collectively bargained terms to unorganised sections of a trade or industry. In order to invoke the statutory machinery for making such extensions a union must be "representative."

b. The Legal Duty to Bargain

The Remuneration of Teachers Act 1965 (section 1) and the Remuneration of Teachers (Scotland) Act 1967 (section 1) require the Secretary of State to secure, for the purpose of considering the remuneration payable to teachers by education authorities, the existence of one or more committees. These must consist of an independent chairman appointed by the Secretary of State, representatives of education authorities,[88] representatives of the Secretary of State,[89] and representatives of "organisations appearing to the Secretary of State to represent teachers or particular descriptions of teachers."[90]

The position in the public services may be contrasted with that in the public corporations. Most of the postwar nationalisation acts laid down a legal duty to bargain. There were several reasons for this, including the ideal of public accountability, the monopoly status of the new corporations, and formal recognition of the fact that the trade unions had been among the chief advocates of nationalisation.[91] The duty imposed on the boards of the nationalised industries led to a rapid expansion of trade union membership among their employees. The transition, in 1969, of the Post Office from the status of a Department of State to that of independent public corporation was also marked by the imposition on the Post Office of a legal duty "to seek consultation with any organisation appearing to it to be appropriate" with a view to the establishment of negotiating and arbitration machinery to deal with a wide variety of matters.[92] This statute does no more than formalise the pre-existing practice of the Post Office which, while a Department of State, went even further in consultations than the act now expressly requires. The purpose of laying down a formal duty in this case was presumably to assure the unions that the new status of the Post Office would not weaken their existing bargaining positions.

88. In the English act these representatives are *directly* appointed by local education authorities and joint education committees; in the Scottish Act the persons are *nominated* by "such bodies as may be determined by the Secretary of State, being bodies appearing to him to represent education authorities."

89. This feature is discussed below in Chap. V.

90. Remuneration of Teachers Act 1965, s.1. The Scottish act, s.1, refers to "persons nominated from time to time by such bodies as may be determined by the Secretary of State, being bodies appearing to him to represent teachers." In the English act the representatives are *directly* appointed by the recognised bodies.

91. See esp. W. A. Robson, *Nationalised Industry and Public Ownership* (London, 1960), chap. XII; and G. D. H. Cole, "Labour and Staff Problems under Nationalisation" in *Problems of Nationalised Industry* (ed. W. A. Robson) (London, 1952).

92. Post Office Act 1969, sch. 1, para 11(1). See below, Chap. V, fn. 4, for a full list of nationalisation statutes.

The remarkable feature of the legal duty to bargain, where it does exist, is that the statutory definitions do nothing to resolve the second and third kinds of recognition problem mentioned at the beginning of this section. The decision to grant or withhold recognition lies solely within the discretion of the Secretary of State in the case of teachers, and of management in the case of the public corporations.[93] Even in the health services, where there is no legal duty to bargain but where statutory effect may be given to the results of negotiations by a "negotiating body,"[94] the constitution of the negotiating body is solely within the discretion of the Minister of Health. For these purposes the statutory regulations define a "negotiating body" as "any body accepted by the Minister as a proper body for negotiating remuneration and other conditions of service for officers or any class of officers."[95] Similarly, in the Fire Services there is no legal duty to bargain but the Secretary of State may give statutory effect to recommendations, in regard to the maintenance of discipline and appeals against dismissals and disciplinary action, made in accordance with "proper arrangements . . . for the consideration by persons representing the interests of fire authorities and of persons employed as members of fire brigades."[96] The Secretary of State must be "satisfied" that the arrangements in force are "proper."

In all these instances no statutory criteria are prescribed as to how the discretion is to be exercised. It is left to the Post Office[97] to determine what organisations "appear to them to

93. Report of a Court of Inquiry under Lord Parson into the dispute between the British Steel Corporation and certain of their employees, Cmnd. 3754 (1968) para. 20, where recognition decisions by the British Steel Corporation were described as being "within the sphere of administration, not adjudication." See too Report of the Inquiry by the Honourable Lord Cameron into the complaint made by the National Union of Bank Employees. Cmnd. 2202, p. 115.

94. National Health Service (Remuneration and Conditions of Service Regulations 1951), S.I. 1951, No. 1373, para. 3.

95. Ibid., para. 2 (1).

96. Fire Services Act 1947, s.17(2) (as amended by Fire Services Act 1959, s.5).

97. In *Gallagher* v. *Post Office, The Times,* 30 July 1970, Brightman J. held that the new Post Office Act gave the Post Office an absolute discretion as to organisations with which it would consult and commented: "It would be strange if it were otherwise." Accordingly he refused injunctions to restrain the Post Office from withdrawing recognition from the National

be appropriate," and to the Secretary of State to determine what bodies "appear to him to represent teachers." The latter formula, in particular, overcomes the difficulties which arose in Scotland over the interpretation of the earlier Education (Scotland) Act, which required the Secretary of State to intimate his intention to make salary regulations to a "council constituted with his approval by agreement between the education authorities and the teachers employed by them, or, failing such agreement, by him. . . ."[98] The National Joint Council to Deal with Salaries of Teachers in Scotland was the body approved for this purpose until 1964. The teachers' side of this Council consisted entirely of representatives of Educational Institute of Scotland (representing 30,000 of the 37,000 teachers in Scotland) and excluded the Scottish Secondary Schoolteachers' Association and the breakaway Scottish Schoolmasters' Association (a body of 2,500 men teachers campaigning against the introduction of equal pay for women). In 1963 some members of the Schoolmasters' Association raised an action in the Court of Session asking for a declarator that the National Joint Council did not comply with the terms of the act. Lord Johnston sustained this contention, holding that "the teachers employed by them" meant "*all* the teachers."[99] As a result the Secretary of State had to withdraw his approval from the National Joint Council. Agreement could not be reached on the constitution of a new body, and so the Secretary of State had to set up a new body under his own hand, in March 1964, consisting of representatives of each of the three teachers' associations, their numbers being roughly in proportion to the respective membership of the associations. Shortly afterwards, however, the Schoolmasters' Association was expelled from the Council for refusing to agree in future to observe the voluntary code of procedure accepted by other members of the Council. (The Association had publicly disclosed certain information, contrary to the provisions of the constitution of the Council. The Association objected to this provision of the constitution because it enabled

Guild of Telephonists (representing about 10,000 of 52,000 telephonists in the P.O.) in pursuance of its policy of negotiating with only one union representing telephonists, namely the larger Union of Post Office Workers.

98. Education (Scotland) Act 1962, s.83(4).

99. *Cannon* v. *Secretary of State for Scotland,* 1964, S.L.T. 91 (C.S., Outer House).

management representatives to block publication of information.) The Remuneration of Teachers (Scotland) Act 1967 replaces section 83 of the 1962 act and brings the law in Scotland into line with that in England.[100] In both countries the test is now "representativeness" as determined by the Secretary of State.

It would be mistaken, however, to assume that the discretion of the Secretary of State is absolutely unfettered. There can be no doubt that the exercise of his powers could be made the subject of judicial review in exceptional circumstances. The Secretary of State could probably be compelled, by way of mandamus (and the equivalent remedy in Scotland), to carry out the duties laid upon him, and it seems likely that the courts would regard a discretion exercised in bad faith or by taking account of irrelevant considerations as a failure to exercise the statutory duties. For example, if the Secretary of State refused to treat a body as "representative" on extraneous political, racial, or religious grounds, this would presumably be treated as a failure to carry out the legal duty and mandamus would lie. However, it is most unlikely that the courts would interfere with any particular numerical formula provided it did not appear to the courts to be grossly unreasonable. There is also the possibility that a formula, rigidly applied without reference to the specific facts of the case under consideration, would be treated by the courts as a failure to exercise the statutory duties. The preincorporation experience of the Post Office, however, makes it most unlikely that there would be any attempt to revert to rigid formulae.[101] The policy adopted by Postmasters-General since 1953 has been to refuse to lay down hard and fast rules and to consider each claim on its merits. In practice this has meant that rival claims to recognition have been settled by the appointment of independent conciliators,[102] and by the processes of trade union amalgamation.[103] The significant feature

100. Remuneration of Teachers Act 1965, s.1.
101. See Report of the Post Office (Departmental Classes)
101. See Report of the Post Office (Departmental Classes) Recognition Committee [Terrington Committee] Cmd. 8470 (1952) and the statement by the Postmaster-General (Earl De La Warr) H.L. Deb. col. 1170 (30 June 1953).
102. For examples see Post Office. Written Evidence to Donovan Commission (1966) paras. 10 et seq. and App. VI.
103. Between 1952 and 1966 the number of recognised unions in the Post Office was reduced by one third mainly by amalgamations.

of the enactment of a *legal* duty to bargain, where this is couched in the language of wide ministerial discretion, is that there is an added deterrent against the adoption of rigid formulae, like the Listowel 40 per cent membership requirement in the Post Office between 1947 and 1953. The *legal* duty, when formulated as it is in the U.K. statutes, encourages emulation of the voluntary practice in the nonindustrial and industrial civil service, where the Civil Service Department (and formerly the Treasury) has never announced any precise percentages (indeed it is not known whether any exist) which would establish a claim to national recognition or raise the question of withdrawal of recognition.[104]

The public corporations may be less amenable to judicial review than the Secretary of State because the duties imposed upon them refer to "appropriate" rather than "representative" unions (except in the coal industry), and this is suggestive of a wider discretion than that which exists under the Remuneration of Teachers Acts. However, even here the courts may be tempted to upset recognition decisions based upon what appear to be extraneous considerations or rigidly applied formulate. Even the Minister's decisions to give effect to the recommendations of "proper" negotiating machinery in the health and fire services could be subjected to a limited degree of judicial control. The fact that no case has been raised under any of these statutes does not imply that possible legal restraints are absent from the minds of those exercising statutory powers. The successful action by members of the Scottish Schoolmasters' Association is evidence enough of the possibilities of judicial intervention in recognition disputes where there is a legal duty to make use of negotiating bodies.

The most important restraint on ministerial and management discretion in these instances is not the threat of legal action, however, but bargaining strength. It is vitally important to appreciate that a *legal* duty to bargain has never been regarded in the U.K. as a compensation for lack of union strength. In each case the legal duty has simply formalised what the unions had already achieved *without* legal intervention. The important practical consequence of this is that the ministers and managements

104. H.M. Treasury, *Staff Relations in the Civil Service* (HMSO, 1965) paras. 12–14.

upon whom a legal duty is laid are usually content to allow the unions to settle their rival claims to recognition among themselves, and to assist this process by supplying independent conciliators, or exceptionally by using statutory powers to set up courts of inquiry.[105] In other words, the apparently wide statutory powers are in practice closely restricted by the willingness of the unions to settle recognition problems among themselves. In this sense the statutory discretions are residual ones, of importance only in those relatively rare instances where agreement is impossible. For practical purposes, then, recognition problems are no differently settled when there is some form of legal duty to bargain than where no such duty exists.

The analysis in the preceding paragraph may be illustrated by the history of the Remuneration of Teachers Act in England and Wales. Standing joint committees to deal with teachers' salaries were voluntarily established in 1919 under the chairmanship of Lord Burnham (and hence the continued reference to "Burnham" committees under modern legislation). These committees (somewhat modified) were first put on a statutory basis by the Education Act 1944, section 89. The Remuneration of Teachers Act 1965, replacing the earlier measure, obliged the Secretary of State to set up committees. Nominally he has an unfettered discretion to decide the number of committees, the classes of teachers to be dealt with by each, the bodies to be represented on the management and teachers' panels of each committee, and the number of representatives each may have. He has the power to remove a body from representation on a panel but only (trivial exceptions apart) by means of statutory instrument which is subject to annulment by resolution of either House of Parliament. When he came to set up the committees the Secretary of State made it clear, however, that he considered this a matter for the teachers' associations to settle among themselves and that he would act upon whatever agreement they reached. They were unable to agree, so the Secretary of State told them that he would leave the balance of representation among teachers' associations as it was immediately before the passage of the act. In 1966, following representations by certain associations, the

105. These may be set up under the Industrial Courts Act 1919, s.4, in order to investigate and publicise the facts of a major dispute: e.g. the Pearson inquiry.

Secretary of State reviewed the composition of primary and secondary school Burnham committees and, after consultations, made certain changes.

In sum, the structuring of management or ministerial discretion by voluntary agreement among rival unions is an explicit part of the philosophy and practice of Whitleyism, which has been retained whenever a legal duty to bargain has been imposed.

c. Current Proposals for New Legal Duties to Bargain

It is perhaps indicative of the strength of the voluntarist tradition that the only large public service union to press the Donovan Commission for the enactment of a legal duty to recognise unions was NALGO, which has a substantial membership in local government service. Even its proposal was confined to a duty to recognise a union "with a significant membership and not in competition with an already recognised union"[106]—an obvious safeguard for its own entrenched position in local government bargaining.

The Donovan Report concluded that there should *not* be new laws aimed at *direct* enforcement of recognition by employers.[107] Instead it proposed that problems of recognition should be investigated by the new Commission for Industrial Relations (CIR) which would have the duty to persuade and encourage reluctant employers to grant recognition, but would have no legal teeth. The Report opposed "detailed intervention by the courts in the processes of industrial relations which appears to us to be a consequence of enforcing recognition by law as in the U.S.A."[108] The law would come in as a last resort, but only to enable a union to take its substantive claims to arbitration before the Industrial Court (a permanent arbitration body), whose awards would be binding on the employer. This form of unilateral arbitration, where recognition was denied or the employer failed to bargain in good faith with a recognised union, would be available only in industries, sections of industry, or undertakings in which the Secretary of State certified that it could contribute to the growth of sound collective bargaining

106. Written evidence to Donovan Commission, para. 64. See below on another legal device successfully used by NALGO to secure recognition.
107. Cmnd. 3623, 1968, paras. 253-56, 273-75.
108. Ibid., para. 256.

machinery, and then only after the CIR had so advised following a full inquiry.

Both major political parties have proposed similar schemes, but have added further legal incidents. The Conservative Party,[109] while in opposition, proposed that an employer should be under a legal duty "to recognise and negotiate with registered trade unions." The Conservatives acknowledged that many large unions are not at present registered (the three examples of this which they cited in a recent publication were all public service unions)[110] but proposed that registration (which would entail detailed control of the union's internal affairs) should be a precondition for the "legal" right to recognition and to bargain. They have not yet considered the legal definition of a "trade union," which might itself be an obstacle to registration by a number of public service workers' organisations.

The former Labour Government's Industrial Relations Bill 1970 (which has now lapsed) proposed adding to the Donovan scheme by enabling the Secretary of State to make orders giving effect to the CIR's conclusions, and by permitting a union to make a complaint to the CIR that an employer is not complying with an order requiring him to recognise and negotiate with that union. The CIR would have been able to arrange for that complaint to be heard by a complaints tribunal, which would then have conducted a semijudicial inquiry and made a declaration whether or not it found the complaint to be justified. If the tribunal found that it was justified the union would have been able to resort to unilateral arbitration of terms and conditions of employment before the Industrial Court. The award of the Court would have become a term of the individual employment contracts of the employees covered by it. There would have been an appeal against the complaints tribunal's declaration (within six weeks) to the High Court in England, or Court of Session in Scotland, confined to points of law.

These provisions would have been applicable to Crown employment and Crown employees, except that there would have been no order and no unilateral arbitration in their case. Instead, where a report of the CIR concluded that a Minister of

109. *Fair Deal at Work* (Conservative Political Centre, 1968), pp. 44-45.
110. Ibid., p. 20 (NALGO, the National Union of Teachers and the Union of Post Office Workers).

the Crown ought to comply with a request for recognition, the Minister would have been obliged to give his answer. Where he gave an undertaking to comply with the Report, the union to which the undertaking was given could have made a complaint of noncompliance to the CIR's complaints tribunal, which could in turn have issued a nonenforceable declaration. However, the Minister need not have given such an undertaking in the first place. These abortive proposals would *not* have applied to recognition in respect of remuneration payable to teachers by education authorities.[111]

In reaching its findings the CIR would have had a wide discretion, because the only statutory definition of "recognition" was one which said that it included "a reference to the taking by the employer of all such action, by way of or with a view to the carrying on of relevant negotiations with a trade union, as might reasonably be expected to be taken by an employer ready and willing to carry on such negotiations."[112]

There is a danger in proposals such as these that the proceedings before the complaints tribunal will assume a legalistic character, particularly because the tribunal's declarations may be upset by the ordinary courts, albeit only on "points of law."[113] The Conservative Party's proposals for a new legal duty of recognition would go even further in introducing lawyers' refinements into this problem, and in particular would require new industrial courts, like the National Labor Relations Board in the U.S., to define the "appropriate bargaining unit."

d. Encouragement of Bargaining by Legal Means

We have so far dealt with the problems of recognition and bargaining solely from the viewpoint of the direct legal duty to recognise and to negotiate. It is now necessary to consider the way in which the law has been indirectly used' in order to secure recognition in the public services.

Wartime legislation,[114] primarily intended to prevent strikes and

111. I.R. Bill 1970, cl.6(4).
112. Ibid., cl.6(6).
113. A warning of the dangers of imposing a new legal duty open to judicial intervention was made by Professor K. W. Wedderburn in *New Society,* 4 December 1969, p. 400.
114. Conditions of Employment and National Arbitration Order No. 1305 of 1940. This was replaced by the Industrial Disputes Order No. 1376 of 1951 (see below).

lock-outs, but which also required the observance of "recognised terms and conditions of employment" by all employers in a particular trade or area, was an important factor in securing the acceptance of trade unionism and collective bargaining in local government. In the Second World War, Order No.1305 obliged all employers to observe terms of employment settled by negotiating machinery covering all or "substantial proportions" of the employers and workers in a particular trade or area, whether they were parties to the machinery or not. Disputes over observance of recognised terms could be referred to the National Arbitration Tribunal established under the Order. The National and Local Government Officers' Association hailed this as a "charter for trade unionism."[115] Before the war some fifteen provincial Whitley Councils for local government employees had been established covering the whole country, but many local authorities had held aloof from these Councils. The effect of Order No.1305 was that every decision by a provincial Whitley Council was a "recognised term" which had to be observed by all local authorities, whether members of the Council or not. Rather than have the terms which they had to observe determined by others, this induced many authorities to join the management panels. Ultimately it led to the formation of a new and improved National Whitley Council in 1943.

For a short time it seemed that judicial interpretation of the Order would prevent its use by local government employees, but, as we shall see in the section on arbitration, NALGO thought the matter sufficiently important to take it to the House of Lords (the highest appeal court) which held that local government employees could be "workmen" for the purposes of the Order, and that a dispute as to whether an employer should make up the salaries of employees who had undertaken war service was sufficiently "connected with the terms of employment" to be justiciable by the National Arbitration Tribunal.[116] Thereafter NALGO referred a large number of disputes to the Tribunal and thereby strengthened its bargaining position.

After the war the order was replaced by a new Order No.1376 of 1951, which established the Industrial Disputes Tribunal (IDT)

115. A Spoor, *White Collar Union* (London, 1965), pp. 193–95.
116. *National Association of Local Government Officers* v. *Bolton Corporation* [1943] A.C. 666.

in place of the NAT but continued the system of securing observance of "recognised" terms and conditions. In this regard the 1951 order introduced its own "recognition" problem by confining access to trade unions which habitually took part in the settlement of terms and conditions of employment in the industry, section of industry, or undertaking concerned, or which, in the absence of negotiating machinery, represented a substantial proportion of the workers concerned in the relevant industry or section of industry. This restriction was designed to prevent break-away unions and bodies which the government did not want to recognise from using the compulsory arbitration machinery. It was for the Minister of Labour to determine the "representativeness" of the trade union. Another important limitation was that under the 1951 order it was no longer a statutory obligation to observe recognised terms and conditions, but the IDT could be asked through the Minister of Labour to order their observance in particular cases. The effect of an order by the IDT was that it became an implied term in the individual workers' contracts of employment.

A study by B. Reiss[117] shows that the civil service organisations did not make use of the Industrial Disputes Tribunal between 1951 and 1959 (it ceased to operate in February 1959). But three public employee organisations did. These were NALGO (157 references), the National Union of Public Employees (74 references), and the Confederation of Health Service Employees (50 references). Like several white-collar unions in private industry[118] these organisations were able, by the actual or threatened use of the IDT, to bring pressure on local authorities to grant recognition.

Not surprisingly, the organisations which had utilised the tribunal for recognition purposes were unwilling to see it dissolved in 1959, and they have pressed for its reintroduction. One feature of the old system has been retained, however. Under section

117. *Compulsory Arbitration as a Method of Settling Disputes with Special Reference to Great Britain since 1940.* B. Litt. thesis Oxford, 1964. See generally W. E. J. McCarthy, *Compulsory Arbitration in Britain.* R.C. on Trade Unions and Employers' Assns. Research Paper No. 8 (HMSO, 1968).

118. The experience in private industry is described by G. S. Bain, *Trade Union Growth and Recognition,* paras. 105–56.

8 of the Terms and Conditions of Employment Act 1959, representative organisations of workers and employers were granted the right to invoke, through the Secretary of State, the adjudication of the Industrial Court (a permanent arbitration body) in cases where recognised terms are not being observed. Orders made by the Court operate as implied terms in the individual worker's contracts of employment. In practice the majority of claims are settled before reference to the Court or are withdrawn before the hearing—a fact which testifies to the continuing importance of the method of "extending" recognised terms as a device for securing recognition.[119]

As may be expected, the requirement of "representativeness" for the purpose of reporting a claim under section 8 of the 1959 act, and the earlier provisions of the Order No.1376 of 1951, have given rise to a case law. This is the only area of collective bargaining in which the grouping of employees has any *legal* effect on the recognition issue. Under section 8 a claim, to be duly reported, must be made by one of the parties to a collective agreement or arbitration award. These parties must "represent (generally or in the district in question as the case may be) a substantial proportion of the employers and of the workers in the trade, industry or section, being workers of the description . . . to which the agreement or award relates."[120] The Secretary of State has the power to require further particulars of the claim (e.g. in regard to representation) to be given; if he cannot bring about a settlement, he is then bound to refer the matter to the Industrial Court which then has the duty to determine whether the claim is well founded, which inevitably includes consideration of the question of representativeness.

The case law is not extensive, nor is it of much importance because the Industrial Court follows the general practice of arbitration bodies in the U.K. of usually not giving reasons for its decisions. Moreover, the Industrial Court does not follow a doctrine of precedent although it aims at some measure of consistency in its awards. Questions of legal definition of the bargaining unit can reach the ordinary courts of law only if

---

119. Other aspects of this provision are discussed below, including the question of coverage of local government and other public employees.
120. S.8(1)(b).

one of the parties alleges that the Industrial Court is exceeding its jurisdiction in hearing a particular case (i.e. an order of prohibition is sought) or that it has wrongfully refused to entertain a claim (mandamus). There is no appeal on questions of fact or law; only review of the extremely narrow question of jurisdiction. Accordingly, those who seek some assistance from the law of the U.K. on questions of "representation" and "bargaining units" will be disappointed. There are perhaps only two general principles to emerge so far. (1) "Section of trade or industry" refers to function rather than geographical situation.[121] To take an example. An agreement negotiated by the National Joint Council for Local Authorities' Services (Manual Workers) could be extended through the statutory procedure to cover a manual worker of a particular description employed by a local authority which has refused to recognise or to negotiate with a trade union which represents a substantial proportion of manual workers employed by other local authorities but has insignificant support in the particular locality. (2) A group of workers in an enterprise may be held to fall within an "industry" or "section of an industry" different from that in which the majority of workers in the enterprise fall.[122] For example, in a single establishment maintained by a local authority the rates of pay and conditions of service of engineering craftsmen will be covered by a Joint Negotiating Committee for that craft; the pay and conditions of building trades craftsmen in that establishment will be covered by another craft committee's agreements; and the pay and conditions of noncraft manual workers will be covered by the agreements of the Manual Workers' National Joint Council (as modified by and elaborated by one of the fifteen provincial manual workers' joint councils). There may even be overlaps with the agreements of other joint councils covering manual workers.

e. Other Means of Reducing Interunion Competition

A variety of other means of an extra-legal character for reducing interunion competition exist. We have found it necessary to refer to some of these means earlier. For example, the system of

---

121. *R.* v. *Industrial Disputes Tribunal*, ex p. *Courage & Co. Ltd.* [1956] 1 W.L.R. 1062.

122. Industrial Court Cases 2808 (*Avon India Rubber Co. Ltd.* and *AESD*) and 2924 (*Parnall Ltd.* and *NUFTO*).

negotiation through Whitley Councils where decisions are reached by the majority vote of each side; interunion agreements on recruitment and negotiating rights; and the work of the TUC Disputes Committee in defining spheres of influence through the application of the Bridlington principles.

It remains for us to mention briefly one method in which legislation has been of importance, namely the movement towards amalgamations and "transfer of engagements." The number of unions in the public services has shown a steady decline. This process has been aided by the Trade Union (Amalgamations etc.) Act 1964, which relaxed the rather unwieldy requirements of earlier legislation.[123] Merger of unions by amalgamation requires a simple majority of the votes recorded in each amalgamating union, but there are elaborate safeguards to ensure that union members are given the relevant facts about the amalgamation, a genuine opportunity to vote, and a fair chance to complain of any irregularity. This procedure has been used by several public service unions. A recent example is the Society of Technical Civil Servants (9,000 members) which decided in May 1969 to merge with the Institution of Professional Civil Servants (75,000 members).

123. See generally Gunfeld, *Modern Trade Union Law* (London, 1966), p. 23, and Donovan Commission, Cmnd. 3623, chap. XII.

·IV·

Organisation and Authority
for Bargaining
on the Employer Side

1. THE CONSTITUTIONAL POSITION OF THE ·GOVERNMENT

BARGAINING in the civil service is bargaining with the State; bargaining in local authorities is bargaining with employers subject to considerable control by the State and largely dependent upon the State for finance; bargaining in the nationalised corporations is bargaining with employers whose general policy objectives are laid down by statute and who are subject to legal and de facto control by the State. In all three cases decisions on questions of wages, etc., may have varying degrees of impact upon the taxpayer.

a. The Executive and Parliament

The classic theory is that Parliament controls the Government in this country. However, the reality, in normal circumstances, is more nearly the reverse. Because of the rigid party system in operation in Britain (the Prime Minister being the leader of the Government party), in reality it is the Government, and in particular the Prime Minister, who controls Parliament. Parliament must approve the raising of all taxes and the expenditure of all money raised in taxes, but so long as the Government has the support of its own party members in Parliament, particularly in the Commons, it need have no fear that Parliament will disapprove its actions. The real discussion of policy today tends to occur within the committee rooms, at meetings of members of the Government party's supporters in Parliament. If the Government's followers in the Commons approve a policy then it is extremely unlikely that such policy will be defeated on the floor of either house of Parliament. Prime Ministers are likelier to resign nowadays because they have lost the support of a significant number of their party members in the Commons than because they have lost the support of the Commons as a whole. In 1940 the Prime Minister, Neville Chamberlain, won a vote of confidence in the House of Commons by a large majority but felt constrained to resign because a significant number of members of his own party failed to vote for him in the Commons on the motion of confidence.

The party is therefore decisive in ordinary matters; the party may normally be relied upon to vote for any policy advocated by the Government, although the Government will keep in contact with its party supporters to ensure that it does not propose to Parliament legislation or other action which at party meetings, or as a result of more informal soundings, it is clear that a considerable number of members of the party will not support. It might appear therefore that the party has the last word, but again in reality this is not so in normal circumstances. The Prime Minister is armed with certain powers which enable him within reasonable limits to carry his party with him. He is leader of his party and controls the party machine, which may determine whether a particular recalcitrant party member may stand for re-election as a candidate of that party at the next election. It is practically impossible for anyone to secure election to Parliament in Britain unless he is adopted as a candidate for one of the three main parties. Whether he may so stand is decided by the central office of the parties concerned, which in the case of the Government party is subject to control by the Prime Minister. The Prime Minister is also able to decide upon the date of a general election; for while Parliaments have a maximum life of five years, the Prime Minister is entitled to call an election at any time he personally chooses. The threat of calling an election has been used by the last Prime Minister, Mr. Wilson, as a means of seeking to ensure the support of party members who were wavering in their support of his policy. It would be a foolish Prime Minister who called an early election and lost it merely because he wanted to discipline his supporters. However, the power and the threat to use it are there, and this has an influence in securing support for the Prime Minister.

Theoretically government in Britain is government by a Cabinet, of which the Prime Minister is merely one member, but the modern reality is that increasing power is exercised by the Prime Minister personally, who may be in a position to take executive decisions, involving the expenditure of money without the Cabinet or even Parliament being aware of what he has done. The money so spent would have had to have been voted by Parliament, but in the past at any rate the amount of detailed information given to Parliament as to how the money was proposed to be spent was so vague that it has been possible for considerable sums to be spent on major projects involving major decisions of policy without either Parliament or the Cabinet being conscious of the way in which the money was spent.[1]

Financial questions, and in particular the initiation of legislation involving public expenditure, are, by an understanding without legal basis but nonetheless rigidly adhered to, regarded as the prerogative of the lower elected chamber, the House of Commons. In practice the initiative to propose the expenditure of money comes not from the Commons itself but from the Government.

b. The Treasury and the Civil Service Department

Traditionally the Treasury was the Government department responsible for the running of the civil service. As a civil service ministry the senior civil servant was directly responsible to the Prime Minister. The Treasury is also the equivalent of a Ministry of Finance and that part of its work is the responsibility of the Chancellor of the Exchequer. In 1969 the civil service side of the Treasury was replaced by a separate ministry under a separate minister who in turn is under the general authority of the Prime Minister. The functions of the Civil Service Department, including the Civil Service Commission,[2] may be broadly classified under three headings: personnel management, administrative and managerial efficiency, and terms of service.

Under the first heading—personnel management—the CSD is responsible for policy and central arrangements for selection and recruitment and the selection process itself; and for policy

1. Cf. Mr. Attlee's decision to order the development of a British atomic bomb. See R. H. S. Crossman's introduction to W. Bagehot, *The British Constitution* (London, 1963).
2. The Civil Service Commission, now part of the Civil Service Department, was formerly an independent public body charged with supervising the qualifications of entrants to the nonindustrial civil service.

and central arrangements on training, promotion, postings and general career management, including problems of staff wastage, welfare, security and retirement policy. It is also responsible for advising on top-level appointments.

Under the heading of administrative and managerial efficiency, the CSD is responsible for the development and dissemination of administrative and managerial techniques; and for the general oversight of the organisation of departments, including the comparative study of the organisational problems and the machinery of government. It is responsible for the provision of central management services such as organisation and methods, computers and operational research, and shares with others a concern for the physical environment in which civil servants work. It exercises a central authority in respect of departmental administrative expenditure generally and departmental manpower requirements in terms of both numbers and grading.

Under the third heading—terms of service—the CSD controls rates of pay and related allowances, procedures for reimbursing expenses incurred in the public service, and the structure of the Civil Service in terms of grade and occupational groupings. It co-ordinates Government policy in relation to pay in the public services generally, including the approval of salaries and allowances for the members and staff of certain public sector organisations. It is responsible for the development and execution of policy on Civil Service superannuation and for the co-ordination of pension arrangements throughout the public sector.[3]

The Civil Service Department's control of pay is exercised of course in consultation with the Treasury, still the department which controls the raising and spending of taxation.

c. The Treasury, Civil Service Department, and other Ministries

Many other ministries are involved in questions concerning the pay, conditions of work, superannuation, etc., of the civil service (and indeed of other workers in the public sector). There is first of all the Department of Employment and Productivity (formerly the Ministry of Labour), charged primarily with the

3. *First Report of the Civil Service Department* (HMSO, 1970), pp. 9–10.

formulation and implementation of the Government's incomes policy. Under the previous Labour Government the Prices and Incomes Acts 1966, 1967, and 1968 gave the Department of Employment and Productivity considerable legal powers to control collective bargaining and the alteration of terms and conditions of employment resulting therefrom. A Prices and Incomes Board, an independent public body, exists whose function it is to advise the Department of Employment and Productivity on certain questions, including in particular the question whether a given wage increase is or is not in the public interest (a concept which the Government has itself defined by statutory regulation). The Government has legal power to delay implementation of any pay increase which conflicts with a recommendation of the Prices and Incomes Board. However, the present Conservative Government has indicated that it is opposed to a statutory incomes policy and now seeks to implement a policy of wage restraint by persuasion. In this effort the Government's own powers over the public sector have an important part to play as restraint in the public sector may influence the way in which private industry behaves.

In any discussion of civil service conditions the ministry to which the particular civil servants who wish an alteration of their conditions belong has a major interest. In the Departmental Whitley Councils the official side consists therefore of representatives of the particular department together with one representative of the Department of Employment and Productivity. It is a general provision in the constitutions of Departmental Whitley Councils that a representative of the Treasury may also attend, and indeed may be summoned. (One assumes that this now would be understood to refer to a representative of the Civil Service Department, but since there has been no formal amendment of the Whitley constitutions this is not certain. The point is academic since most negotiation and discussion in the Whitley system takes place very informally, very often between individuals.)

d. Central Government and Local Authorities

Local authorities are subject to central control in many ways, although it is not easy to describe the working of this relationship with any precision. The working relationship between central government departments and local authorities in England and Wales can be regarded in terms which are formal, informal, statutory, non-statutory, legal, extra-legal, financial, official, personal, political, functional, tragical-comical-historical-pastoral. Seneca cannot be too heavy nor Plautus too light. Any generalization evokes shouts of protest.[4]

Central Government departments, most commonly the Ministry of Housing and Local Government, exercise considerable control over the activities of the local authorities. Of most relevance to us is the control exercised over the staff of local authorities.

The appointment, dismissal, discipline, pay and conditions of service of some local authority staff is subject to the influence and control of government departments. Thus the salary of county clerks although fixed by the relevant county council is subject to the approval of the Minister of Housing and Local Government;[5] more importantly, a county clerk cannot be dismissed without the consent of the same Minister.[6]

The dismissal of a county, county borough or county district medical officer of health is subject to the consent of the Minister of Health, as also is the dismissal of a county borough or county district public health inspector.[7] Similarly, the appointment of a children's officer closely involves the Home Secretary, the local authority being required to submit their short list to the Home Secretary who is able to prohibit the appointment of anyone considered unsuitable.[8] The appointment of a chief education officer involves the Secretary of State for Education and Science in exactly the same way.[9] These powers to prohibit are still used occasionally.

The Home Secretary is empowered to make regulations governing the maintenance of discipline, pensions, appointment, promotion and standards of training of members of fire brigades; and governing certain matters relating to equipment.[10] Fire authorities are required to obtain the approval

4. J. A. G. Griffith, *Central Departments and Local Authorities* (London, 1968), p. 1.
5. Local Government Act 1933, s.99(1).
6. Ibid., s.100(1).   8. Children Act 1949, s.41(2).
7. Ibid., ss.103(3), 110.   9. Education Act 1944, s.88
10. Fire Services Act 1947, ss.14, 17, 18, 21, 26; and Fire Services Act 1959, ss.5, 6, 8.

of the Home Secretary to their appointment of a chief fire officer.[11]

The police service represents an extreme example of central control over local authority staff.[12] The powers of the Home Secretary are considerable over the appointment, dismissal, discipline and conditions of service police officers in England and Wales. His general power is to make regulations as to the government, administration and conditions of service of police forces.[13]

Financial control is exercised by central Government, by the giving or withholding of authorisation where such is necessary, by the giving of grants for general or specific purposes, and above all by means of auditing of the accounts of local authorities by the district auditors of the Ministry of Housing and Local Government. Their duty is to disallow every item of account contrary to law and to surcharge the persons responsible for such unlawful expenditure.[14] It is worth noticing that although

11. S.I. 1965, No. 577, reg.i.

12. Legally, the police are not employees of local authorities and appointments to ranks below that of assistant chief constable are made by the chief constable and not by local authority: Police Act 1964, s.7(2).

13. Police Act 1964, s.33(1). The powers of the Police Council and the Police Advisory Board affect the exercise by the Secretary of State of his general power (see ss.45, 46). Quote is from Griffith, op.cit., pp. 59–60.

14. One of the strangest cases arising out of the activities of district auditors was *Roberts* v. *Hopwood* [1925] A.C. 578 in which the auditor, exercising his power under s.247(7) of the Public Health Act 1875 to "disallow any item of account contrary to law," disallowed wages paid by the Labour-controlled London Borough Council of Polar, on the grounds the amount paid was unreasonable and therefore unlawful. The Council decided to fix wages in the light of three considerations: (1) that men and women should be paid the same wage, (2) that no employee should receive less than a reasonable wage, and (3) that as a model employer, the Council should pay good wages, notwithstanding that they were above the rates fiixed by the National Joint Industrial Council. The House of Lords decided that the District Auditor had acted correctly; the wage rates fixed by the Council were unlawful, because they fixed rates without considering the market rate for similar work in private employment. Equal pay was lawful but only if it was equal pay for the same work. The cost of living was falling and therefore by failing to take this into account the Council again had acted unlawfully. At least one member of the House of Lords, Lord Buckmaster, seemed to think (notwithstanding that this would involve a violation of the contracts of employment of its employees) that the Council ought unilaterally to have reduced wages as the cost of living fell. The idea of being a model employer did not appeal to Lord Atkinson, at p. 595:

this power is exercised with some strictness in one area of public employment it was never applied in the case of police. Until the Police Act 1964 local authorities had no power to make grants of money to members of local police forces who had costs or damages awarded against them in respect of unlawful acts by such policemen committed while performing their duties as policemen. However, it became the practice before 1964 for local authorities to refund such damages and costs virtually automatically, so much so that it became a matter of complaint by the police when such local authority payments were unreasonably delayed.[15] These payments which were generally made were unlawful, but there is not a single example of a district auditor disallowing such expenditure by a local authority—a nice example of the practical understanding between public officials of the problems of maintaining good labour relations in the public service!

e. Distinction between the Formal Employer and the Financing Authority

In many areas, particularly local government, the body which in law may be the employer may not be the body which is wholly responsible for the payment of the wages concerned, e.g. the relationship between teachers and the local authorities. Finance may come in whole or in part from the central Government.

An example of the distinction between the formal employer and some other public body which may control wages, or other aspects of the employment relationship, may be seen in *Hannam* v. *Bradford City Council*.[16] Education at the secondary level in Britain is either wholly public, wholly private, or mixed. "Mixed" education takes several forms, of which one is a system whereby the local authorities maintain schools originally provided and established by some private body. In such circumstances a teacher, formally employed by the governors of the school, can be dismissed

---

"The indulgence of philanthropic enthusiasm at the expense of persons other than the philanthropists is an entirely different thing from the indulgence of it at the expense of the philanthropists themselves. The former wears quite a different legal as well as moral character." All this was with reference to a statute, the Metropolis Management Act 1855, s.62, which provided that the Council might "pay such wages as [the Council] may think fit."

15. B. Whitaker, *The Police* (Harmondsworth, 1964), p. 76.
16. [1970] 2 All E.R. 690.

only if the local authority, who provides his salary, does not withhold its approval of the dismissal, in accordance with the provisions of the Education Act 1944. The local authority in such a situation has the power to require that a teacher be dismissed, the power to specify the qualifications that teachers appointed must have, and the power to lay down terms and conditions of employment, including length of notice. The subcommittee of the local authority concerned with education, which met to decide whether the local authority should withhold its consent to a dismissal of the teachers by the school governors, included three of the school governors. It was obvious that a risk of prejudice occurred, of a kind which might entitle the dismissed teacher to challenge the validity of the subcommittee's decision. The teacher sought damages for breach of contract between himself and the local authority, the term alleged to be broken being that the committee of the local authority considering his dismissal by the governors should be properly constituted. Although one judge would have been willing to hold that on the facts there was a tripartite contract agreement governing the employment of the teacher, the court by a majority held that the teacher had only a contract with the school governors, and not with the local authority. This therefore is an example of a public body having wide legal power to require or prohibit dismissal, and to regulate the conditions of employment of someone who is in law not the employee of the public body concerned.

f. Representation of Employing Authority

Representation of the employer in the civil service raises a difficulty because all civil servants are "employees." In practice this difficulty is more apparent than real. In local government because there is not a single unified local government employer there are real difficulties of coordination, but these have been partly overcome by establishing machinery for consultation between different local authorities on questions of negotiations with their employees.

2. CENTRALISATION OF BARGAINING

Centralisation helps to obtain uniformity of working conditions, and therefore in the local government area especially we find joint negotiating bodies established for particular grades of workers on a national basis. On the other hand the work of Government departments may vary so much, particularly when an industrial worker or a skilled professional man is employed only by a particular department, his conditions must be dealt with on a local basis.

3. THE AUTHORITY FOR DECISION-MAKING

Enough has been said earlier about the relations between Prime Minister 'and Parliament, between central and local Government to indicate that precise answers may often be lacking with respect to the question of who has authority to make decisions in the field of public employment.

We shall see in Chapter V that collective agreements arrived at by bargaining between employers and workers' organisations do not themselves usually give rise to contractual relations between the parties to such agreements. Nor do collective agreements automatically become enforceable at the instance of the employees to whom they apply.[17]

The general view, and it must surely be correct, is that agreements or awards arrived at by joint negotiation in the public sector are not themselves more than recommendations to the authority responsible for making payment. This is so notwithstanding the provision in the constitution of the National Whitley Council that "The decisions of the Council shall be arrived at by agreement between the two sides, shall be signed by the Chairman and Vice-Chairman, shall be reported to the Cabinet *and shall thereupon become operative."* There is a similar provision in the constitutions of Departmental Whitley Councils that their decisions "shall be reported to the Head of Department *and shall become operative."*

The National Council subsequently agreed the position to be as follows:

The establishment of Whitley Councils cannot relieve the Government of any part of its responsibility to Parliament, and Ministers and Heads of Departments acting under the general or specific authority of Ministers, must take such ac-

17. We shall see in Chap. V, however, that the decided cases are difficult to reconcile in regard to the effect of a past practice of giving effect to collectively agreed terms.

tions as may be required in any case in the public interest. This condition is inherent in the constitutional doctrines of Parliamentary Government and ministerial responsibility, and Ministers can neither waive nor escape it.

It follows from this constitutional principle that, while the acceptance by the Government of the Whitley system as regards the Civil Service implies an intention to make the fullest possible use of Whitley procedure, the Government has not surrendered, and cannot surrender its liberty of action in the exercise of its authority and the discharge of its responsibilities in the public interest.

·V·

The Scope of Bargaining

1. THE SUBJECTS OF BARGAINING

a. Introduction

i. ABSENCE OF EXPRESS EXCLUSIONS

APART from the case of the police, there has never been any attempt to limit, by express enactment, the matters which may be the subject of discussion between public employee organisations and employing authorities. On the contrary, the list of topics has continuously expanded as a result of union strength and not through legislation. This has led to complaints from management, voiced by the Post Office in 1966, that "some trivial matters are taken to unnecessary lengths so overloading management and union machinery" and causing unnecessary delays in decision-making.[1] To this the staff side of the Post Office Whitley Council has responded that the extension of negotiation into areas which were previously regarded as the sole prerogative of management has led to the Post Office being exceptionally free from disputes (those which have occurred are attributed to National Incomes Policies) and to the peaceful introduction of technological change.[2]

ii. "NEGOTIATION" AND "CONSULTATION"

The critical distinction in the U.K. is sometimes considered to be that between matters appropriate for "negotiation" and "consultation" respectively. Yet there is no agreed definition of these terms either in statute law or by usage. The Nationalisation Acts[3] and the Post Office Act 1969 all require the managements in question to "seek" or "enter into" "consultation" with "appropriate" organisations with a view to the "conclusion . . . of such agreements as appear to the parties to be desirable with respect

1. Post Office, RCWE (November 1966) para. 44
2. Post Office Dept. Whitley Council (staff side) RCWE.
3. Coal Industry Nationalisation Act 1946, s.46; Gas Act 1948, s.57; Iron & Steel Act 1949, s.39 (as amended by Iron & Steel Act 1967, s.31); Transport Act 1947, s.95; Electricity Act 1947, s.53; Atomic Energy Authority Act 1954, s.7. In the Coal Act this wording is different.

to the establishment and maintenance"[4] of joint machinery. The Coal Industry Nationalisation Act 1946[5] (and in fairly similar terms the Gas Act 1948)[6] then goes on to elaborate two separate functions of this machinery:

> (a) the *settlement by negotiation* of terms and conditions of employment, with provision for reference to arbitration in default of such settlement in such cases as may be determined by or under the agreements.

> (b) *consultation* on—(i) questions relating to the safety, health or welfare of such persons; (ii) the organisation and conduct of the operations in which such persons are employed and other matters of mutual interest to the Board and such persons arising out of the exercise and performance by the Board of their functions.

The other Nationalisation Act and the Post Office Act repeat in more or less similar words the first of these functions ("settlement by negotiation") but drop the word "consultation" in regard to the second. They refer simply to the "promotion and encouragement" of matters such as safety, health and welfare, efficiency, training, and "other matters of mutual interest." The only meaningful difference between these functions, as they appear on the face of the statutes, appears to be that the settlement by negotiation of terms and conditions may be referred to arbitration in default of settlement, whereas there is no *duty* to seek an arbitration agreement in respect of the "other matters." This means that the distinction between negotiation and consultation in the nationalised industries can only be of importance when the parties *disagree*.

The acts themselves recognise that the consultation aimed at establishing negotiating machinery must be with a view to *agreement*. So too the DEP's *Industrial Relations Handbook* (1961) refers to "joint consultation" as "management and employee cooperation," and cooperation seems to imply some form of agreement and joint action. In other words, "consultation" sometimes means far more than simply allowing the other side to tender

4. These words are used in the Post Office Act 1969, sch. 1, para. 11. Fairly similar words are used in the other acts.
5. S.46(1). Italics added in quotation.
6. S.57(1)(b); the other matters in this case expressly include "efficiency."

advice.[7] Nor is it adequate to suggest that "consultation" inevitably implies cooperation while "negotiation" involves haggling. Economic sanctions have on occasion been applied in regard to matters such as individual dismissals or promotion, technological change, and so on, which are usually regarded as "consultative" rather than "negotiable" topics.

Despite the absence of statutory definitions of these terms, an attempt to establish their ordinary usage was made in the Report of a Court of Inquiry under Lord Pearson (a Lord of Appeal in Ordinary) into a recognition dispute between the nationalised British Steel Corporation and some of its employees:[8]

> *"Negotiation,"* it was said, "means a joint decision by two sides after discussion which may involve bargaining; the items where a negotiated decision is required are normally those included in the management-union contract."[9]

> *"Consultation"* "means one side or group asking advice of the other side or group before taking a decision (this decision will normally then be made by either management or the unions but there will be occasions when, after consultation, it might be appropriate for negotiations to take place leading to a joint decision)."

> *"Communication"* "means giving or receiving information especially about decisions which have been taken and the reasons behind them."

Other attempts have been made to draw the distinction by reference to factors such as subject matter, parties, and the nature of the process involved in "negotiation" and "consultation" respectively.

As regards subject matter, the DEP offers a negative definition by saying that consultation is limited to "matters of joint concern which are not the subject of joint negotiation with trade unions." This simply begs the question for the precise topics of negotiation vary from industry to industry, from enterprise to enterprise,

7. This is the ordinary legal construction of the word "consultation" in other statutory contexts, e.g. *Rollo* v. *Min. of Town & Country Planning* [1948] 1 All E.R. 13, 17.

8. Cmnd. 3754 (1968), App. 1.

9. The word "contract" seems inappropriate because elsewhere the report supported the traditional view that collective labour agreements in Britain are usually not intended to give rise to contractual relations.

and from sector to sector of the public services. For example, only the remuneration of teachers is a subject for *negotiation* within the Burnham committees, while all other topics are the subject of *consultation* with teachers' associations. On the other hand, the range of matters discussed on the National Civil Service Whitley Council is extremely wide and includes general conditions of service, new working methods and general questions such as the organisation of the service.

"Consultation" requires at least two parties. But is the employee side to be represented by unions, or does consultation, unlike negotiation, involve some form of direct discussion between management and the workers in an establishment or department? At national and departmental level in the public services the phrase "direct consultation" is often used simply as being synonymous with negotiation with individual unions in contradistinction to negotiation with several unions organised as a united "staff side" on Whitley Councils. Yet "consultation" within enterprises or departments may imply direct employee involvement.

Consultation is often seen as a means of localising agreements. Do the unions have a role in this process? If so, what are its precise limits? The establishment of joint works committees was an important part of the recommendations of the Whitley Committee which regarded them as a means for improving industrial democracy. The Whitley Committee was conscious, however, of the danger of undermining trade union development and so envisaged that the workers' representatives would be trade unionists. Moreover, local consultative machinery was not to interfere in matters settled by national negotiations, although it was considered that they could discuss issues of interpretation in the light of local conditions. During the interwar years joint consultation did not progress rapidly in private industry because of management fears that its "prerogatives" would be undermined, and trade union suspicions that bargaining strength and national policies would be subverted. During the Second World War "joint production committees" at plant level were established under a number of national agreements. These were thought of as means for utilising the ideas and energies of workers, and not as a place where bargaining led to a compromise agreement binding on both sides. After the war a number of private firms responded to a new government philosophy of consultation which went beyond the wartime experiments. It was this philosophy which lay beneath the statutory distinctions between consultation and negotiation in the Nationalisation Acts. As Clegg[10] has said:

> The essence of the philosophy was that joint consultation was the means to produce a new industrial society. To this end it emphasised the differences between collective bargaining and joint consultation. Collective bargaining was appropriate in the narrow area in which the interests of managers and workers conflict. Joint consultation was to be used in the wide area in which these interests coincided (particularly increasing productivity). Joint consultation required different qualities from workers' representatives than did collective bargaining (and perhaps even different men as representatives). . . . It was a continuous process of so informing the workers of the facts through their representatives, and of conveying the attitudes of the workers to management, that the decision of the firm would become the expression of a "general will" of the whole body of those who worked in the firm, from the directors to the unskilled labourers.

This philosophy was undermined and the character of joint consultation transformed by a major postwar development, namely the growth of shop steward influence. This change is well researched in private and nationalised industries. In the nationalised gas and electricity industries McCarthy and Coker found that shop stewards had realised that more substantial gains could be won by exploiting disputes procedures than by using the purely "advisory" consultative machinery. (In electricity supply shop stewards did not attend the Local Advisory Committee which they termed the "Let's All Cuddle"!; there is similar evidence in respect of colliery consultative committees).[11] McCarthy advances two propositions about the relationship of joint consultative machinery to shop steward bargaining:

> First, plant consultative committees, in the strict sense of bodies intended simply to advise management on how to raise

10. H. A. Clegg, *A New Approach to Industrial Democracy* (1960), p. 36.
11. W. E. J. McCarthy, *The Role of Shop Stewards in British Industrial Relations,* R.C. Research Paper No. 1 (1967), p. 33.

efficiency and discuss other matters of assumed "common interest" without reaching binding agreements, cannot survive the development of effective shop floor organisation. Either they must change their character and become essentially negotiating committees carrying out functions which are indistinguishable from the formal processes of shop floor bargaining, or they are boycotted by shop stewards and, as the influence of the latter grows, fall into disuse. Secondly, shop stewards themselves do not subscribe to the assumptions which lay behind the provisions of separate institutional arrangements for the purpose of dealing with so-called "conflicting" and "common interest" questions, and any committee on which they serve which cannot reach decisions, albeit informal ones, they regard as essentially an inferior or inadequate substitute for proper negotiating machinery.[12]

This indicates that the distinction between "negotiation" and "consultation" is less important than it was when the Nationalisation Acts were framed, and that interpretations depend not upon the divinations of lawyers but the actual state of shop floor relationships. The recent attempt to distinguish "negotiation" of terms and conditions from "promotion" of efficiency (by consultation?) in the Post Office Act 1969 may be of little importance in practice. Joint Production Councils and Committees were set up in the Post Office after the war, but the Engineering Council was suspended in 1961 because of the withdrawal of two unions following the rejection of a pay claim in the Whitley Council. The Non-Engineering Council appears to have limited itself to the consideration of staff suggestions, and all the major matters relating to efficiency and technological change have been considered as matters for bargaining on the Whitley Councils. In other words, the only bodies which were obviously "consultative" have ceased to be of importance, and all other procedures have been used equally for "negotiation" and "consultation" matters. The Post Office rules on local Whitley Councils procedures attempt to distinguish between "prior notification" by management of impending changes and "prior consultation," but in practice the unions have limited the use of the former and have expected "consultation"

12. Ibid.

(with a view to agreement) even in respect of relatively minor matters.

In the public services, unlike the nationalised industries, there is no formal statutory distinction between "negotiation" and "consultation." Matters which are considered appropriate for negotiation in one sector may be dealt with by consultation in another. A case in point is superannuation, which is regarded as a subject for negotiation through Whitley-type machinery in the industrial and nonindustrial civil service and the police, but is the subject of direct consultations with appropriate organisations of health service employees and teachers. Some matters, such as efficiency, may be the subject of negotiation at the national level and consultation at the local level. Yet even locally, "consultative" bodies may be spurned as office or shop-floor productivity bargaining gains in popularity.

In some sectors of the public service "consultation" has been formalised through special advisory bodies, such as the Police Advisory Boards and the Fire Services Advisory Council. These bodies may deal with the residue of subjects which are not specifically "reserved" to negotiating bodies; yet the negotiating bodies are not expressly precluded from discussing the "nonreserved" subjects, and the tendency has been for the scope of negotiable (i.e. "reserved") topics to expand.

iii. DETERMINANTS OF THE SCOPE OF BARGAINING IN THE PUBLIC SERVICES

The scope and nature of bargaining in the public services is the product of piecemeal development and compromise. There are wide variations between different sectors of the public services and these defy logical explanation. Within each sector the boundaries of negotiation and consultation are usually vague and flexible; the precise limits of bargaining are decided pragmatically. In other words, the definition of subject matter is open-ended and is itself a matter for bargaining.

Nevertheless, it is possible to isolate four structural determinants of the scope of bargaining:

(1) *The type of machinery used.* Some matters are considered appropriate for Whitley-type negotiating machinery (which involves agreement by a majority of both sides of the negotiating body), some for direct discussion with employee organisations, some for

agreement by joint standing conferences, and others for consultation with advisory bodies. The only subject which is dealt with by the Whitley method throughout the public services is remuneration, and even in this regard there are isolated exceptions—for example, the county clerks (chief executive officers of administrative counties) in Scotland who have no negotiating machinery, engineers and builders in hospitals whose wages are fixed in accordance with outside trade rates, and a few employees of local government such as bakers and catering staff whose wages are fixed by Wages Councils orders.

General conditions of service are usually dealt with by the Whitley method, the most significant exception being teachers, for whom model terms of employment are agreed by joint standing conferences. Individual cases are nearly always dealt with by direct discussions with the appropriate employee organisation. General questions about training, efficiency, redundancy, and superannuation are dealt with by a variety of methods.

(2) *The status of the employees.* This affects the type of machinery used and the scope of bargaining. For example, salaries of the higher nonindustrial civil service are not the subject of negotiations through the Whitley method but are the outcome of recommendations by an independent advisory body. In the industrial civil service, negotiations take place, through Whitley machinery, on a trade basis, and in local government services there is separate machinery for craft and noncraft manual workers, for administrative and clerical staffs, and for senior officers. In the health services the constitutional limits of negotiating bodies are determined on an occupational basis, and in educational services they depend on the kind of institution in which the teachers are engaged. In the police and fire services there are also limitations on the jurisdiction of negotiating bodies depending on the status of employees.

(3) *Geographical and departmental limits.* The scope of bargaining is often limited by the structure of the public service. For example, in the nonindustrial civil service there is a division of functions between National and Departmental Whitley Councils; in the industrial civil service there may be resort to direct negotiations with appropriate unions in regard to matters of con-

cern to a single department and use of the Whitley method when more than one department is involved or where departmental negotiation does not yield a settlement; in local government the National Whitley Councils for noncraft manual workers and for administrative and clerical staffs each have a number of provincial or district councils arranged on a geographical basis.

(4) *The form of agreements and advice.* Two basic forms are to be found. The first is a *recommendation* to the *employing* authority.[13] The second is a *recommendation* to the Secretary of State (i.e. Central Government department) which, if approved by him, is embodied in statutory regulations and then binds all employing authorities. For convenience, the first may be called the voluntary method and the second the statutory method. But it must be stressed that even the first method may receive statutory support. Provided they have been negotiated by "representative" organisations the terms and conditions may be regarded as "recognised" ones which can then be extended to other employing authorities (whether parties to the machinery or not) under section 8 of the Terms and Conditions of Employment Act 1959. Whichever method is used, the agreements always take the form of recommendations. They are not of automatic contractual effect between the parties. But once recognised by employers under the first method they take legal effect as part of the individual employee's contract of employment. This is not always the case, however; for example, disputes procedures and some vague aspirational agreements of joint negotiating machinery may never acquire legal effectiveness. Terms and conditions approved and made the subject of statutory regulations under the second method also take effect as part of the individual contract of employment.

The following is a summary of the matters dealt with by the second, i.e. "statutory," method—after negotiation.

13. Our insistence on treating all Whitley decisions as *recommendations* may be regarded by some as an indication of the difference between the *legal* and *nonlegal* approaches to this question. For example, the Treasury memorandum No. 31 to the Fulton Commission on the Civil Service (vol. IV, p. 500) states: "Whitley Councils are not merely advisory; their decisions become operative. But the official sides are responsible to Ministers, and, unless Ministers have authorised official sides to agree, no agreements can be reached on the Councils." From the lawyer's viewpoint this is untenable. For a full discussion see Chap. IV above.

> Health services—remuneration and conditions
>> Police—remuneration and certain conditions, except promotion and discipline, which may *not* be the subject of negotiation or consultation
>
> Fire services—discipline and appeals against dismissals
>
> Teachers (primary—remuneration and secondary)
>
> County clerks—remuneration

There are also certain matters which become the subject of statutory regulation after consultation. These include the "non-reserved" subjects in the police and fire services, and superannuation for teachers and health service employees.

It is not possible to provide any rational grounds for preferring one method to another. However, it may be observed that in certain sectors there has been pressure from employee organisations in favour of the voluntary method. In the fire services this resulted in 1959 in the removal of pay and conditions from the matters requiring ministerial approval and regluation, and in the educational services some associations wish the present statutory method to be replaced by voluntary observance of agreements without ministerial intervention.

This general picture is subject to much detailed variation in each sector of the public services. We shall now describe the situation in each sector, concentrating on those in which the "statutory" method is used. Then we shall consider the legal results of bargaining.

b. Nonindustrial Civil Service

Here there are no statutory provisions about the subjects of negotiation and consultation. It is important to notice that "consultation" is used in the nonindustrial civil service to describe direct *negotiations* with associations as distinguished from negotiations through the Whitley machinery. According to the Treasury's *Staff Relations Handbook*, "a substantial proportion of present-day negotiation of civil service conditions of service is done by direct discussions with associations and not by Whitley machinery." The formal constitution of the National Whitley Council says that "the scope of the National Council shall comprise all matters which affect the conditions of service of the staff." The Report on the Application of the Whitley Report to the Civil Service (1919)[14] took the view that it would be inadvisable to lay down a close definition of subjects; yet the principle seems to have been followed that "the only joint body at which questions of remuneration affecting a particular class common to the service should be discussed" is the National Whitley Council. This avoids a series of separate concurrent discussions with each of the associations representing the affected classes, or the discussion of the same question at a number of departmental meetings, or the discussion of remuneration by classes who have no interest in the matter.

The formal constitutions of National and Departmental Whitley Councils in no way limit discussion of remuneration and conditions of service to matters affecting the lower grades. But a convention exists (reaffirmed in 1956) that on pay and certain other subjects it is expedient to exclude the highest grades. The purpose of this is to obviate the difficulties which would arise if members of the official side on the Whitley Councils, drawn from the higher grades, were called upon to negotiate their own pay and conditions. Both the staff side and the official side were agreed on the need for some form of independent review of the remuneration of staff above the financial limit for the reference of disputes to arbitration. This limit is now set at the maximum of the Administrative Principal without reference to a specific figure so that it varies with the maximmum of the Principal. As a result there was established in 1957, on the recommendation of the Priestley Commission on the Civil Service,[15] a Standing Advisory Committee on Salaries of the Higher Civil Service, appointed by the Prime Minister and supposed to reflect "a cross section of informed opinion in the country at large." (The present membership of six consists mainly of senior academics who have experience of government.) The Advisory Committee acts as an independent body, submitting its recommendations directly to the Prime Minister. (At present its recommendations affect about 8,000 civil servants of whom 1,200 are in the administrative class

14. Cmd. 9 (1919) para. 24.
15. Cmd. 9613 (1955) paras. 284–86.

and the remainder in the executive, professional, scientific and other specialist classes.) It has been said that the "independent position of the Committee should, and should be seen to be, maintained."[16] Its third review (1966) was vetted by the Prices and Incomes Board, but the Government defended this submission on the grounds that it had submitted the matter in its capacity as "custodian of the public interest" rather than as employer. "Minor" matters affecting the higher grades are not dealt with by the Committee but by direct negotiation with the staff associations representing those grades. The scope of "minor" matters is itself a subject for negotiation.

Apart from remuneration, there is a large number of other matters dealt with by negotiation on National and Departmental Whitley Councils. The formal constitution of the National Whitley Council lists the following as examples of what may be discussed:

(i) Provision of the best means for utilizing the ideas and experience of the staff.

(ii) Means for securing to the staff a greater share in and responsibility for the determination and observance of the conditions under which their duties are carried out.

(iii) Determination of the general principles governing conditions of service, e.g. recruitment, hours, promotion, discipline, tenure, remuneration and superannuation.

In the National Council the discussion of promotion shall be restricted to the general aspects of the matter and the principles upon which promotions in general should rest. In no circumstances shall individual cases be taken into consideration.

It shall be open to the National Council to discuss the general principles underlying disciplinary action, but there shall be no discussion of individual cases.

(iv) The encouragement of the further education of civil servants and their training in higher administration and organisation.

(v) Improvement of office machinery and organisation and the provision of opportunities for the full consideration of suggestions by the staff on this subject.

16. National Board for Prices and Incomes, Report No. 11, *Pay of the Higher Civil Service* (1966), para. 3.

(vi) Proposed legislation so far as it has a bearing upon the position of civil servants in relation to their employment."

The model constitution for a departmental Whitley Council lists all the same matters ((i) to (vi) above) but in regard to promotion and discipline does not contain the same rigid exclusion of discussion of individual cases:

Promotion and discipline. Without prejudice to the responsibility of the head of the Department for making promotions and maintaining discipline, it shall be within the competence of the Council:

(a) to discuss any promotion in regard to which it is represented by the staff side that the principles of promotion accepted by or with the sanction of the National Council have been violated; and

(b) to discuss any case in which disciplinary action has been taken if it is represented by the staff side that such a course is desirable.

Cases about individual civil servants, however, are generally negotiated directly with the association concerned and not by the Whitley method. This includes, in addition to promotion and discipline, discussion about superannuation and sick leave in individual cases (general policy being a matter for the Whitley Councils).

In practice the list of matters actually discussed is even wider than those specified in the formal constitutions. It includes policy on the political affiliations of civil servants (the National Council) and staff welfare problems (Departmental Councils).

c. Industrial Civil Service

The subjects of bargaining in this sector, like the nonindustrial civil service, depend on custom and usage and not on legislation. Wages and other conditions of service (such as normal hours and overtime, sick absence and holidays) in their relation to workers' pay are dealt with on a trade basis. There are three Trade Joint Councils (Shipbuilding, Engineering, and Miscellaneous). The Shipbuilding Council is mainly concerned with employees of the Navy Department. Each of the others is concerned with workers employed in a number of departments (e.g. Air,

Army, Works, etc.). The formal constitutions of these three Councils contemplate negotiations on the following topics:

1. The regular consideration of the rates of wages of persons in the trade employed in the various establishments concerned, including the fixing of time and piece rates, together with their re-adjustments as may be necessary, subject to due consideration being given to such national or other agreements as may be fixed for the trade from time to time.

2. The consideration of methods of determining wages, and of adjusting wages to new conditions.

3. The collection of statistical and other information relating to output, costing, etc.

4. The consideration of questions relating to working conditions generally (including hours, sick absence, holidays and superannuation), in their relation to wages, so far as these questions may specifically concern the employees in the . . . trade in the various establishments concerned.

5. The consideration, in conjunction with the Departmental Councils where necessary, of the conditions of entry into the various establishments, and training therein in the trade, and of educational questions in relation thereto.

6. The consideration of the local and other machinery for the speedy settlement of differences in the various establishments; the creation of machinery under which, in the event of failure to settle matters in dispute in the Trade Joint Council, they can be referred, by agreement between the Government and the Trade Unions concerned, to arbitration.

7. The consideration of arrangements for setting up and adjusting local machinery by way of Trade or other committees in the Works under the Departments concerned, to deal with the local aspects of any or all of the above matters, and the consideration of matters referred to the Council by such committees.

8. Co-operation with other Trade Joint Councils or with Departmental Councils or with Joint Industrial Councils for private industry, where necessary, to deal with matters of common interest.

It will be noted that, apart from wages and fringe benefits, the Councils discuss matters such as trade entry qualifications, training, and disputes procedures. In the case of Engineering and Miscellaneous Trades, questions of concern to a single department are frequently negotiated directly with the unions concerned; the Council procedure being resorted to when more than one department is involved or where it has been impossible to reach a settlement by departmental negotiation.

There are Departmental Joint Councils in departments which employ substantial numbers of industrial staff. The subjects for discussion are those domestic to the department concerned. Examples are the interpretation of departmental regulations, welfare, the arrangement of working hours and holidays, the provision of tools, meals and work breaks, staff transfers, and security questions. The departments with such councils are H.M. Stationery Office, Air Force, Army, Navy, Technology, Public Building and Works, and the Royal Mint. There is also an Industrial and Trade Council for employees of the Forestry Commission. In departments with small industrial staffs all matters are settled by direct negotiation with the unions concerned.

There is also a Joint Coordinating Committee which performs very much the same function as the National Whitley Council for the Non-Industrial Civil Service, that is the consideration of general conditions of service common to all industrial civil servants, including sick pay, leave, superannuation, and expense allowances. It is also concerned with implementation of the general policy of according all government workers (industrial and nonindustrial) equality of status and the removal of the "staff" "blue overall" distinction. This is a matter of vital concern to all the industrial and craft unions organising workers in the industrial grades only; they are anxious to negotiate new definitions of work in order to prevent loss of members to the nonindustrial civil service unions as technological change leads to the "nonindustrialisation" of many key jobs.[17]

These three levels of joint machinery are all concerned with full negotiation of agreements. "Consultation" in the industrial civil service is normally used to refer to the activities of local consultative committees, established at factory and shipyard level.

17. National Board for Prices and Incomes, Pay of Industrial Civil Servants. Cmnd. 3034 (1966) paras. 29–51.

To some extent these bodies are concerned with traditional "consultation" matters such as productivity and efficiency. But they are also involved in discussing the application of national agreements.

d. Health Services

There is a distinct legal advantage, from the unions' point of view, in negotiating remuneration and conditions of employment through Whitley machinery. This is because the National Health Service (Remuneration and Conditions of Service) Regulations 1951[18] provide that

> the remuneration of any officer who belongs to a class of officers whose remuneration has been the subject of negotiations by a negotiating body and has been approved by the Minister after considering the result of those negotiations shall . . . be neither more nor less than the remuneration so approved whether or not it is to be paid out of moneys provided by Parliament.

The regulations also give the Minister power to direct that other conditions of service which have been the subject of negotiations by a negotiating body shall be observed. The tendency has been for an increasing number of topics to be negotiated on Whitley Councils and, after consultation by the Minister, to be included in the subsequent regulations. For example, although the Redundancy Payments Act 1965 does not apply to National Health Service (NHS) employees other than those employed by local authorities, a Whitley Council agreement provides for a scheme of lump sum compensation for displaced NHS employees, and also for periodical payments where redundancy results from reorganisation. These arrangements are at least as favourable to NHS employees as those provided for in the Redundancy Payments Act.

It will be observed that the regulations do not define "negotiating machinery," but in practice this is the General Whitley Council for the health services and the nine functional councils dealing with particular groups of health service employees. Since the approved results of negotiations by this method *must* be observed

18. S.I. 1951, No. 1373, reg. 3.

by all hospital authorities, there is a strong incentive for unions to participate in the Whitley machinery. Between 1946 and 1966 the Minister in fact approved all except one of the agreements reached by Whitley Councils. In appropriate cases he has the power to authorise a hospital authority to vary the approved remuneration or conditions in the case of an individual officer or group of officers. But there is an understanding with the staff side that this power will never be used to *worsen* pay and conditions of service.

Where there is no Whitley agreement, the pay and conditions of employees are such as the hospital authority "may determine," although the Minister has a residual power to give written directions in this regard to the employing authority. Not all unions have availed themselves of the Whitley procedure. For example, engineers in hospitals are paid rates directly negotiated with their unions, and electricians are paid the usual trade rates negotiated *outside* the health services. The Minister's power to issue written directions ensures that these nonparticipating grades are not worse off than those in similar employment outside the hospital service.

The agreements of the nine functional councils all relate to pay and conditions of employment. Those of the General Council are wider in scope. They include agreements on the constitutions of functional councils, the establishment of appeals machinery to deal with individual cases, and other procedural matters, in addition to general conditions of service on matters where standardisation is required (e.g. mileage and subsistence allowances, leave for special purposes). The agreed procedures for dealing with individual conditions of employment, dismissals and disciplinary action, and complaints of racial discrimination all emanate from the General Council. We shall consider the nature of each of these procedures in Chapter VIII.

There is *consultation* with the staff sides of Whitley Councils on matters other than pay and conditions of service. These matters are discussed on the Council, but are not made the subject of agreements. This kind of "consultation" may often be intertwined with negotiation. For example, consultation on a new grading structure may be allied with negotiation on remuneration. Sometimes, however, there are "consultations" on Whitley Councils for the health services on matters which, following usage, cannot lead to agreements, such as the rents paid by nurses for lodgings provided by the employing authorities and help with expenses for training courses.

There is also direct consultation between employing authorities and individual unions on a flexible range of topics. For example, check-off arrangements, training, and qualifications for a particular grade may be discussed by this method. Superannuation of health service employees is determined by regulations approved by Parliament. Wherever changes in these regulations are contemplated there is direct consultation with affected unions.

One other type of consultation is that conducted through Joint Consultative Committees, established at many hospitals in terms of an agreement of the General Whitley Council for the Health Services, dated April 1950. The staff representatives on these committees must be members of a nationally recognised negotiating body. The management sides have regarded this as a serious limitation on the effectiveness of the machinery, but the unions have insisted on its retention. Hospital medical staff have declined any form of representation on these committees. The Consultative Committees deal with "matters requiring cooperation and coordination," for example arrangements for reduction of working hours of nurses, the staffiing implications of reorganisations and hospital closures, and work studies. According to the Ministry of Health, these committees "have . . . not been as successful as had been hoped. In some hospitals they have still not been set up."[19] Among the criticisms which have been expressed are that the management side includes members of hospital boards and committees who are not conversant with the day-to-day running of the hospital, and that the committees pay too much attention to individual complaints rather than developing "positive ideas on management and organisation."[20]

There are intricate arrangements for direct negotiations between the Minister of Health and professions which are in contract with the NHS, which we cannot describe in detail here. The early discussions on the NHS envisaged that the Whitley Councils would cover the remuneration of these professions. Only the opticians and pharmacists elected to be so covered, and during

19. Ministry of Health, RCWE (April 1966).
20. Ibid.

the 1960s even the pharmacists in England and Wales preferred direct negotiation to Whitleyism. Doctors and dentists in general practice have never participated (hospital medical and dental practitioners are covered by Committee B of the Medical Whitley Council, and medical practitioners employed by local authorities by Committee C of that same Council).

e. Educational Services

i. PRIMARY AND SECONDARY SCHOOL AND TECHNICAL COLLEGE TEACHERS

The negotiating (Burnham) committees which the Secretaries of State are obliged to set up in England and Wales,[21] and the similar committees in Scotland,[22] are empowered to consider only the remuneration payable to teachers by education authorities. The reasons for this limitation are historical, in that the standing joint committees voluntarily established under the chairmanship of Lord Burnham in 1919 confined their attention to salaries. When the committees were put on a statutory basis by the Education Act 1944, section 89, and (with various changes) by the Remuneration of Teachers Act 1965 in England and Wales (and correspondingly the Remuneration of Teachers (Scotland) Act 1967), no attempt seems to have been made to expand their subject matter. The basic elements of this system are that there is free negotiation on the committees and that approved salary settlements are mandatory on local education authorities. The statutory basis of this negotiation has come under much recent criticism, particularly from the National Association of Schoolmasters, who believe they could achieve better representation if the Burnham structure was settled on a voluntary basis. But none of the criticisms has suggested widening the scope of the machinery to deal with questions other than remuneration.

The terms and conditions of employment of teachers, other than remuneration, are governed by the contracts of employment of individual teachers with local education authorities. Certain minimum requirements are laid down by the Secretary of State for Education and Science in regulations of national application.[23] These are: (1) a teacher must be employed under a written

21. Remuneration of Teachers Act 1965.
22. Remuneration of Teachers (Scotland) Act 1967.
23. Schools Regulations S.I. 1959, No. 364, sch.II.

agreement or minute of authority; (2) this must define his conditions of service and state whether he is employed full-time or part-time; (3) the agreement must provide "that the teacher shall not tbe required to perform any duties except such as are connected with the work of the school or to abstain outside the school hours from any occupations which do not interfere with the performance of his duties"; (4) the teacher must be furnished with a copy of the agreement. The regulations also require the Minister to give a hearing to a teacher before he exercises his power to determine that a teacher shall not be employed in any school on grounds of misconduct or grave professional default, or to suspend or terminate the employment of a teacher on educational or medical grounds. (The general power of appointment and dismissal of teachers is in the hands of local education authorities in county, i.e. state, schools, and is regulated by the rules of management or articles of government in state-aided schools.[24]

A large degree of uniformity has been achieved in regard to terms and conditions by means of model agreements drawn up by a standing joint conference of teachers' organisations and local education authorities. Among the main matters covered by the model agreement for an assistant master/mistress in a county school are these:

1. Time and manner of payment of salaries.
2. Notice of termination (two calendar months before the end of the spring or autumn term and three months before the end of the summer term, to terminate at the end of the term).
3. Retirement at 65 years of age.
4. Right to a personal hearing before termination by employer.[25]

24. Education Act 1944, s.24(1, 2); Education (Scotland) Act 1962, s.82 (education authority), and s.85 (protection against arbitrary dismissal—petition to Secretary of State for Scotland).
25. Unless the teacher can establish a contractual right of this kind he may have no remedy for dismissal without a hearing. Thus a teacher at an aided voluntary school may be unable to obtain damages against a local authority which maintains the school if the governors of the school fail to observe the articles of government by disregarding the rules of natural justice: *Hannam* v. *Bradford City Council* [1970] 2 All E.R. 690. Possibly, however, the governors could be ordered by mandamus to hear his complaint of wrongful dismissal (ibid., p. 698).

5. Right of head master/mistress to suspend for adequate cause; but with right to personal hearing by Committee.

The central government is in no way concerned in the establishment of these model agreements, or with the practice of local education authorities in regard to appointments of teachers, and accordingly the Secretary of State does not participate in negotiations about these matters.

Teachers' superannuation and pensions were until 1965 governed mainly by acts of Parliament. In 1965 most of the earlier legislation was repealed and provision was made for the Secretary of State to make superannuation regulations and to introduce pensions for teachers' widows and other dependents. The 1965 measure was repealed and consolidated in the Teachers' Superannuation Act 1967 and regulations made thereunder. The act expressly provides that "Before making regulations under any provision of this Act, the Secretary of State shall consult with representatives of local education authorities and of teachers appearing to him to be likely to be affected by the proposed regulations."[26] This is simply a duty to "consult" and not to negotiate; in particular, it should be noted that the consent of the Treasury is required to any regulations, and that the regulations are subject to annulment by resolution of either House of Parliament.

Individual cases are dealt with by direct discussion between local education authorities and the teachers' organisation involved; matters of general interpretation of model agreements are referred to a joint standing conference for consideration.

ii. TEACHING STAFF IN COLLEGES OF EDUCATION

In 1945 a committee (still known as the Pelham Committee after its first chairman) was established to consider the remuneration of teaching staff in institutions for the training of teachers. This was not brought within the scope of the statutory machinery in 1965 because of the fact that the management side includes not only the representatives of local authorities but also other bodies, such as churches, which maintain voluntary teachers' training establishments. This was considered to give rise to certain legal difficulties. However, the recommendations of the Pelham Committee are usually made mandatory by the Secretary of State

26. Teachers' Superannuation Act 1967, s.15(4).

when he exercises his discretionary powers under the Training of Teachers (LEAs) Regulations 1959, which state: "The teachers [at these institutions] shall be paid salaries in accordance with scales approved by the Minister."[27] A corresponding requirement is laid on voluntary colleges under the Training of Teachers (Grant) Regulations 1959.[28]

Other matters are discussed directly with the authorities concerned by the Association of Teachers in Colleges and Departments of Education.

iii. UNIVERSITY TEACHERS

There is no distinction in the U.K. between "public" and "private" universities. Constitutionally, the institutions of higher (i.e. tertiary) education are of two kinds: those which have individual charters or acts of Parliament conferring their autonomy, which includes the right to appoint and dismiss staff, and those which are maintained or assisted by local authorities. In the first category are all those institutions which are usually described as "universities." But within this broad framework there are numerous divergences of constitution and control. At the one end of this category Oxford and Cambridge universities are governed entirely by their senior members. The constituent colleges of these ancient universities are self-governing but are in some respects subordinate to congregation (Oxford) or Regent House (Cambridge), consisting of all resident senior members of the universities. The London colleges, on the other hand, have their own governing bodies and are under the university senate in academic and financial matters. In the civic universities (mainly a development of the late nineteenth century in industrial cities) the most important body in financial matters is the Council, an executive body analogous to a board of directors usually composed of a majority of laymen (e.g. local businessmen, representatives of local government). In the University of Wales it is the Council which acts in matters of finance. In Scotland there is a distinctive structure in which the equivalent body to the Council is known as the "Court."

In the second category are the technical colleges and polytechnics. These are bodies which cannot award their own degrees

27. S.I. 1959, No. 395, reg. 18.
28. S.I. 1959, No. 396.

and, in the past, usually prepared students for the London external degrees, or the awards of professional bodies. Since 1964, however, degrees have been made available to these institutions through a Council for National Academic Awards. The distinctive feature of all these technical colleges and polytechnics is that they are maintained by local authorities and their governing bodies are composed of representatives of local education authorities as well as local industry and commerce. Their staff are employees of the local authority.

Today about 90 percent of the capital cost and 74 per cent of the current income of universities (out of which staff are paid) is provided by the central government through a body known as the University Grants Committee (UGC). This body falls under the Department of Education and Science and has direct access to the Secretary of State and his junior ministers. They in turn are responsible to Parliament. Since 1948 the Parliamentary Committee on Public Accounts has been pressing the Treasury to regularise the system of university grants and to ensure that the comptroller and auditor general examines their capital expenditure. Following a report by the Committee on Public Accounts in 1966, the Secretary of State announced that with effect from 1968 the comptroller and auditor general would be given access to the books and records of the UGC and the universities. This did not, however, entail any alteration in the grants system itself, nor did it give the parliamentary committee authority to question policy decisions. There is at present an uneasy truce on the issue of parliamentary control of university expenditure. The main task of the UGC is to fit the plans of each university into national plans, taking account of the global sum made available by the central government. In the result, therefore, it is the Secretary of State and Treasury who have the decisive voice in agreeing to salary increases because it is the central government which alone can increase the global sum available for this purpose.

The remainder of the capital cost and income of universities is provided by private endowments and fees. But the fees themselves (making up about 10 percent of current income) are, in the case of most students resident in Britain, paid in whole or part by local authorities in the form of grants to individual students. Local authorities' revenue for this purpose, in turn, comes largely from the central Government and to a lesser extent from local ratepayers.

One of the most important developments of recent years has been the strengthening of liaison between the various institutions with university status. In particular the Committee of Vice-Chancellors and Principals has adopted common policies on many matters affecting terms and conditions of staff. The first move in this direction was in 1952 when the Universities' Committee on Technical staffs was established in order to provide central machinery for the determination of salaries of university technicians. This committee played an important part in the establishment of new bargaining machinery in 1970.

There are no statutory arrangements regarding the negotiation of remuneration of academic and administrative staff in universities. Before 1970 the Association of University Teachers (AUT) had to rely on ad hoc methods of settling salaries or had to go through the process of submitting its representations to an independent review body, such as the Prices and Incomes Board. After a highly unpopular report had been published by the Board in 1968, the AUT pressed for national negotiating machinery.

A scheme was agreed on in 1970. This envisages two stages of bargaining: (1) first, the AUT will negotiate with a body representative of the universities and colleges as employers, operating under the general guidance of the heads of the universities. (2) Second, the universities and the AUT will then negotiate with the Government. The University Grants Committee (which allocates government-provided funds to the universities) will be represented at meetings held during the first stage.

In the event of failure to reach agreement at the second stage there may be reference to arbitration (to which consent has been given in advance) by a specially constituted arbitration tribunal. The Government are expected to abide by arbitration awards (although there will be no legal compulsion to do so) subject to the overriding authority of Parliament. This new machinery became operative late in 1970.

Negotiating machinery for nonteaching staffs in the universities was set up in June 1970, after negotiations between the Committee of Vice-Chancellors and Principals and the TUC. The new Central Council for nonteaching staffs in universities consists of fifteen representatives of universities (they will in fact be members of the executive committee of the Universities' Committee for Non-teaching Staffs, which will decide on "management policy") and two representatives from each of six participating unions. Wages of technical staff will be negotiated nationally, but those of clerical and manual staff will continue to be settled locally unless otherwise agreed. Problems of union representation will be solved by an agreement between the interested unions (under TUC guidance) on "spheres of influence." Oxford and Cambridge universities and their colleges will not join directly in this new body (largely because of the satisfaction of their staffs with local negotiations) but will send observers to its meetings, and it seems clear that pay and conditions at these universities will be closely influenced by agreements reached on the national body.

f. Police

The Police Act 1919 established Police Councils (one for England and Wales and another for Scotland) which were purely consultative bodies including representatives of local authority associations and the Police Federations. The last word always lay with the Secretaries of State, who had the power to make regulations and could disregard the advice of the Councils (which in any event met in England only fourteen times between 1919 and 1939). The representatives of the lower ranks of policemen objected to this arrangement on the grounds that in round-table talks they were always outnumbered and their views tended to be submerged under those of the official side, and that it was wrong for the Secretary of State to have the final word because he, as an "employer," tended to side with the local authority associations rather than the men.

These objections were considered in 1948-49 by the Oaksey Committee on Police Conditions of Service.[29] According to its report difficulties arose because a purely consultative body was being asked from time to time "to perform functions which could be satisfactorily performed only by a properly constituted negotiating body, with recourse to arbitration in the case of failure to reach agreement."[30] As a result of the Committee's recommenda-

29. Cmnd. 7676 and Cmnd. 7831.
30. Cmnd. 7831, para. 371.

tions a Police Council for Great Britain was established in 1953. It functioned on a nonstatutory basis until the enactment of the Police Act 1964.[31]

The constitution of the Police Council is the result of "consultations between the [Home Secretary] and organisations representing [the] interests" of police authorities and members of police forces.[32] The Council has a Whitley-type structure: there is an independent chairman; the Secretary of State has six representatives, and the local authority associations twenty. On the staff side there is the Commissioner of Police of the Metropolis, and twenty-six representatives of the Police Federations, the Chief Police Officers', and the Superintendents' Associations. The Council works through five standing committees—"A" for ranks above that of chief superintendent; "B" for ranks of chief superintendent and superintendent; "C" for ranks below that of superintendent; "D" for matters which by reason of the ranks affected do not fall to be considered by any one of the other standing committees; and "E" for pension matters. Questions as to demarcation of subjects between these committees are resolved by negotiations on the Council.

The Police Act 1964, which places the practice since 1953 on a statutory basis, limits the matters which may be "considered" with a view to making "recommendations" to the Secretary of State. These are all topics which were considered by the Oaksey Committee to be "negotiable subjects": (1) hours of duty; (2) leave; (3) pay and allowances; (4) the issue, use, and return of police clothing, personal equipment, and accoutrements; (5) pension matters. Questions of the Council's internal procedure are also regarded as "negotiable." These are all customarily referred to as "reserved subjects" outside the scope of the Police Advisory Boards which were also set up by the 1964 act.[33] Any question whether a particular subject is a "reserved subject" is itself a matter for negotiation.[34]

The Police Advisory Boards (one for England and Wales, the other for Scotland) have somewhat different constitutions from

31. S.45. Between 1953 and 1964 its agreements required formal ratification by the Police Councils set up by the act of 1919.
32. Police Act 1964, s.45(1).
33. Police Act 1964, s.46.
34. This follows a recommendation of the Oaksey Committee, para. 376.

the Police Council. The Secretary of State is chairman and he may appoint other members. In addition, in terms of the constitution approved by the Secretary of State after "consultations," the local authority associations, the Commissioners of Police of the City of London, and the Metropolis and the Police Federations and Chief Officers' and Superintendents' Associations nominate representatives, with the police associations in the majority. The Boards are precluded from advising on subjects "reserved" to the Police Council, but may advise the Secretary of State on draft regulations relating to any other matters, and "on general questions affecting the police."[35]

The Oaksey Committee rejected a proposal for local negotiating machinery. In practice the representatives of Branch Boards of the Police Federations are normally given personal hearings by police authorities and chief officers of police on matters such as rotation of shifts, tours of duty, canteen and welfare facilities and operational methods. The Federations are expressly precluded from representing policemen on "questions of discipline and promotion" affecting individuals.[36]

It will be observed that matters for negotiation are reserved to the Police Council ("consideration" is the word used in the act, but this is a hospitable expression encompassing both negotiation and consultation),[37] while residual advisory functions are allocated to the Advisory Boards. At the local level there is direct access to the police authorities and chief officers. However, the final word, even in respect of "negotiable" matters, rests with the Secretary of State. He must take the recommendations of the Council into account when making regulations;[38] and it appears that he has never refused to do so.

g. Fire Services

The arrangements in respect of local authorities' fire brigades afford an interesting example of a movement away from statutory regulation of terms and conditions to free collective bargaining.

35. Police Act 1964, s.46(1, 3).
36. Police Act 1964, s.44(1).
37. See the discussions on the Police Bill in H.C. Standing Committee D, 30 January 1964, cols. 522 et seq., when the Home Secretary (Mr. H. Brooke) said it would be "retrograde" to substitute the word "negotiate" for "consideration."
38. Police Act 1964, s.45(1), 45(4).

The Fire Services Act 1947 permitted the Secretary of State to make regulations as to ranks, pay and allowances, hours of duty and leave, the maintenance of discipline, and appeals against discipline or disciplinary action. Before making regulations he was obliged to take into consideration the recommendations made in accordance with "proper arrangements . . . for the consideration, by persons representing the interests of fire authorities and of persons employed as members of fire brigades . . . or any class of persons so employed, of questions arising as to the conditions of service of persons so employed."[39] The Secretary of State approved the National Joint Council for Local Authorities' Fire Brigades as a "proper arrangement" for considering the terms and conditions of service of all personnel below the rank of chief officer, and the National Joint Council for Chief Officers of Local Authorities' Fire Brigades was approved in respect of chief officers. The official side of both Councils is drawn from local authorities' associations; the employees' representatives come from the National Association of Fire Officers, the Fire Brigades Union, and the National Union of General and Municipal Workers. (In the case of the Chief Officers' Council the only union represented is the Chief Fire Officers' Association.)

In 1959 the act was amended so as to delete those matters which related to pay and conditions of service. The result is that since September 1959 the only matters which have to be submitted by the Councils to the Secretary of State are those relating to the maintenance of discipline and appeals against dismissal or disciplinary action.[40] All other matters are now negotiated and are the subjects of agreements of the Councils. Local authorities may be compelled to implement decisions of the Councils through the obligation to observe "recognised terms and conditions of employment" under the Terms and Conditions of Employment Act 1959.

The formal constitutions of the Councils provide that they may take any action falling within their defined functions. "Conditions of service" are defined as including rank, pay and allowances, hours of duty and leave, maintenance of discipline, procedure

---

39. Fire Services Act 1947, s.17(2)(a).
40. Fire Services Act 1959, ss.5, 14(4) and sch. The current regulations are the Fire Services (Discipline) Regs. S.I. 1948, No. 545 am. by S.I. 1949, No. 2161, and S.I. 1965, No. 578.

for appeals against dismissal or disciplinary action (including dismissal on disciplinary grounds) other than questions of discipline affecting individuals, and welfare arrangements.

The Councils do not discuss the method of appointment of chief officers, nor the qualifications for appointments to a brigade or promotion into any rank.[41] These matters are the subject of regulations made by the Secretary of State after consultation with the Central Fire Brigades Advisory Council. The latter is a purely consultative body whose members are appointed by the Secretary of State. These members represent the interest of fire authorities and persons employed as members of fire brigades.[42] Apart from qualifications and promotion, the Secretary of State *must* consult this body before making regulations as to the provision of fire hydrants and as to the standards of training for firemen and the design and performance of their equipment. The Advisory Council *may* advise the Secretary of State on any other matter (other than those reserved to the approved negotiating bodies) whether or not he has made a reference to them.[43]

h. Other Local Government Services

There is only one other group of local government employees in respect of whom there is ministerial (central government) regulation of remuneration. This is the numerically small and relatively unimportant group of clerks (chief executive officers) to county councils. The Local Government Act 1933, section 99(1), provides that a county council "shall pay to its clerk such reasonable salary as may be determined by the Council, *subject to the approval of the Minister.*" In effect the Minister is expected to approve the salary of each individual county clerk. In this respect county clerks are in an exceptional position because the salaries of the two other major groups of chief and senior officers in local government service (the town and district council clerks, and other chief officers) are determined by the employing authority, without ministerial approval.[44]

41 Fire Services Act 1947, s.18. The current regulations are S.I. 1965, No. 577, am. by S.I. 1967, No. 1689.
42. Fire Services Act 1947, s.29.   43. Ibid.
44. Local Government Act 1933, ss.102(1), 103(1), 104(1), 105(2), and 106(2), which requires county, borough, or district councils to pay "such reasonable remuneration as it may determine" to each of its chief or senior officers (e.g. chief education officer, county planning officers).

However, in practice the Minister will give effect to the results of joint negotiation. Although two permanent joint negotiating bodies, one for town and district council clerks and the other for chief officers, were set up in 1948, the county clerks felt no need for formal negotiating machinery until 1957, and even then they decided that their "exceptional position" put it "out of the question" for them to become incorporated in the framework of the other two negotiating bodies. (Before 1957 their representatives had been "consulted" about salaries.) Accordingly, their own negotiating body was set up. This body meets less regularly than the other two negotiating bodies and its practice (like the Greater London Council which has no formal machinery) has been to adopt salary increases already negotiated by those other bodies. In Scotland there is a separate negotiating body for all senior officers, excluding county clerks.

It should be noted that each of these joint negotiating bodies prescribes a range of starting salaries and a set of annual increments. It is then left to each local authority, within the range, to determine the commencing salary of each of its principal officers. Because annual increments then follow automatically, the salary agreements in effect also fix *maximum* salary levels. By adopting wide general salary ranges the joint negotiating bodies deliberately confer a considerable degree of discretion on the employing authorities. (In areas with populations over 600,000 the authorities have an even wider discretion.) In recent years the salary structure determined by the four bodies has broken down, with many authorities choosing to pay starting salaries near the maximum and others exceeding the maximum. This, according to the National Board for Prices and Incomes,[45] has made a "mockery" of the avowed aim of the joint negotiating machinery, which is to ensure that equal responsibilities are equally rewarded. This led the Prices and Incomes Board to propose a "fundamental change in the method of determining salaries" of these officers. In particular the Board wants the discretion of the employing authorities to be limited and insists that there should in future be a single negotiating body to cover all principal officers, in order to avoid the "wasteful and inefficient" duplication of effort.

45. Report No. 45. *Pay of Chief and Senior Officers in Local Government Service and the GLC* (November 1967). Cmnd. 3473, para. 17.

(There is a degree of common membership of the three bodies on the authorities' side; meetings are held on the same dates and discussions largely duplicated; and the recommendations of each body are usually similar.) The Board also wants the county clerks in Scotland to be brought within the existing negotiating body there. The negotiation of general conditions of service is also within the purview of these bodies, but each of them has regard to the conditions recommended by the National Joint Council for Local Authorities' Administrative, Professional, Technical and Clerical Services.

The remaining manual, craft, clerical, administrative, and professional groups have their remuneration and other terms and conditions of employment negotiated, without legislative intervention, on some thirteen national joint negotiating bodies. The scope of each of these bodies depends primarily on status: administrative and clerical staffs have separate machinery from manual workers, and craft workers (e.g. in building and engineering) have separate machinery from noncraft workers. The two major bodies—one for administrative, professional, technical, and clerical services, and the other for noncraft manual workers—each have provincial or district councils covering the whole of England and Wales. (Scotland was brought into this structure in 1969.) The scope of each of these two National Councils is "to secure the largest possible measure of joint action for the consideration of salaries, wages and service conditions of the officers within the scope of the Council, and to consider such proposals in reference to these matters as are submitted to it from time to time by provincial councils." The National Councils are concerned with the proper functioning of local machinery; each has an appeals committee, consisting of representatives of both sides, which deals with differences between the two sides on provincial councils. Decisions of the appeals committees do not require confirmation by the appropriate National Council. The National Councils spend much of their time negotiating amendments to the agreed national Scheme of Conditions of Service.

The provincial councils consider matters referred to them by their respective National Councils, act as conciliation boards (at the request of both the parties) in disputes between local authorities in their area and trade unions, and give decisions on the correct zoning of local authorities within their area and of the grading and classification of work. (In Scotland there is a National Joint Industrial Council for Local Authority Services' Manual Workers and a National Joint Industrial Council for Local Authority Staffs Administrative Clerical and Technical Staffs; although their constitutions provide for district councils, none has so far been established.)

The Joint Negotiating Committees covering building, civil engineering, and engineering craftsmen cover all craftsmen within their scope employed by local authorities. The subjects of bargaining extend beyond wages and conditions and include such matters as training, health, and safety.

Finally, it must be noted that there is a small but unknown number of local government employees whose wages are determined not by collective bargaining but by Wages Councils orders. These include catering, baking, and laundry workers. Wages Councils are successors to the Trade Boards which were first set up in 1909 to protect unorganised workers in the "sweated trades." Each Council consists of an equal number of representatives of employers and workers respectively together with not more than three independent members (the latter are usually university teachers or lawyers) and all of whom are appointed by the Secretary of State for Employment and Productivity. The Council must allow persons affected to make representations, and it makes proposals for fixing statutory minimum remuneration (including holidays and holiday remuneration) to be paid to workers within its jurisdiction. The Secretary of State must give effect to the proposals, although he may give the Council an opportunity to reconsider. When he does so, in the form of a Wages Regulation Order, all employers and workers concerned must observe the prescribed rates. The orders are enforceable by criminal proceedings, and a worker may recover arrears of remuneration by civil proceedings.

The Donovan Commission made various proposals for the early abolition of a number of Wages Councils and for their replacement by satisfactory collective bargaining arrangements.[46] Accordingly, this method of wage regulation—less satisfactory than collective bargaining in controlling pay and conditions—is likely to be of diminishing importance to local government employees. In parti-

46. Cmnd. 3623, paras. 262–66.

cular, the proposed amendment to section 8 of the Terms and Conditions of Employment Act 1959, to allow a claim that "recognised terms and conditions" are not being observed to be reported in respect of workers in Wages Councils industries, will result in wider effect being given to voluntarily agreed standards.[47]

2. THE LEGAL RESULTS OF BARGAINING

The striking feature of the British system is that collective labour agreements do not, in general, give rise to legal proceedings between the bargaining parties. This does not mean, however, that the decisions of Whitley-type negotiating bodies or ad hoc agreements between employing authorities and employee organisations in the public services are devoid of legal consequences. On the contrary, many but not all of the collective standards take effect through the individual employees' contracts of employment, and sometimes (particularly important in parts of the public services) through statutory promulgation by the central government. Moreover, collective standards may be extended by legal process to unorganised sections of a trade or industry, a legal device which is relevant to local government employment.

a. Absence of Legal Proceedings between the Bargaining Parties

The philosophy of voluntarism, so deeply embedded in the British system, is reflected in the general belief that collective labour agreements do not have contractual effect between the parties.[48] There is nothing in the law to prevent employers and employee organisations from giving legal force to their agreements. It is true that a statutory provision—section 4 of the Trade Union Act 1871—says that agreements between one "trade union" and another cannot be "directly" enforced in a court of law and damages cannot be recovered for their breach. An employers'

47. Ibid., para. 265; *In Place of Strife,* Cmnd. 3888, paras. 63–64. Generally on Wages Councils see F. J. Bayliss, *British Wages Councils* (Oxford, 1962), and C. W. Guillebaud, *The Wages Councils System in Great Britain* (2nd ed., London, 1962).
48. The Whitley Committee (Cd. 9099, 1919) para. 15, concurred in the views of a Report on an Inquiry into Industrial Agreement by the Industrial Council in 1913 (Cd. 6953), para. 61, that collective agreements were more likely to be fulfilled "by an increased regard for moral obligation, respect for an instructed public opinion, and reliance on the principles of mutual consent rather than by the establishment of a system of monetary penalties."

THE STRUCTURE OF BARGAINING

association may be a "trade union" in law and so could not, if it wished, make its collective agreements with other "trade unions" "directly" enforceable or through an action for damages. They could, however, make them "indirectly" enforceable, for example, by obtaining a declaration from a court as to the interpretation of the agreement. Moreover, this provision of the 1871 act, whatever its effect in relation to private employment, is irrelevant to collective agreements in the public services. It is highly doubtful whether local government associations represented on the official sides of some Whitley-type bodies are "trade unions" in law.[49] Even if they are, there are nearly always other parties (such as the Secretary of State) to their agreements who are certainly not "trade unions"; and, as was shown earlier, several employee organisations in the public services may not be "trade unions" in law. In any event, section 4 cannot affect an agreement between an individual employing authority and a trade union.

The fact that collective agreements are not legally enforced is not due, therefore, to the law; it is because the parties have *freely chosen* that they should remain outside the law. There is nothing to prevent them from expressly stipulating that their agreements shall be legally enforceable. In practice they have never done so in the public services, and only rarely in private industry. This practice, as rationalized by academic commentators,[50] has in turn led the courts to adopt a presumption that collective agreements are not intended to give rise to contractual relations.[51]

49. It can be shown, we believe, that "the regulation of the relations between workmen and masters . . . or between masters and masters, or the imposing of restrictive conditions on the conduct of any *trade or business*" are not the "principal objects" of these associations under their constitutions. For a discussion of the definition of trade union see above, Chap. III.

50. Principally O. Kahn-Freund in *The System of Industrial Relations in Great Britain* (ed Flanders & Clegg) (London, 1954), pp. 55–58, and several other writings. For a critique and select bibliography see B. A. Hepple, "Intention to Create Legal Relations" (1970) *Camb. L.J.* 122.

51. An interesting problem might arise, for those who rest the non-contractual nature of collective agreements on the intention of the parties to the bargain in the constitution of the Joint Negotiating Committee for Clerks of County Councils, which in Clause 3, after saying that the parties to the negotiations shall be the County Councils Association (the employers) and the Association of Clerks of County Councils (the employed), says "The organisations named in this clause are hereafter collectively referred to as 'the Contracting Parties.' "

This presumption may be rebutted by an express declaration to the contrary or by implication from all the circumstances. In effect the courts, following industrial practice, have indicated their reluctance to treat collective agreements as justiciable.[52] The former Labour Government proposed in its Industrial Relations Bill 1970 to make the presumption irrebuttable by providing that collective agreements could in future be made legally binding only by an express written clause to that effect in the agreement. The Conservative Government plans to *reverse* this presumption so as to make it necessary for the unions to buy *non*enforceability.

The absence of contractual effect of collective agreements in Britain is not simply a matter of ideology. It is, as the Donovan Commission said, "deeply rooted in its structure."[53] This is nowhere better evidenced than in the form by which decisions of Whitley-type negotiating bodies are taken. A resolution, agreed to by a majority on both sides, is recorded in the minutes, signed by the chairman (and, in some Councils, by the vice-chairman), and forwarded by him to the appropriate executive authority. This may be the employing authority, in which event the agreement does not become operative until approved by that authority.[54] Or it may be the Secretary of State, if there is provision for regulations to be made by him. In that event the agreement only becomes operative when approved by him and embodied in statutory regulations. In other words, the resolutions of Whitley-type bodies are always, in effect, *recommendations* to executive authorities. Thus their resolutions or decisions can scarcely be called contracts.

There is an even more fundamental objection to the application of the categories of contract to Whitley-type decisions. This is that these bodies are permanent joint institutions whose function is to formulate standards and adapt them to ever-changing circum-

52. The only litigation on this issue in recent times, *Ford Motor Co. Ltd.* v. *Amalgamated Union of Engineering & Foundry Workers* [1969] 1 W.L.R. 339, was decided on the basis of absence of intention to create legal relations: for doubts see Hepple, "Intention to Create Legal Relations."

53. Cmnd. 3623, para. 471.

54. This is the case, e.g., with the Joint Industrial Council for Government Industrial Employees whose decisions require the sanction of a Treasury minute and the authority of a Director Establishment (see *Dudfield* v. *Ministry of Works, The Times,* 24 January 1964) and the Shipbuilding Trades Joint Council where an Admiralty Fleet Order is required (see, *Faithful* v. *Admiralty,* ibid.).

stances. In Kahn-Freund's words, they represent a "dynamic" method of collective bargaining which differs from the "static" bargaining which prevails on the European continent and in much of the U.S.[55] Bargaining in the Whitley system is "a continuous process in which differences concerning the interpretation of an agreement merge imperceptibly into differences concerning claims to change its effect."[56] The decisions of Whitley-type bodies are variable at any time and, in particular, in the light of difficulties of interpretation. There is a continuous process of amendment and reformulation. A process of this kind is incapable of legal enforcement as a "contract" and, it may even be argued, is sufficiently flexible to obviate the need for legal interpretations. The absence of lawyers either at the negotiating table or in the process of "interpretation" is regarded by the parties as one of the most valuable characteristics of the system. The decisions themselves are often expressed in the terminology of compromise with a degree of vagueness which would lead lawyers to treat many of their provisions as "void for uncertainty." Yet the parties, by reference to unwritten "custom and practice" and in the light of their bargaining positions, are able to operate them and, where necessary, redefine them.

There are other structural features of the Whitley system which make contractual enforcement difficult to contemplate. Agreements are reached by the vote of a majority of each side. The system works because dissidents voluntarily accept the majority decisions. But if it came to a question of legal enforcement the dissidents could argue, with considerable force, that there was no binding agreement until the decision of the Council was ratified by the executive body of each constituent union. (These points were raised but not decided in the *Ford* case (above), where a decision of a National Joint Negotiating Committee had been accepted by only a slender majority—7-5—of 19 unions on the body.)

In the case of ad hoc agreements negotiated outside the Whitley system other obstacles to legal enforcement present themselves. The fragmented nature of shop floor bargaining in government industrial enterprises makes it difficult to identify the parties on the workers' side. If these are shop stewards they may lack

55. In "Intergroup Conflicts and Their Settlement," 5 (1954) *Brit. Journal of Sociology* 193.
56. Cmnd. 3623, para. 471.

the authority of the union to enter into agreements on its behalf. Moreover, these shop floor "understandings" are often informal and their contents difficult to ascertain.

The case for legal enforceability of collective agreements in the U.K. usually rests on the belief that unions should be made liable for the breach of "peace" obligations which are frequently expressed in collective agreements. According to the Donovan Commission, "official" strikes (those sanctioned or ratified by the union and which are often "unconstitutional" as well, in the sense that they occur in breach of agreed settlement procedures) are not a serious problem in the U.K.[57] The overwhelming majority of stoppages, in public and private sectors, are due to "unofficial" (wildcat) strikes. Unless, as the Conservatives have proposed,[58] unions were obliged to repress wildcat strikes (which, in turn, might lead to the rapid growth of militant splinter groups), legal enforceability would not lead to a reduction in the number of unofficial stoppages. This is because of three important features of collective labour law in Britain. First, it is generally agreed that unions do not negotiate as "agents" for their members.[59] This means that they do not automaically bind individual members (and much less nonmemebrs) to observe "no-strike" obligations. Second, a union is not liable (in the absence of an express stipulation to this effect) for unauthorised breaches of an agreement. This means that it cannot be liable for an *unofficial* stoppage in breach of a procedure agreement. Third, English law (although not Scots law) knows nothing of the doctrine of the "third party beneficiary" contract. This means that an employer, even if a member of an association which agreed to a Whitley decision, could not take advantage of the collective "contract" and sue the union party for damages for breach of that "contract," except on the view that the associations act as agents for their members, a view which is generally discredited.[60] Because of the composition of Whitley-type bodies, it is therefore obvious that legal enforceability would be of no help to individual employers.

57. R.C. Cmnd. 3623, para. 367.
58. This is not spelt out in *Fair Deal at Work* (1968), but emerges from speeches by Mr. Heath and others: LIX: 5 *Labour Research* (May 1970) 69.
59. See the discussion in Wedderburn, *The Worker and the Law*, p. 112, and below.
60. Kahn-Freund in *Labour Relations and the Law* (London, 1965), p. 26.

These considerations indicate that collective agreements in the British public services could be made legally enforceable only by means of a statute which attached the force of law to a bargain *against the will of the parties*, and by a fundamental restructuring of the Whitley system, including fixed-term agreements in legalistic language, a system of contract interpretation and grievance arbitration, employers' associations and trade unions being designated as bargaining "agents," and being made responsible for defined breaches. This would be an unprecedented step in the British system and is not advocated by either of the main political parties.[61] It could be justified only if it could be shown that it would lead to a decisive improvement of industrial relations. This has certainly not been proved in the case of the public services, where wildcat strikes, the major complaint against the system of industrial relations in British private industry, are of relatively minor importance.

b. The Normative Effect of Collective Bargaining

The primary effect of collective agreements in Britain is that they operate as a code for the industry or sector of the public services. This means that Whitley Council decisions or ad hoc agreements between employers and unions are either expressly or impliedly incorporated into the individual contract of employment. This, of course, presupposes that the individual has a *contract* with his employer. We have seen that in the case of Crown servants this is by no means certain. So far, in all those reported cases in which individual civil servants have sought to enforce Whitley decisions, the courts have carefully managed to sidestep this fundamental issue, leaving open for future decision the precise status of employees of the Crown and, consequently, the normative effect of Whitley decisions in relation to individual civil servants.[62]

The normative effect of collective agreements on the contracts of other categories of public employees has one important peculiarity in Britain which immediately distinguishes it from the kind

61. The only difference between Labour and the Conservatives in this regard is that while the former would make employers buy enforceability (by means of an express provision), the latter would make the unions buy non-enforceability (by an express "honourable pledge" clause): *Fair Deal at Work*, p. 32. Both sets of proposals would apply to public employees.

62. E.g. *Dudfield* v. *Ministry of Works*, The Times, 24 January 1964; *Rodwell* v. *Thomas* [1944] ! K.B. 596.

of normative effect recognised in many Continental countries. This is that, apart from isolated legislation (to be discussed in the next section), collective agreements have no *compulsory* normative effect. The English and Scottish common law doctrine is that no term can be implied in a contract which is repugnant to an express term in the same contract. This means that the employer and employee can, by an express term, provide for a wage higher or lower than that laid down in a collective agreement which would otherwise be implied into the individual contract. Individual bargaining therefore can, and sometimes does, displace the results of collective bargaining.

Express incorporation of collective terms in the individual contract has been encouraged and facilitated by section 4 of the Contracts of Employment Act 1963, which enables an employer to refer his employee in an obligatory written statement of particulars of certain terms of employment to "some document which the employee has reasonable opportunities of reading in the course of employment." This statutory provision also overcomes the problem of changing collective terms (especially important in Britain because of the "dynamic" nature of bargaining arrangements) by allowing the employer to notify the employee, in advance, that this other "document" will change from time to time. Employers have not made as much use of these provisions as had been hoped; but, without having specifically researched this matter, our impression is that *express* incorporation by the use of the 1963 act is fairly widespread in local government employment. In the case of teachers, the model agreements between education authorities and individual employees expressly provide for the payment of Burnham (negotiated) scales as promulgated by the Minister. The 1963 act does not apply to Crown servants.

If the employee's contract is silent about the collective agreement then its provisions may be incorporated in the individual contract by means of the implied term theory. This is still the most usual way for collective standards to take effect. For comparative purposes it must be stressed that this theory, as understood in England and Scotland, is wholly distinct from the problem whether the union can be regarded as the "agent" of its members. An implied term is something "that goes without saying" or is "necessary to effectuate the intention of the parties." It may sometimes be difficult to incorporate *new* collective terms into an employee's contract, particularly where he is ignorant of them (a problem which may now be solved by use of the 1963 act), but it plainly makes no difference to the implied term approach whether the employee is a trade unionist. The "agency" view is generally not favoured by English lawyers,[63] precisely because of the problems which would arise, if it were adopted, in applying collective terms to nonunionists and to those who were not members of the union at the time of the agreement or had withdrawn their authority from the union "agent." It is true that at least one civil service union has, since 1963, purported to bargain for its members *alone,* and in recent claims the largest local government union (NALGO) has demanded that increases be paid to *union members only.* The only relevence of such claims to the English lawyer would be as an indication that the employer and the individual employee did not "intend" the resulting agreement to be implied in the contract. But the *union's* intentions would not be decisive, either in regard to its own members or to nonunionists. A more sophisticated approach, suggested by a case in 1964,[64] would be to treat the terms of the collective agreement as a standing offer open to acceptance by individual employees. If the agreement refers only to union members it would be possible to confine "acceptance" to such members. However, this approach has not yet won general approval and is far more akin to the implied term theory than the "agency" view.

Implication of collective terms in the individual contract, irrespective of whether the employee belongs to a union party to the collective agreement, is thus the principal link between collective bargaining and the law. However, it is not without its own difficulties and uncertainties, several of which have come to light in cases in which public employees have sought to enforce collective standards as terms of their individual employment contracts.

First, it would seem that the terms of a new or amended collective agreement will not be impliedly incorporated into the

63. See the discussion in Wedderburn, *The Worker and the Law,* pp. 112–14.

64. *Edwards* v. *Skyways Ltd.* [1964] 1 W.L.R. 349 (Megaw J.).

individual's employment contract before the employing or other executive authority has approved the collective terms. This emerges from a case in 1964[65] in which a lift attendant member of the TGWU was employed by the Ministry of Works as an established chargehand. He received a copy of the Ministry's *Industrial Handbook* and signed a document to the effect that he understood that the rules in it applied to him. One of these rules was that the wages to be paid to him were those as agreed by the Miscellaneous Trades Joint Council for Government Industrial Employees. In 1952 the Council agreed on new rates which were regularly revised in terms of the agreement. In October 1961, an increase of two shillings per week was agreed. Two months earlier the Treasury had informed the unions and the Council that the Chancellor of the Exchequer's policies meant there could be no further wage increases in the industrial civil service during a "pay pause." The lift attendant instituted proceedings in the High Court for the increase which the Ministry of Works refused to pay. The Judge held that the functions of the Council were "purely consultative" and not "executive." Accordingly, its decisions did not create legally enforceable rights. But it was argued that the long-standing practice by which the Ministry and employees had recognised the rates agreed by the Council gave rise to an *implied* obligation on the Ministry to observe the new agreement of the Council. This contention was rejected on the ground that every increase required the double sanction of a Treasury minute and the authority of the Director of Establishment in the Ministry of Works. In another case heard at the same time, the same judge refused to imply a term in the contract of a storehouse assistant employed by the Admiralty that he should be paid the rate agreed or awarded in a voluntary arbitration (after disagreement) by the Industrial Court. He was entitled only to such sums as were directed to be paid in Admiralty Fleet Orders.[66] As Wedderburn has pointed out, these decisions

65. *Dudfield* v. *Ministry of Works, The Times,* 24 January 1964. See however *Brand* v. *Greater London Council, The Times,* 28 October 1967 (Southwark County Court), in which a decision of the NJC panel for local authority employees was held to be binding on an employing local council, which had regularly observed such awards, "as soon as the award of the NJC was made." Such *automatic* incorporation must be rare, and the *Dudfield* case represents the more general practice.

66. *Faithful* v. *The Admiralty, The Times,* 24 January 1964.

"diminish severely the possibility of using implied, or even express, incorporation as a mechanism for closing the gap between collective agreements and individual contract."[67]

A second difficulty, on which there is so far little guidance from the courts, is the not infrequent conflict, particularly in times of wages drift, between national and local collective agreements. Can an employee enforce a local agreement more favorable to him than a national one? Conversely, may his employer pay him locally agreed rates which are *lower* than those agreed nationally (the reverse of the modern wage drift situation)? At present the answer to the first of these questions appears to be in the negative, and to the second in the affirmative. In a 1964 case[68] an ambulance driver was employed by the West Riding County Council. His contract referred to both national and local agreements and said that he was entitled to additional payments for "stand-by" duties according to the "scheduled rates." It was held that he was entitled only to the local "stand-by" rates which the employer had negotiated in order to avoid paying higher nationally agreed "stand-by" rates. Other recent cases, however, have denied the employee's right to enforce local agreements which contain more favourable terms than national ones.[69] This is a highly unsatisfactory situation from the point of view of local union officials and shop stewards who have won increases for their members.

A third difficulty about incorporation in the individual contract is that not every collective term is appropriate for individual enforcement. Wage rates and other benefits in so-called price-list agreements are readily implied as terms in individual contracts. But there is far more uncertainty about procedure agreements, including dismissals and disciplinary arrangements, and "no strike" provisions. In general it seems that the judges are disinclined to imply procedural arrangements into an individual's contract so as to extend his rights. In the leading case, decided in 1944, a High Court judge said that the National Whitley Council agreed disciplinary procedures which had been circulated to all departments by a Treasury circular could not be enforced by a dismissed civil servant.[70] It was held that even if there had been a breach

---

67. *The Worker and the Law*, p. 118.
68. *Clift* v. *West Riding C.C., The Times,* 10 April 1964.
69. These cases are discussed by Wedderburn in (1969) 32 M.L.R. 99.
70. *Rodwell* v. *Thomas* [1944] 1 K.B. 596.

of the agreed procedures, and even if his status as a Crown servant did not preclude him from challenging the Crown's right to dismiss him at pleasure, he had failed "to get within measurable distance of establishing that the recommendations of the joint committee enclosed with the Treasury circular . . . form part of [his] contract of employment." On the other hand, in another case, in 1958, it was held that a clause in a memorandum, circulated by the Minister ·of Health to Regional Hospital Boards after consultations with representatives of the medical profession, which allowed a dismissed hospital consultant a hearing by the Minister, was "clearly appropriate to inclusion in the contract of a consultant, just as appropriate as the clauses relating to his terms of remuneration, leave and other matters of a similar kind."[71] Accordingly, a consultant dismissed without such a hearing was entitled to recover damages from his employer (the Regional Hospital Board) on grounds of breach of contract. Unfortunately, this decision did nothing to clarify the legal status of procedural agreements because the learned judge added that there were "certain other [unspecified] paragraphs in the [Minister's memorandum] which really contain directions to the Board rather than directions which may be incorporated in any contract between either a whole-time or part-time officer and the Board."

The legal enforceability of "peace" obligations against individual employees is even more ambiguous. In the important case of *Rookes* v. *Barnard* in 1964,[72] it was conceded by defendant's counsel that draughtsmen employed by the state-owned British Overseas Airways Corporation were individually bound by the terms of a "no-strike" clause in a collective agreement between two sides of a panel of the National Joint [Whitley] Council for Civil Air Transport. This concession would not be binding in a future case, and it should be observed that the relevant clause in the collective agreement stated: "The employers . . . and the *employees* . . . undertake that no lock-out or strike shall take place." The concession might not so readily have been made had the clause read "the *trade union* . . . undertakes" etc. Accord-

71. *Barber* v. *Manchester Regional Hospital Board* [1958] 1 W.L.R. 181 at 190; cf. *McClelland* v. *N.I. General Health Services Board* [1957] 1 W.L.R. 594 (dismissal procedures made *express* terms).
72. [1964] A.C. 1129 (H.L.); and see [1963] 1 Q.B. 623 (Donovan L.J. in the Court of Appeal) and [1963] 2 All E.R. 825 (Sachs J.).

ingly, the incorporation of the "no strike" clause in *Rookes* v. *Barnard* was, as Kahn-Freund has said, "quite exceptional."[73] Moreover, it is difficult to reconcile this case with statements in two Court of Appeal decisions concerning public employees, in which the Court refused to incorporate procedural arrangements for the settlement of disputes into individual employment contracts. In one of these cases,[74] the employer, the Portland Urban District Council, argued that the question whether a scheme of conditions of service approved by a Whitley Council applied to a workman should be dealt with in accordance with a paragraph of the scheme which provided machinery for settling a question whether or not an employee was within the scheme. Instead of using this machinery the trade union had referred the dispute straight to the Minister as an "issue" under the Industrial Disputes Order 1951. The only matter that could be reported to the Minister under this order as an "issue" was whether an employer should observe "recognised terms and conditions." The local authority argued that so long as they were observing the procedural paragraph in the scheme it could not be said that they were failing to observe recognised terms and conditions. This argument was rejected by the Court on the ground that the local authority had repudiated the scheme altogether by refusing to regard the workmen as within the scheme; but the Lord Justices of Appeal went on to say that the procedural paragraph was not, properly speaking, one of the "terms and conditions of employment" at all. Lord Denning called it "only machinery for settling a difference" and Romer L.J. described it as "administrative machinery." In a series of awards, the Industrial Court (a permanent arbitration body) has in effect followed this Court of Appeal decision and declined to treat procedural arrangements as "terms and conditions of employment," with the consequence that they cannot be extended (by the use of section 8 of the Terms and Conditions of Employment Act 1959, which will be discussed later) to unorganised sections of a trade or industry.[75]

73. *Labour Relations and the Law*, p. 27.
74. *R.* v. *Industrial Disputes Tribunal, ex p. Portland UDC* [1955] 1 W.L.R. 949.
75. I.C. Cases 3059 and 3069 (the latter "reinterpreting" and in effect reversing Case 3026 in which the Court had enforced on employers "recognition" and procedure clauses).

The second relevant Court of Appeal decision concerned a dispute between a teacher and his employer, the Sunderland Corporation, whether he was entitled, under scales set out in a Burnham report incorporated in a statutory order made by the Secretary of State, to an additional payment for teaching deaf children.[76] A clause in the Burnham report, all the terms of which were included in the statutory order, provided that "any question relating to the interpretation of the provisions of this report brought forward by a local education authority acting through the authorities' panel or by any association of teachers acting through the teachers' panel or by consent of the Chairman of the Burnham committee shall be considered and determined by the joint committee." It was argued for the Corporation that this was an arbitration clause written into the contract of service between the teacher and his employer by the statutory order. The Court of Appeal rejected this contention. This was not an arbitration clause because it did not confer bilateral *rights* of reference, and Parliament had not expressed a clear intention to deprive teachers of their ordinary common law right to come to the courts. Davies L.J. went on to say: "There is a great deal to be said for the submission [by the teacher's counsel] that really this is not primarily designed to deal with individual claims at all.... What is it really meant to deal with is a question brought up by the teachers' side ... or the local authorities' body ... in order to obtain a decision on a broad question of interpretation which may affect a large number of teachers up and down the country."[77] Similarly, Salmon L.J. thought that the procedure for interpretation had no relevance to "the case of a teacher suing his employers."[78]

One must conclude, therefore, that public employees, like other workers, are unlikely to have procedural arrangements used against them, either as clogs on their right to take individual employment disputes to the courts, or in order to penalise strikers in breach of collective "peace" obligations. On the other hand, they find it difficult to enforce procedural arrangements regarding matters such as recognition, dismissal, and disciplinary action.

76. *Baron* v. *Sunderland Corporation* [1966] 2 W.L.R. 363.
77. Ibid., p. 367.
78. Ibid., p. 368.

c. Statutory Regulation

We have seen that remuneration and certain conditions in the health services and police, dismissals and disciplinary matters in the fire services, and the remuneration of primary, secondary, and technical college teachers are regulated by statutory orders made by central government Ministers after negotiations. In addition, a large number of other matters are the subject of statutory regulation, usually after consultation with recognised unions. These include superannuation in most parts of the public services, health, safety and welfare in factories, offices, shops, etc., redundancy payments for local government employees, training, and control of racial discrimination.

The legislative process, manner of enactment, degree of parliamentary control, and method of enforcement for each of these statutory measures is richly varied. Some are contained in acts of Parliament (e.g. Redundancy Payments Act, some Superannuation Acts, Factories Act, the latter with special orders relating to Crown factories), others in subordinate legislation made by Ministers (e.g. remuneration). In some cases there may be individual enforcement through the courts based on breach of statutory duty (e.g. breach of factory legislation) or breach of contract; in others individual enforcement through industrial tribunals (e.g. redundancy payments), or special domestic tribunals (e.g. police and fire service dismissals). Remedies such as these may in some cases be supplemented or displaced by administrative inspection (e.g. factories and offices legislation) or public enforcement (e.g. antidiscrimination legislation). Ministers acting in excess of power when purporting to make subordinate legislation, and local authorities "abusing" their powers to pay "reasonable" remuneration, may find themselves subject (as appropriate) to court orders of certiorari, mandamus, injunction, and declaration. Some subordinate legislation has to be laid before Parliament which may annul it.

It is beyond the scope of this study to itemise each one of these large number of statutory measures and to describe their peculiar provisions. We shall confine ourselves to those statutory orders which give effect to agreements relating to remuneration, and to a summary of consultation before statutory regulation of pensions.

A problem common to all the statutory instruments (i.e. subordinate legislation made by Ministers) on this issue is whether an individual employee has the legal right to enforce payment of the amount stipulated in the instrument. In the case of teachers this presents no practical difficulty because the model agreement for individual teachers states: "The Committee shall pay the teacher for his/her services an annual salary in accordance with the Scale and Regulations for the time being in force and in accordance with such Orders as may be made from time to time by the Minister of Education." A teacher paid less than the stipulated amount could, therefore, bring an action for breach of contract against the employing authority. Where the agreement does not contain an express provision of this kind, the employee may seek to rely on the common law doctrine that "wherever an Act of Parliament creates a duty or obligation to pay money, an action will lie for its recovery, unless the Act contains some provision to the contrary."[79] It seems clear that a National Health Service employee, whose remuneration has been approved after negotiation and embodied in a statutory order, may rely on this doctrine because the relevant regulations provide that his remuneration "shall be neither more nor less than the remuneration so approved, whether or not it is paid out of moneys provided by Parliament."[80] In effect, the courts would treat this simply as an action for breach of contract, the terms of which would, in Lord Wright's words, be "reconstituted by striking out the rate of wages where it is lower than it ought to be, and by inserting the proper rate of wages in accordance with the statute."[81]

In the case of the police, however, the position is not quite so clear. The Police Act 1964 authorises the Secretary of State to make regulations relating to the conditions of service of members of police forces, including pay, but neither the act nor the regulations which have been made[82] expressly avoid any agreement

79. Per Parke B. in *Shepherd* v. *Hills,* 11 Exch. 55,67.
80. National Health Service (Remuneration and Conditions of Service), Regulations S.I. 1951, No. 1373, para. 3.
81. *Gutsell* v. *Reeve* [1936] 1 K.B. 272,283 (dealing with the effect of minimum wage legislation in agriculture). See too, *Aylott* v. *West Ham Corporation* [1927] 1 Ch. 30.
82. The current regulations on pay are the Police Regulations, S.I. 1968, No. 26 (as amended).

with an individual police officer to pay him either more or less than the amount specified in the regulations. (The same difficulty could arise with a teacher whose contract of employment did not include the model clause mentioned above.) The matter has never been tested, but if it were the court might be persuaded that the statutory rates could be ousted by an express agreement to that effect.[83] In practice, police forces appear to adhere to the letter of the regulations.

Another matter of general interest in relation to the statutory regulation of remuneration is parliamentary control. One of the major differences between this method of enforcing agreements and the voluntary method is that (1) Ministers who make regulations are responsible to Parliament under the general constitutional doctrine of ministerial responsibility, and (2) in some instances the enabling legislation requires the Minister's regulations to be "laid" before Parliament. The first of these methods of parliamentary control may be exercised through Questions to a Minister, motions of censure moved on the responsible Minister, or a debate or motion when the House of Commons is in Committee of Supply and on certain other occasions. All of these are rather unwieldy and, apart from Questions, do not appear to have been used in respect of regulations concerning the remuneration or conditions of those classes of public employees to whom the statutory method is applicable.

There is no consistency in the enabling acts in regard to "laying" before Parliament. Regulations for the conditions of service of members of police forces are subject to annulment

83. This approach is supported by *Hulland* v. *Sanders* [1945] K.B. 78, in which it was held that a requirement in the Conditions of Employment & National Arbitration Order 1940 (since repealed), that all employers "shall observe" recognised terms, did not confer an individual right to sue for the difference between the (higher) trade rates and those stipulated in his contract of employment. But it is submitted that this decision ought to be distinguished on the ground that the Court of Appeal was strongly influenced by the other provisions of the statutory scheme, which enabled a trade union to report an employer who had failed to pay trade rates to the Minister, who then had to refer the matter to a tribunal whose award became an implied term of the individual's contract of employment. To allow an individual to sue before reference to the tribunal would have rendered these other provisions nugatory, i.e. the basis of the scheme was to give precedence to collective action. These considerations do not apply in the case of the Police Regulations.

in pursuance of a resolution of either House of Parliament.[84] The same applies to regulations regarding the fire services,[85] and health services.[86] However, there is no requirement of "laying" before Parliament in respect of ministerial directions concerning the remuneration of county clerks.

Parliamentary control of remuneration of teachers takes a special form under both the English and Scottish legislation. There is no procedure for "laying" and annulment by Parliament of an order made by the Secretaries of State in pursuance of an agreement of the Burnham Committees. However, where as a result of disagreement there is a reference to arbitration, each House of Parliament may resolve that effect should not be given to the recommendations of the arbitrators because national economic circumstances so require.[87] Where such a resolution has been passed by each House of Parliament, the Secretary of State must consult with the Burnham Committee in question and proceed to revise the pay scales by means of a fresh order.[88] To date, Parliament has not sought to exercise these powers.

One of the best-known examples of statutory regulation is the determination of pensions. But even in this area there is extensive consultation with employers and public employee organisations, as the following breakdown will show:

How pensions determined

Civil service	Main features in act of Parliament (especially Superannuation Act 1965). All benefits are payable at the discretion of the Minister for the Civil Service (in Scotland, the Secretary of State for Scotland), who is empowered to determine all questions. But the National Joint Council has a Joint Superannuation Committee on which these issues are discussed.

84. Police Act 1964, s.33(6).
85. Fire Services Act 1947, s.35.
86. National Health Service Act 1946, s.75(2). Treasury consent to such regulations may be required by the Treasury: s.75(3).
87. Remuneration of Teachers Act 1965, s.4(2); Remuneration of Teachers (Scotland) Act 1967, s.4(2).
88. Remuneration of Teachers Act 1965, s.4(3).

National Health service	Main features in regulations made in terms of National Health Service Act 1946 by Secretary of State for Social Services with consent of Minister for Civil Service, after consultation with employers and representatives of employees.
Teachers	Main features in regulations made by Secretary of State for Education and Science, after consultation with representatives of teachers and local authorities.
Police	Main features in regulations made by Home Secretary with consent of Minister for Civil Service, after consulting Police Council.
Fire services	Same as for Police except Central Fire Brigades Advisory Council give advice.
Other local government employees	Many regulated by Local Government Superannuation Acts 1937–53 and parallel Scottish legislation. Minister of Housing and Local Government makes regulations and determines questions under these acts. Proposals for changing arrangements are always discussed with representatives of employees and local authorities.

In summary, it may be said that the main advantage of the statutory method is that it avoids most but not all technical legal difficulties about "implied" terms, especially in regard to the enforcement of rights of appeal against dismissal and disciplinary action. The main disadvantage, from the viewpoint of the collective parties, is that it increases the possibility of "external" control, both from central government Ministers and Parliament. This has led to some pressure, particularly in the case of schoolmasters, for the replacement of the statutory method of fixing remuneration, but not other conditions, by voluntary enforcement.

d. Statutory Extension of Recognised Terms

We have already described, in the context of union recognition, the use made by public employee organisations of section 8 of the Terms and Conditions of Employment Act 1959 and its predecessors. It will be remembered that the conditions which must be satisfied in order to invoke the current procedure are: (1) the terms and conditions must have been established in a trade or industry (an expression which is expressly defined, section 8(5), so as to include the activities of public and local authorities), either generally or in any district by agreement or arbitration award; (2) the parties to the agreement, or to the proceedings in which the arbitration award was made, must be "representative"; (3) an employer engaged in the trade, industry, section (and, where appropriate, district), whether a party to the agreement or award or not, is not observing the recognised terms and conditions; (4) the claim must be reported to the Secretary of State by one of the "representative" parties above. The Secretary of State is empowered to require further particulars of the claim and to take "any steps which seem to him expedient to settle" the claim. If this fails he may refer it to the Industrial Court (a permanent arbitration body). The Industrial Court, if satisfied that the claim is well founded, must make an award requiring the respondent employer to observe the recognised terms or conditions.

In view of the comparisons which may be made between this procedure and the extension procedures under French, German, and certain other Continental law, some significant features of the U.K. legislation must be stressed. The first is that there is no such thing as a *general* extension order made by the Secretary of State. The procedure can be invoked only against individual employers. Second, the procedure cannot be invoked by individual employees, despite the quasi-judicial nature of the proceedings before the arbitration body, but only by "representative" organisations, and they themselves cannot directly approach the Industrial Court but only through the Department of Employment and Productivity, which first seeks to settle the matter amicably. Indeed, many claims are settled or withdrawn even after reference to the Industrial Court but before an award has been made. Third, as we saw in the section on recognition, the legislation, in marked contrast to that in other countries, leaves the determination of the "representative" character of the organisations to administrative authorities. Fourth, once the matter reaches the Industrial Court, that court must be satisfied (1) that there are recognised terms or conditions which the employer has failed to observe, and (2) that the terms or conditions which that employer is in fact observing are not less favourable than the recognised terms or conditions.

Finally, the effect of the Industrial Court's award is not limited to the particular employee or employees whose conditions have given rise to the claim. The award applies to all persons "of the relevant description" employed by that employer both at the time of the award and in the future. The award may have retrospective effect but not beyond the time when the employer was first informed of the claim against him, which has led organisations of local government employees to give immediate notice of new Whitley Council agreements to all local authority employers. The award ceases to have effect on the coming into operation of a new agreement or award varying or abrogating the recognised terms or conditions. When that happens it is necessary to obtain a fresh award from the Industrial Court.

The sanction for breach of an award is a purely civil one, namely an action before the ordinary courts by an employee whose terms or conditions are covered by the award. The award has effect as an implied term of the individual contract of employment, and the general view is that the award *must* remain in the contract until overtaken by a new collective agreement or award.[89] The employer who pays less than the amount required by the award does not commit a criminal offence, nor is there any machinery for the inspection of books or otherwise for the enforcement of the award. This detracts from its usefulness, particularly in the case of workers who are not members of trade unions and are ignorant of their legal rights.

The extension procedure is of importance, in the public employment field, only to local government employees. Even in this field its significance is severely limited by the fact that it cannot be used where there is in operation any minimum wages legislation applicable to the employees concerned (e.g. the catering,

89. However in *Fox v. Pianoforte Supplies* [1964] 4 Current Law 106, a County court judge held that an employer could "contract-out" of an award. This decision was probably wrong in law. The matter awaits authoritative interpretation.

baking, and distributive employees of local government)[90] or where there is statutory machinery for the settlement of remuneration. This excludes from the extension procedure teachers in primary and secondary schools and technical colleges, National Health Service employees, and members of police forces. Since 1959 members of fire services have fallen within the scope of the extension machinery because their statutory wage settlement machinery was dropped in that year.

Even without the use of the legal machinery, however, collectively agreed wages have been treated as minimum *standards*. The real difficulty is that employers have not treated collective standards as laying down *maximum* amounts of payment. In other words, statutory extension machinery is concerned exclusively with protecting lower-paid workers, and not with preventing "whipsaw" tactics. This is illustrated by the Report of the Chief Inspector of Fire Services:

> There must, however, be some sympathy for members of fire brigades who feel that through no fault of their own and for no logical reason they are paid less than their colleagues in some other brigades who perform similar duties. When they ask me why this should be so I am unable to supply a satisfactory answer. It is more than a pity that some fire authorities do not abide by the recommendations of the National Joint Council of which they are members and instead decide to give their own firemen some higher remuneration. This leads to other fire brigades, particularly those adjacent and who provide reinforcements to the brigades referred to, becoming dissatisfied and expecting similar additional pay. Unless what is happening is checked it will undoubtedly result in a growing uneven spiral which could well have an effect on efficiency. I hope therefore that a way will be found to put this matter right and to prevent its occurrence in future.[91]

90. The Donovan Commission (and the ex-Labour Government) proposed a limited extension of s.8 so as to permit claims to be reported in respect of workers subject to Wages Councils Orders.

91. *Report of Her Majesty's Chief Inspector of Fire Services (Counties and County Boroughs, England and Wales and Greater London Council) for the Year 1969* (HMSO, 1970. Cmnd. 4397), para. 123.

·VI·

Negotiating and Financing Authorities

THERE is no relationship of any direct kind between the bargaining and budget-making cycle. On the other hand, certain pay increases are automatic, the employees concerned being on an incremental scale whereby increases of specified amount are granted annually, the date being dependent not upon the budget year but upon the date of appointment or promotion to a new grade. In addition regular reviews of pay are carried out, for example the work of the Pay Research Unit in the Civil Service.

The negotiating bodies in the civil service will not reach agreement unless and until it is known that the Civil Service Department approves the new agreement. Similarly in local authority bargaining there can be no agreement unless a majority on the employers' side agree (and of course a majority on the trade union side must also agree), and they will not agree unless they know that the financing authority will authorise payment. Sometimes this may mean that both sides, as in the case of teachers' pay in 1970, will make it publicly known that they would be willing to agree on an increase but that the local authority side could not formally agree to this because of its knowledge that the Ministry of Education was not willing to approve the proposed agreement. The National and Local Government Officers' Association complained to the Donovan Commission that when they were negotiating with local authorities about the wages and conditions of health service employees, they found that the Treasury was a backdoor influence.

3855. Mr. Anderson: We think it ought not to be a backdoor influence. It is an influence we feel both sides of the negotiating committee should have fairly put on the table when they are negotiating. The present system is, as you have said, both sides may agree and then possibly unknown to either, certainly unknown to the Staff Side, there is some movement

158

behind the scenes from the Treasury which can upset that agreement and the course of the negotiations.

3856. That must be very frustrating at times.—It is indeed.

3857. But when you say the influence should be open, do you mean the Treasury should come to the bargaining table, or what?—Yes, we feel it would be better if the Treasury has a point of view, that point of view should be stated at the bargaining table so both sides know what obstacles there are to the course of negotiations and indeed have a chance to challenge them.

3858. The Treasury I suppose could not effectively intervene at the bargaining table until it knew what it was that was going to be asked?—Negotiations normally start, do they not, with a claim from the Staff Side, so from that stage the Treasury know what the claim is. They no doubt have in their own minds some idea of what may be conceded, if anything. Let it come straight out in negotiations, we say, rather than the Chairman of the Management Side be told after the negotiations that he has limits within which he can work. A similar situation arises in regard to gas and electricity where, in the background, is the Ministry of Power. Let this all come out, let us have free negotiations and if there are some questions, some difficulties in the way, let the Staff Side who are claiming, be told during the neotiations the reasons for it and have an opportunity to challenge them.[1]

However, as it was felt that the presence of the Treasury might stultify discussion right at the very outset, Mr. Anderson, speaking for the National and Local Government Officers' Association, did not recommend a change.

Very often payment may involve action taken by a public authority under some statutory authority, as in the case of the teachers as a result of which statutory authority exists for the payment of monies which nationally may not have been approved by Parliament. In practice this does not occur. The voting of money for State purposes is a continuous process and is not decided once and for all for the whole year when the budget is approved. Departments frequently return to Parliament for sup-

1. RCME, Day 26, p. 1031.

plementary votes. Nor does payment of sums by Government departments have to wait on the passing of a supplementary vote. It is an increasing practice generally to incur liability to pay money, and even to pay it, in advance of statutory authority to do so. It is not known how often this occurs in the field of wages and salaries of public employees but it does occur here. Because the Cabinet stands behind the acts of Ministers, and because the Cabinet is able in normal circumstances to secure parliamentary approval for whatever is done with its, or the Prime Minister's, authority, it would be inconceivable in present circumstances that Parliament would disapprove of liabilities incurred by Ministers in advance of their being given authority by Parliament to pay the money concerned.

More difficulties might arise in local government if local authorities paid money which they had not lawful authority to pay over. Therefore local authorities do not in practice commit themselves to alterations in wages and salaries unless they have made provision themselves to raise the money by rates. Where the charge falls upon the central government and not local rates, then they will not make an agreement until they have the approval of the Government department concerned.

Part Three

Disputes Settlement: Policies and Procedures

·VII·
General Features of Disputes Settlement

THE separation of "disputes settlement" from "collective bargaining" in this monograph is, in many respects, a highly artificial division.

In the first place, British labour law and practice show little concern for the distinction—so vital in many European countries—between "conflicts of interest" and "conflicts of right." Nor do they know the distinction established in the United States between negotiation and grievance procedure. As Allan Flanders has said: "So long as the agreed disputes procedure is followed through its various stages we are not particularly interested in whether new substantive rules are being made or old ones applied; the main thing is to find an acceptable and, if possible, a durable compromise by means of direct negotiation between representatives of the two sides."[1]

In the processing of disputes, therefore, "economic" claims merge imperceptibly with questions of "interpretation." This is nowhere better illustrated than in the practice of the various institutions provided by law for purposes of conciliation, inquiry, and arbitration. In general neither the *choice* of institution nor the *procedure* followed is determined by the *content* of the dispute. Even more fundamental than this is the fact that the stage of reference to conciliation, inquiry, or arbitration is not sharply delimited from the bargaining process. On the contrary, it is seen as no more than an aid or prop to the successful conclusion of negotiations. The results must be voluntarily agreed and accepted by both sides to the dispute. The law, in general, does no more than provide means by which the State can help the parties reach a compromise. The wisdom of the British system, some would think, rests precisely on its recognition that industrial peace is best secured, not by compulsion, but by the freely evidenced intentions of both sides to make collective bargaining "work." In this public employers, in particular the Crown (i.e. central

1. *Industrial Relations—What Is Wrong with the System?* (London, 1965), p. 28.

government), have for the past fifty years been "models," excelling their counterparts in private industry and setting an example in their willingness to reach negotiated settlements and to act upon those settlements without legal sanction.

The main weakness of this system has been its inability in private industry to provide an adequate standard of job security for all employees and to protect various "minorities"—such as women, children, and coloured workers—from gross exploitation. The "Method of Legal Enactment" (as the Webbs called it) has been utilised since the nineteenth century to correct this weakness. The Factories Acts and similar legislation have guaranteed certain minimum standards of health, safety, and welfare; the Race Relations Act 1968 has provided means of redress for members of ethnic minorities who allege discrimination; the Contracts of Employment Act 1963 has provided certain minimum periods of notice of termination of contracts of employment; and the Redundancy Payments Act 1965 has entitled certain workers to obtain lump-sum compensation for loss of job caused by rationalisation and technological change. These legal standards operate, in many cases, through the individual worker's contract of employment, and in their enforcement they resemble "disputes of right."

The individual worker will often be assisted by his union in enforcing these rights, but he need not be. His claim will in some cases go through the ordinary courts (e.g. claims for damages for wrongful dismissal or for injuries sustained at work due to the employer's fault) and, in the case of some more recent statutory rights, before the industrial tribunals. The latter are specialist bodies consisting of a legal chairman, one member drawn from a panel of employers' representatives, and another from representatives of work people. The main criticism of this system of tribunals has been that the legal chairman (who usually has had little experience in industry) overshadows the "wing" members, and that the ultimate legal control over these tribunals, exercised by the ordinary superior courts, has made them adhere to literal interpretations of statutes and rigid legal doctrines.[2]

In other words, the attempt to establish "rights" enforceable by legal process has been regarded by some commentators as

2. Wedderburn and Davies, p. 258.

being somewhat less satisfactory than the process of voluntary dispute settlement which relies on a mixture of conciliation and mediation. This adherence to the flexible, voluntary system is evidenced, for example, in proposals by the Donovan Commission for a law against "unfair" dismissals, which would give primacy to satisfactory voluntary dismissals procedures.[3] Another example is antiracial discrimination legislation which makes approved voluntary bodies responsible, in the first instance, for the "settlement" of complaints of unlawful discrimination.[4]

Another weakness of the traditional system has been said to be the frequency of short-duration strikes in breach of voluntary "peace" obligations (unconstitutional stoppages). The Donovan Commission diagnosed the source of this, in private industry, as the conflict between the formal industry-wide system of bargaining and informal plant-level negotiations which permit a high level of "wages drift" in response to militant shop floor action. It recommended the reform of bargaining so as to formalise the informal system. It rejected, for the time being, the legal enforcement of collective agreements, in particular the "peace" obligation. Although it has not been alleged by any commentators that the public services suffer from a similar problem of unconstitutional stoppages, those who would make procedural obligations legally enforceable between the collective parties apparently contemplate that this should apply to the public services as well as to private industry. We have already indicated in Chapter V our reasons for doubting the efficacy of such proposals.

Since British labour law is not at present concerned with the breach of collective agreements as an aspect of disputes settlement, it will be asked how the law defines the legitimacy of "means" and "ends" in industrial conflict. (We shall indicate below, however, that "unconstitutionality" affects the attitudes of the parties and courts of inquiry etc. to the propriety of stoppages.) One basic feature of the British system is its apparent lack of concern with the "ends" of a dispute. Since the 1920s the British courts have regarded practically all honestly held trade union objectives as legitimate and have denied legal protection only to those who pursue personal grudges. The position of "political" strikes

3. Cmnd. 3623, Chap. IX.
4. Bob Hepple, *Race, Jobs and the Law in Britain.*

remains obscure, but it would seem that the mere element of political pressure on the government does not expose strikers to legal sanctions.[5] On the whole, the policy of the law has been to protect the State and the courts from having to become embroiled in the *merits* of any particular dispute.

The law has, however, sought to regulate the means used by the parties. Physical violence of any sort is obviously not countenanced and has not in this century presented any problem, particularly in the public services. How far may economic pressures be exerted? Legislation between 1871 and 1906 aimed (like the 1935 Wagner Act in the U.S.) at equalising the economic powers of capital and labour. By contrast with U.S. legislation, however, the British statutes do not provide positive rules on what is permitted and what is forbidden. The British legislation is entirely negative: it simply removes the disabilities which judge-made law had imposed on collective action. This means that while the courts have been inclined to widen the area of civil liability in tort for causing economic loss, Parliament has been concerned to maintain the equality of labour's bargaining position by conferring negative immunities on those engaging in industrial action. The means therefore are those permitted by the judges, mainly through the application of tort law, within the limits of immunities defined by Parliament. The settlement of 1871-1906 was achieved only after a long period of sharp conflict between the law and the unions, and, needless to say, any attempts to reopen it are likely to be bitterly resisted.

It will thus be seen that British labour law has little in common with those systems which are concerned with "unfair labour practices" which can be suppressed through administrative action and court injunctions. Moreover, questions such as whether the strike is in breach of a contract of employment, or whether as in France a strike terminates or simply suspends a contract of employment, are theoretically debated but not of vital practical significance. Nor is social security law used to the extent it is in some countries, such as Belgium, to secure compliance with certain standards of conduct. We would not ascribe to the orthodox view that British social securiuty law is wholly neutral

5. See A. L. Goodhart in *Essays in Jurisprudence and the Common Law,* p. 241.

in industrial disputes, because the striker is in fact penalised by being denied unemployment benefit and supplementary benefits unless he shows that *he* is not participating or directly interested in a trade dispute. One curious effect of the definition of "trade dispute" is that certain public employees (e.g. Crown servants) may not be engaged in "trade disputes" when they strike, and so in a superior position to unemployed workers in private industry. However, it should be pointed out that no person can be denied unemployment benefit simply because he refuses to accept work because of a trade dispute.

Perhaps the most striking feature of the law on this subject in Britain is that it is uncodified, resting on a patchwork of isolated judicial decisions and several acts of Parliament spanning a century. There is, moreover, no constitutional guarantee of a "right to strike." Nor—and this is vital in the context of our monograph—is there in Britain any separate category of public employees such as the *fonctionnaires* or *Beamten* of Continental countries, who owe a special duty of fidelity. The hotly disputed controversies of Continental lawyers whether this duty excludes the right to strike is no part of the English or Scottish lawyer's stock-in-trade. The separate problem, which features in much American literature, of protecting the "public interest" against public employee strikes has received little attention in Britain. It is true that a few categories of public employees—policemen, postmen, and certain public utility employees and those engaged in "dangerous" activities—have been arbitrarily singled out for special legal prohibitions enforced through the criminal law. But it is impossible to rationalise these special prohibitions in any consistent way. They are exceptional and serve only to emphasise that the majority of public employees are in a similar legal position to their counterparts in private industry (although we shall emphasise certain distinctions) when it comes to industrial warfare.

167

·VIII·
Economic Sanctions

1. THE STRIKE PATTERN

PUBLISHED statistics do not give a clear picture of the nature and incidence of strikes among those whom we have chosen to classify as public employees for the purposes of this study. The Department of Employment and Productivity's annual figures group workers according to the Standard Occupational Classification which does not contain a separate category of public employees akin to the one we have used in this study. However, it seems that a large proportion of those whom we have grouped as public employees would be included in the standard classification "administrative, professional, and technical services." This would cover not only white-collar workers but also manual workers employed by local authorities. However, it does not cover those in government industrial establishments, local authority transport services, and postal services. Moreover, the "administrative, professional, technical services" category is not confined to employees of government but includes as well many employees in the private sector (e.g. entertainments, sport, catering). Within these important limits the figures in Table 6 give some indication of the *trend* in the number of stoppages involving public employees in the period 1967-69.

It will be noted from this table that strikes among administrative, professional, and technical workers form a relatively small number of the total of stoppages and working days lost, but that the *rate* at which these stoppages have grown is much greater than that for employees in all industry groups. This reflects the growing militancy among white-collar workers in general and public white-collar workers in particular, as well as several lengthy disputes involving local authority manual workers in 1969.

Table 7 indicates the nature of the most important and lengthy strikes in 1969 and the ways in which they were resolved. Several features of these strikes ought to be noted. First, all except one of these were "official," that is they were sanctioned or ratified by the unions whose members were on strike. Since we do not have overall statistics of strikes among public employees

Table 6.

Public Employee Stoppages of Work, 1967–1969

Group[1]	1969			1968			1967		
	Number of Stoppages	*Workers*	*W/Days lost*	*Number of Stoppages*	*Workers*	*W/Days lost*	*Number of Stoppages*	*Workers*	*W/Days lost*
Administrative, Professional Services	75	140,100	309,000	53	9,700	44,000	20	5,700	11,000
Gas, Electricity, Water	31	10,700	18,000	14	3,000	7,000	13	3,700	9,000
All Industry Groups	3,021	1,619,600	6,772,000	2,378	2,257,600	4,690,000	2,116	733,700	2,787,000

1. As defined in the Standard Occupational Classification, 1958.
Source: Department of Employment and Productivity *Gazettes* (1968–70)

Table 7.

Major Strikes of Public Employees Commencing in 1969

Group	Cause	Outcome
Teachers		
1. Official "work to rule" and one-day selective strikes (Feb. 1969) (National Association of Schoolmasters)	Salary claim	Negotiated settlement (improved offer)
2. Official selective one-day and half-day stoppages (Nov. 1969) followed by 8-day selective stoppages (National Union of Teachers, 87,000 involved)	"Interim" salary claim	Negotiated settlement (improved offer after arbitration refused) (March 1970)
Ambulance personnel		
Official indefinite stoppage, London and Home Counties (Federation of Ambulance Personnel, 300 involved)	Recognition of union (opposed by three existing unions)	Agreed reference to joint negotiating body for manual workers leading to independent inquiry and report
Hospital electricians		
Official indefinite (Electrical Technicians' Union) 12 cities (June)	Wage claim	Negotiated settlement (improved productivity-pay offer)
Firemen		
1. Official (ballot) (Dec. 1968)	Wage claim (undermanning allowance)	Strike notice withdrawn after negotiated settlement (improved offer)
2. Official. Ban on all except emergency calls (Oct.-Nov.). Threat of full stoppage.	Rent allowance claim	Negotiated settlement (improved offer)

Local authority dustmen

Unofficial, Hackney. Unofficial sympathetic strikes in other boroughs (25 Sept.-18 Nov.). 150,000 work days lost.	Wage claim	Sporadic return to work after settlement negotiated by unions (improved offer)
Admiralty dockyard employees One-day official. (All Britain) (Oct.)	Wage claim (against delay in negotiations)	Negotiations held
University technicians Official. One day and three days. (March)	Wage claim	Negotiated settlement (improved offer)
Post Office[1] 1. *Overseas telegraphists.* Official. Indefinite (3,900 between 20 Jan.-1 Feb.). Official sympathetic after general overtime ban. 103,000 work days lost	Wage and productivity claim	Negotiated settlement (improved offer)
2. *Engineering workers.* Official. One-day. 84,000 work days lost	Wage claim	Negotiated settlement (improved offer)

Sources: D.E.P. *Gazette.* British Journal of Industrial Relations Labour Research.

1. Became a public corporation after these stoppages.

we are unable to say whether the strikes in this table are "typical" of public employee strikes generally. It should be noted, however, that both the Donovan Commission[1] and a Government White Paper[2] take the view that a great majority of strikes (about 95 per cent), in the economy as a whole, is unofficial,[3] and that these

1. Cmnd. 3623, para. 368.
2. Cmnd. 3888, p. 39.
3. The assumptions of these reports have been questioned by H. A. Turner, *Is Britain Really Strike Prone?* Cambridge Dept. of Applied Economics. Occasional Paper, No. 20 (1969).

unofficial strikes are nearly always unconstitutional, i.e. they take place in breach of the appropriate voluntary procedure for dealing with disputes. Official strikes, although fewer in number, tend to last longer and involve more workers than unofficial strikes.

Second, all but one of the strikes in the table were about wages. This does not necessarily represent a typical pattern and certainly does not in respect of unofficial stoppages. Dismissals, redundancy, suspension, working rules, and other individual employment grievances are a frequent cause of unofficial stoppages. (There were 972 unofficial stoppages in respect of these matters in 1964-66 in all industries compared to 1,072 in respect of wages in the same period.)

Third, all these strikes were ended by negotiation and not by the use of legal sanctions, either in the form of compulsory arbitration or injunctions. This we would regard as fairly typical of the way in which strikes are resolved. It will also be noted that all the wage claims were settled, after the strike or threat of strike, by means of an increased offer. In other words, strikes were regarded as an integral part of the bargaining process and, in 1969 at least, always paid off. The one recognition dispute (involving the Federation of Ambulance Personnel) was ended by an agreement to refer the matter to a joint negotiating body, which in turn appointed an independent (academic) expert to conduct an inquiry. His report rejected the claim for recognition but made a number of far-reaching proposals for the reorganisation of collective bargaining for ambulancemen which might eventually resolve the underlying causes of the dispute.[4] At the present writing, however, the Federation of Ambulance Personnel has threatened further militant action to achieve recognition.

Finally, it will be seen that the tactics used ranged from full indefinite work stoppages, through selective one-day and half-day stoppages, to bans on overtime, "work to rule," and other forms of "go-slow" action. Picketing is nearly always employed in stoppages together with such other forms of protest as processions, rallies, and mass deputations to Parliament.

---

4. W. E. J. McCarthy, *Representation and Collective Bargaining in the Ambulance Service* (National Joint Council for Local Authorities' Services [Manual Workers], May 1970).

2. THE LAW AND STRIKES

The "right to strike" is basically a right to withdraw labour in combination without being subject to legal consequences. In Britain this right is widely regarded as an essential part of free collective bargaining. In the nineteenth century it was threatened by a hostile judiciary which developed various common law doctrines (such as criminal and tortious conspiracy) in order to illegalise strikes and picketing. The extension of the franchise in 1867 and 1885 and the gradual emergence of a political arm of the labour movement resulted in the passing of various statutes—in particular the Trade Union Acts 1871 and 1876, the Conspiracy and Protection of Property Act 1875, and the Trade Disputes Act 1906 (supplemented by a further act in 1965)—which grant "negative" immunities against the illegalities threatened by the judiciary. They do not establish a positive right to strike, but they do aim to give trade unions and individuals liberty of action within the confines of "trade disputes." As we shall see later, it is doubtful whether public employees enjoy these immunities to the same extent as other employees (largely because of the vague definition of "trade dispute"), and judicial innovations in the 1960s have to some extent frustrated the original aims of the statutes. The indirect judicial attack on the right to strike has been largely overtaken by a frontal political onslaught, mainly evidenced in the proposals of the Conservative Government (elected in June 1970) for industrial reform. These developments may in the future be of great importance to those public employee unions which are in the process of adopting increasingly militant tactics and have shown their willingness to utilise economic sacntions.

The law has not singled out public employees for special treatment, with the exception of the police, postal employees, and those engaged in public utilities and in occupations where stoppages would result in serious dangers to life or property. In those exceptional cases the law provides criminal sanctions against some, but certainly not all, strikes. The most important legal consequence of strike action, for both public and private employees, is that it usually exposes the striker to disciplinary measures (including summary dismissal) by his employer. The criminal sanctions, as we shall see, have not been used for at least twenty years. Disciplinary action by the employer is relatively rare in practice. However, like the criminal sanction, it may exert psychological effect on those contemplating strike action.

Another legal vehicle which may be available to an employer is the private civil action (before the ordinary courts) in respect of torts committed or threatened in the course of strike action. The main attraction of this, from the employer's viewpoint, is the possibility of obtaining a "labour injunction." However, this possibility is severely restricted in two ways. First, section 4 of the Trade Disputes Act 1906 purports to prohibit any action in tort "in respect of any tortious act alleged to have been committed" by, or on behalf of, a trade union. This immunity for trade unions[5] extends beyond trade disputes, but, as we shall see, it has been eroded by judicial interpretations, and it does not protect those public employee organisations which are not "trade unions" in law. Second, although nothing in this section protects union officials, they are immune from liability for most of the torts which are likely to be committed in the course of a trade dispute. This is an immunity which extends not only to union officials but to "any person," with the result that the law draws no distinction between "official" and "unofficial" strikes. Nor is any distinction drawn between disputes of "rights" and disputes of "interest"; nor, subject to certain esoteric legal qualifications, between constitutional and unconstitutional action. It is these "negative" protections which enable a wide range of economic pressure to be exerted in trade disputes. This has been rationalised by the view that in Britain the law "abstains" from industrial relations. As we shall see, this view has become increasingly untenable as the courts in the 1960s and the threat of parliamentary action in the 1970s have reopened the settlement of 1871-1906.

---

5. This was enacted in consequence of the controversial House of Lords decision in *Taff Vale Ry. Co.* v. *Amalgamated Socy. of Ry. Servants* [1901] A.C. 426 that tort actions could be brought against trade unions, despite the fact that they are voluntary unincorporated bodies, by reason of their *voluntary registration* under the act of 1871.

3. CRIMINAL SANCTIONS AGAINST PUBLIC EMPLOYEES

a. Police

Section 53(1) of the Police Act 1964 provides:

Any person who causes, or attempts to cause, or does any act calculated to cause, disaffection amongst the members of any police force, or induces or attempts to induce, or does any act calculated to induce, any member of a police force to withhold his services or to commit breaches of discipline, shall be guilty of an offense and liable—

(a) on summary conviction, to imprisonment for a term not exceeding six months or to a fine not exceeding £100, or to both;

(b) on conviction on indictment, to imprisonment for a term not exceeding two years or to a fine or to both.[6]

An offence of inciting disaffection among the police had first been introduced in the Police Act 1919, following the Metropolitan and City of London police strike of 1918. There had been earlier strikes of police in 1872 and 1890, and while the Police Bill was being debated in 1919 an unsuccessful attempt was made to call out the police throughout the country.[7] The then Home Secretary, E. Shortt, denied that the disaffection provision was aimed at the trade unions; he insisted that he was seeking to punish "the agent of disaffection and of revolution and the agent of real mischief."

The Police Act 1964 dropped that part of the 1919 act which provided that a policeman convicted under it would forfeit all his pension rights and become disqualified from membership of any police force. However, the 1964 act retains the wording of the 1919 act which enables the prosecution to obtain a conviction for "doing any act calculated to" cause disaffection without proof of a guilty intention. This is generally regarded as a "surprising" example of strict criminal liability.

The disaffection provision was used on a few occasions between the two world wars but, it seems, has not been the basis of a prosecution since the end of the Second World War. Wartime

6. This covers special constables as well: s.53(2).
7. Reynolds and Judge, *The Night the Police Went on Strike* (London, 1968).

175

emergency regulations contained specific provisions in respect of incitement of the police. The 1918 police strike occurred in wartime and was sometimes described as a "mutiny." There were even veiled suggestions that the police were subverting soldiers. But no prosecutions resulted. The prosecutions arose out of the activities of the movement of unemployed workers. These included two cases in 1921, a time of severe industrial unrest. During the 1926 general strike there was no trouble. Wal Hannington, a leader of the National Unemployed Workers' Movement, was convicted and jailed for three months in 1932 for a speech in which he sought to associate the police with the unemployed in opposing the Government's economy measures.[8]

b. Postal Employees

The Post Office Act 1953, section 58, provides that any officer of the Post Office who "wilfully detains or delays" any postal packet commits an offence.[9] The main significance of this is in relation to "go-slows," "work to rule," and "overtime bans," because it means that a Post Office worker who engages in any one of these forms of action may commit a crime, irrespective of any breach of contract on his part. In this the offence is rather different from the criminal liabilities which may be imposed on others engaged in essential services, as we shall see below.

This provision has not, it seems, been used against postal strikers. In its evidence to the Donovan Commission the Post Office pointed out that part of the trouble was that "slow working is hard to detect and bring home to the individuals responsible."[10] The Post Office has not been plagued by unofficial action, partly because the national officers of the postal unions have gone to great trouble to discipline local representatives threatening or taking such action. The relatively low incidence of industrial action has been attributed to extensive local consultations over matters other than pay, the effectiveness of the Whitley system, and a "sense of responsibility to the public" on the part of postal unions.[11]

8. See Wal Hannington, *Unemployed Struggles 1919–36,* and David Williams, *Keeping the Peace* (London, 1965), pp. 192–95.
9. See too s.59, which penalises certain other forms of misconduct. These provisions have survived the conversion of the Post Office into a public corporation by the Post Office act 1969.
10. RCWE (Post Office) (1966), para. 42.
11. Ibid.

c. Public Utilities and Dangers to Life or Property

Sections 4 and 5 of the Conspiracy and Protection of Property Act 1875 create what is, in effect, a cooling-off provision in respect of certain strikes.

Section 4 makes it a criminal offence for any person to break a contract of service in the following circumstances: (1) He is employed by a municipal authority or by any company or contractor which has the duty of supplying any city, borough, town or place with gas or water; (2) he wilfully and maliciously breaks his contract of service with that authority, company, or contractor; (3) he knows or has reasonable cause to believe that the probable consequences of his so doing, either alone or in combination with others, will be to deprive the inhabitants concerned wholly or to a great extent of their supply of gas or water.

This provision was extended by section 31 of the Electricity (Supply) Act 1919 to persons employed by an electricity authority. The punishment laid down is a fine of £20 or imprisonment not exceeding three months. The gas, water, and electricity supply undertakers are obliged by the statute to post and keep posted a printed copy of the section in some conspicuous place where it may be conveniently read by the persons employed.

It will be noticed that the section does not make the lawful termination of the contract of service a criminal offence, even though this is done in combination with other employees and with the intention of depriving the public of gas or water or electricity supplies. Generally speaking, one week's notice suffices to terminate lawfully the contracts of employees of these public utilities. This means that, at its highest, the section imposes a one-week cooling-off period before strike action may lawfully be taken. Nor does the section restrict forms of industrial action which do not involve breaches of individual employment contracts. For example, in the electricity supply industry overtime work is voluntary, so a ban on overtime, even without notice, could not result in criminal liability.

In the period since the Second World War, section 4 has been used only once. That was in 1950 when the Attorney-General prosecuted gas strikers. However, the charge under section 4 was withdrawn and the strikers were convicted under emergency regulations then in force. In their evidence to the Donovan Commission both the Gas[12] and Electricity Councils[13] favoured the retention of section 4, although they conceded that it had had little effect on negotiations. The arguments for its retention (accepted by the Donovan Commission[14]) were its psychological value on men contemplating lightning strikes, and the danger that its repeal would be interpreted as indicating new public policy which did not regard it as serious to cut off power supplies. Only one large public employer—London Transport—asked the Commission (unsuccessfully) for the extension of section 4 to cover other employees (i.e. those in public transport). The grounds for this were that "one is entitled to ask [a man entering public employment] to accept certain responsibilities, perhaps certain restraints, because he is in public employment."[15] But under cross-examination London Transport's witnesses admitted that they had never used the legal sanctions available to them of suing individual strikers for damages for breaches of contract, and that this was because of the difficulty of taking proceedings against so many men.

Section 5 of the 1875 act is on similar lines to section 4 but is of wider application. It applies to any person who wilfully and maliciously breaks a contract of service or of hiring, knowing or having reasonable cause to believe that the probable consequences of his so doing, either alone or in combination with others, will be to endanger human life, to cause serious bodily injury, or to expose valuable property to destruction or serious injury. The punishments are the same as those under section 4.

Like section 4, there has to be a breach of contract (and hence this is another cooling-off provision), but unlike the earlier section it is not confined to "employees" nor to public utility undertakings. Among those whom it may cover are those engaged in emergency work such as ambulancemen, hospital staff, sewage and garbage workers, drivers, firemen, and a host of other public and private employees, the breach of whose contracts would in some circumstances put life or valuable property at risk.

Again like section 4, this provision has not been used in modern times. For example, its use was not even suggested during the strikes of dustmen, ambulance employees, and firemen in 1969

12. RCME, Day 11, p. 379.   13. RCME, Day 21, p. 779.
14. Cmnd. 3623, paras. 838–39.   15. RCME, Day 5, para. 894.

(Table 7). Indeed, during a strike in 1970 of 400 craftsmen whom the Greater London Council employs to control pumps and sludge boats, it was a spokesman for the men who asserted that the strike could cause a serious health hazard.[16] Apparently the possibility that this might constitute an offence under section 5 had not acted as a deterrent. Nevertheless, there has been no movement for the repeal of the section, and the Donovan Commission did not recommend any alteration the existing law.[17]

Between 1927 and 1946 there was an addition to section 5 in the form of section 6(4) of the Trade Disputes and Trade Unions Act 1927. This made it a criminal offence for employees of local or other public authorities to break their contracts of service "knowing or having reasonable cause to believe that the probable consequence of so doing, either alone or in combination with others, will be to cause injury or danger or grave inconvenience to the community." In practice this was not used, and it was repealed in 1946.

Apart from these provisions, there have been criminal sanctions against strikers in times of war and in peacetime national emergency. In regard to the latter it should be noted that the Emergency Powers Act 1920 (which was used during the 1926 general strike, the docks strike of 1949, and the railway strike of 1955) allows the government to take over and maintain "essential services" but in express terms protects the right to strike.

d. Current Proposals to Extend Criminal Sanctions

There has been remarkably little public discussion of the basic issues involved in controlling strikes by use of the criminal law; and even less about strikes in "essential" services. The Labour Government, against the advice of the Donovan Commission, mooted criminal sanctions against unofficial strikers who disobeyed a cooling-off order made by the Secretary of State, but these proposals were abandoned under trade union pressure. The Conservative Government (elected in June 1970) does not, it seems, propose an extension of the *criminal* law.

The only prominent proposal for rtaionalising the criminal law has been that made by Mr. Andrew Shonfeld in his Note of Reservation to the Donovan Report.[18] He argued that there

16. *The Times,* 1 June 1970.   17. Cmnd. 3623, paras. 840–45.
18. Cmnd. 3623, pp. 291–92.

were no grounds for singling out gas, water, and electricity employees for special treatment, and accordingly he proposed the repeal of section 4 of the 1875 act. However, he was in favour of extending section 5 to make it apply to "people who act dangerously, regardless whether they are formally breaking their contracts or not." He seemed to contemplate criminal proceedings against *trade unions* ("or any other group of persons") because he proposed that unions should be bound to refrain from lightning strikes of a "dangerous" character and also to avoid impeding the employer in his efforts to minimise the risks to life and health. The reference by Mr. Shonfeld to "lightning" strikes in this context is difficult to understand in view of his suggestion that lawful termination of contract should not preclude criminal liability. His proposal would mean that even official strikes of which long notice had been given would give rise to criminal liabilities.

4. DISCIPLINARY ACTION BY THE EMPLOYER

The most likely legal consequence of strike action is summary dismissal or other disciplinary measures by the employer. In practice this is a weapon which is not often used, because of union insistence on "no victimisation" as a term of negotiated settlements.

In the case of Crown servants, successive governments have made it clear that they feel free to take "any disciplinary action that any strike situation that might develop demanded."[19] In the case of firemen and policemen there are elaborate statutory disciplinary codes under which strikers could be charged before domestic tribunals and, after a fair hearing, dismissed or otherwise disciplined.

In the case of other public employees strikes very often are in breach of their individual employment contracts. Only one modern judge[20] has been prepared to countenance the idea that a contract of employment can be *suspended* by giving notice of strike equivalent in length to notice to quit. In the case

19. H.M. Treasury, *Staff Relations in the Civil Service,* para. 73.
20. Lord Denning M.R. in *Morgan* v. *Fry* [1968] 2 Q.B. 710.

of indefinite stoppages, where no notice is given, it is clear that employment contracts will be broken. If the employees give due notice to *terminate* their contracts, the contracts end when the strike begins so there is *no* breach (the usual practice in the public utilities because of the risk of criminal sanctions; see above). But the judges have recognised that men giving strike notice usually do not wish to terminate their contracts. This implies that in many instances the giving of strike notice is nothing less than notice of an intention to break contracts.[21]

Throughout the public services an employee engaged in a lengthy strike might find that he loses his pension rights, either because of a disciplinary penalty imposed by the employer or simply because of a break in the "continuity" of employment required to gain entitlement to certain pensions. In the case of industrial and nonindustrial civil servants this particular sanction may take various forms. Each department has an established complement. An established civil servant might have it decided, as a disciplinary penalty for going on strike, that he is to be disestablished and so lose his entitlement to pension. A Treasury witness told the Donovan Commission that he could remember only one occasion on which this sanction had been applied against unofficial strikers in the established industrial civil service, and then it had later been decided to restore their pensions.[22] Even if disestablished, an industrial civil servant would continue to be entitled on retirement or resignation to a gratuity which is paid to all employees with sufficiently long service, but is not as advantageous as a pension.[23] In theory payment of gratuities and pensions is discretionary, and there is statutory authority to reduce the amount of a pension or gratuity if the "default" or "demerit" of the employee justifies such a course.[24] The same Treasury witness could not remember a case in which a pension had been refused.[25]

21. This was the view of Russell L.J. in *Morgan v. Fry* (above), and see generally the discussion in Wedderburn, *Cases and Materials on Labour Law,* p. 525, and by Paul O'Higgins in [1968] Camb. L.J. 223.

22. RCME, Day 10, paras. 1616, 1629, 1633, 1642, 1669, 1672.

23. It is calculated on a basis which means that it can never exceed the equivalent of one year's pay, and might be substantially less for a person with less than ten years' service.

24. Superannuation Act 1965, s.11.

25. RCME, Day 10, para. 1665.

5. LABOUR INJUNCTIONS AND OTHER ACTIONS IN TORT

a. Trade Union Immunity

The object of section 4 of the Trade Disputes Act 1906 was to reverse the *Taff Vale* case and prevent the use of labour injunctions against trade unions. However, between 1963 and 1969 a majority of the judges interpreted the section to mean that unions were protected only in respect of *past* acts.[26] This meant that an injunction could be obtained for *threatened* torts. The Court of Appeal reversed this trend in a decision in 1969,[27] but it would still be open to the House of Lords to restrict the immunity in this way.

Public employee organisations which engage in strike action will nearly always be "trade unions" in law, and so be entitled to the protection of section 4. In other words, their funds will not be put at risk as a result of strike action. However, as we have seen in Chapter III, there are several organisations whose legal status is uncertain so that they may not enjoy this protection.

b. Immunities of "Any Person" Engaged in "Trade Dispute"

After the Conspiracy and Protection of Property Act 1875 had effectively put an end to criminal prosecutions for strike action, the judiciary developed certain forms of civil liability. Immunities were granted in respect of these in the Trade Disputes Act 1906. Civil conspiracy, peaceful picketing (regarded by some judges as a common law "nuisance"), inducing breach of contracts of employment, or interfering by lawful means with the trade, business, or employment of some other person were all protected by the 1906 act, provided only that those committing any of these wrongs acted "in furtherance or contemplation of a trade dispute." In a liberal wave of judgments between 1920 and 1961 these immunities were interpreted so as to protect a wide variety of industrial actions, including strikes in support of a closed shop,[28]

---

26. *Boulting* v. *ACTAT* [1963] 2 Q.B. 606, and Wedderburn, op.cit., p. 530.
27. *Torquay Hotel Co. Ltd.* v. *Cousins* [1969] 2 Ch. 106.
28. *White* v. *Riley* [1921] 1 Ch. 1.

sympathetic strikes,[29] recognition disputes[30] (provided "interunion" prestige was not the predominant motive),[31] and actions by trade union officials on their own initiative even where no members were employed by the employer with whom the dispute arose.[32]

The English and Scottish courts have never been called upon to decide directly, in the context of a strike, whether these immunities apply to a dispute involving public employees. The Trade Disputes Acts 1906-65 are far from clear in this regard. There are several unresolved problems. First, do the acts bind the Crown? There is a general presumption that the Crown is not bound unless expressly named in a statute. The Crown is not named in the Trade Disputes Acts, nor for that matter in other statutes dealing with trade unions, and this suggests that the immunities are not available as a defence against the Crown suing as plaintiff (i.e. employer) for an injunction or damages arising out of torts threatened or committed in the course of industrial conflict. The Donovan Commission proposed that this point should be clarified.[33]

Second, it is controversial whether the statutory definition of a "trade dispute" in the Trade Disputes Act 1906, section 5(3), is wide enough to cover all public employees. It provides that

"trade dispute" means any dispute between employers and workmen, or between workmen and workmen, which is connected with the employment or non-employment, or the terms of the employment, or with the conditions of labour, of any person, and the expression "workmen" means all persons employed in trade or industry, whether or not in the employment of the employer with whom a trade dispute arises.

Although the term "workmen" has been held to include white-collar workers (such as managers, clerks, and actors), it is by no means settled that it covers every employed person. In some modern statutes it is expressly provided that "the carrying on

29. *Conway* v. *Wade* [1909] A.C. at 512 (even though not confined to the same industry).
30. *Beetham* v. *Trinidad Cement Ltd.* [1960] A.C. 132; *Bird* v. *O'Neal* [1960] A.C. 907.
31. *Stratford* v. *Lindley* [1965] A.C. 261; provided also that the claim was not "extravagant," ibid. at 341.
32. *NALGO* v. *Bolton Corporation* [1943] A.C. at 176.
33. Cmnd. 3623, para. 901.

of the activities of public or local authorities shall be treated as the carrying on of a trade or industry."[34] This has been taken as illustrating that the functions of local authorities come within the expression of "trade or industry";[35] but it has also been argued that in the absence of an express reference to local authorities their functions do not fall within that expression.[36] Moreover, although it has been judicially suggested that everyone who seeks to dispose of his services is engaged in a "trade,"[37] it is also the case that the judges have tended to interpret the words "trade or industry" narrowly when they appear together. This narrow interpretation has been carried furthest in the Irish Republic where it has been held that the employees of a public authority, not engaged in profit-making, could not be engaged in a trade dispute with it.[38] If the profit-making nature of the employer's activity were accepted as a valid criterion of a "trade dispute" in the United Kingdom, the result would be that all those public employees who are not employed in "trading" or "industrial" undertakings (such as teachers, nurses, hospital doctors, and nonindustrial civil servants) would not be within the definition.

Apart from the meaning of "workmen" the existence of the words "of any person" in the definition may also give rise to difficulties. Does "person," like "workmen," mean "any person employed in trade or industry"? Can there be a dispute as to the employment of persons outside "trade or industry"? For example, can officials of a union which includes industrial and nonindustrial workers claim the benefit of the immunities if they organise industrial action in connection with the terms of employment of their nonindustrial members? An Irish judge has held that they may not do so,[39] but the point remains open in the U.K.

34. E.g., Terms and Conditions of Employment Act 1959, s.8(5); Conditions of Employment & National Arbitration Order (S.R. & O. 1940, No. 1350).
35. *NALGO v. Bolton Corporation* [1943] A.C. at 184–85 (Lord Wright).
36. Ibid. at pp. 175–76 (Viscount Simon), 181 (Lord Atkin), and 182–83 (Lord Thankerton).
37. Ibid. at 185 (Lord Wright).
38. *British & Irish Steampacket Co. v. Branigan* [1958] I.R. 128. Great caution must be exercised in relation to this and other Irish cases, because of the different economic, social, and constitutional position in Britain.
39. *Smith v. Beirne* [1954] 89 I.L.T. 24, 33, 34. As Citrine (p. 608, n. 14) says, "it is difficult to escape the conclusion that the status of the employee was determined solely by the nature of the employer's activities."

We would contend for a liberal interpretation of the definition of "trade dispute" so as to cover the activities of unions of all public employees. Although courts in the U.K. would not look at the legislative history of the statutory immunities when interpreting them, it is significant that before 1906 disputes between local authorities and their employees were commonly described as "trade disputes."[40] Moreover, there were "trade" unions of municipal employees and civil servants on the register of trade unions before 1906, and at least one Law Lord has said: "If there can be a *trade* union to which the higher grades of officers of a municipal corporation can belong, it does not seem an impossible use of language to say that a dispute concerning their conditions of service can be a trade dispute."[41] Finally, a broad interpretation would avoid the anomalies which inevitably arise from attempts to distinguish trading and nontrading activities, since in a single dispute with, say, a local authority employees engaged in both kinds of activity may be involved. According to the narrow interpretation there would be immunity in respect only of those employees engaged in "trade or industry."[42]

The general point which emerges from this discussion is that the legal position in regard to strikes of public employees is extremely uncertain. This has not given rise to any major litigation as yet,[43] but the increasing militancy of public employee unions may lead public employers to test the limits of the statutory immunities in the near future.

c. The Reopening of the Settlement of 1906

The legislation of 1906 served as the basis of legal "abstention" in industrial conflict until the early 1960s. Then, in a situation of wage drift and a growing number of unofficial strikes, and middle-class criticism of union strength, there occurred what has

40. Citrine, p. 611.
41. *NALGO* v. *Bolton Corporation* [1943] A.C. at 175 (Viscount Simon).
42. The High Court of Australia in *Federated Municipal and Shire Council Employees' Union* v. *City of Melbourne* (19.8-19) 26 C.L.R. at 564-5, 574, 588 (of persuasive authority in England) refused to distinguish between the trading and nontrading functions of a municipal corporation in determining whether there was an "industrial" dispute. In West Pakistan in *Management of Municipal Committee, Mianwali* v. *General Secretary, Municipal Muharrirs' Union P.L.D.* 1968, Lahore 395, the distinction was based on regal and nonregal functions of public employees.
43. See generally O'Higgins and Partington 32 (1969) Modern L.R. 53.

been called "a sharp twist" in judicial policy.[44] This became evident first in *Rookes* v. *Barnard (1964)*[45] in which the House of Lords extended the tort of intimidation, in a way which could not have been visualised in 1906, by holding that a threat to strike in breach of contract was no different than a threat of violence, and that nothing in the act of 1906 provided a defence against this new form of tortious liability. *The outcry which this produced from the trade union movement resulted in the passing of the Trade Disputes Act 1965, which grants an "immunity" in trade disputes to any person who threatens to break a contract of employment or induces another to break such a contract. The 1965 act did not reverse the major innovation of the judges in *Rookes* v. *Barnard* (the equation of violence with breach of contract), and so several forms of "economic" intimidation remain unprotected. The Conservative Government elected in June 1970 is pledged to repeal the 1965 act.

Second, in a series of decisions beginning with *Stratford* v. *Lindley* (1965)[46] the tort of "inducing breach of contract" was expanded by the courts, and the statutory immunities correspondingly reduced.[47] The immunities have been questioned in other ways as well, for example throwing into doubt and confusion the legality of recognition disputes particularly where more than one union is involved.[48]

The Donovan Commission,[49] appointed by the Labour Government in 1965, expressed itself, in the main, as being satisfied with the status quo. It favoured a widening of the statutory immunities in some respects (e.g. to cover conspiracy to break contracts, and inducing breach of commercial contracts), but a majority of the Commission also wanted to restrict the immunities to those acting on behalf of registered trade unions and employers' associations so as to deprive unofficial strikers of legal protection from common law liabilities.

44. Wedderburn and Davies, op.cit., p. 14.
45. [1964] A.C. 1129 and generally Wedderburn, *Worker and the Law*, p. 255. In *Morgan* v. *Fry* [1968] 2 Q.B. 710, Russell L.J. suggested that the "breach" must be a flagrant one (e.g. in defiance of a no-strike obligation) for the tort to be committed.
46. [1965] A.C. 269.
47. For a survey of these developments see [1966] ASCL 628, [1967] ASCL 634, [1968] ASCL 701, [1969] ASCL.
48. Ibid.   49. Cmnd. 3623, paras. 816–911.

The Conservative Government proposes to go much further than this.[50] The definition of a trade dispute is to be narrowed to exclude sympathetic strikes or action; disputes between trade unions; strikes to enforce a "closed" or "union shop," and strikes to prevent the employment of certain types of workers.

6. THE TUC'S ROLE IN DISPUTES

We have already examined in Chapter III the role of the TUC Disputes Committees in reducing interunion competition in the context of freedom of association. In the present context it ought to be noted that the price which the trade unions have agreed to pay in return for the retention of the existing legal status quo is a considerable growth in the powers of the TUC over affiliated unions.

In 1969 a special conference of the TUC agreed to an amendment of the TUC's rules so as to empower disputes committees to intervene in official and unofficial disputes and to make recommendations to affiliated unions. In the case of interunion disputes the Disputes Committees may make awards which are binding on affiliated unions. The ultimate sanction for disobedience is expulsion from the TUC. Another part of this new *Programme of Action* is an acceptance of the competence of the TUC to make recommendations to affiliated unions on procedures regarding admission to, and expulsion from, membership—a matter of some importance in regard to "unofficial" strikes. To date these powers have not been used in regard to disputes involving affiliated public employee unions.

50. *Fair Deal at Work*, pp. 30–31.

·IX·

Machinery Provided by Law for Disputes Settlement

THE law provides a basic structure in which three forms of dispute settlement take place. These are (1) conciliation, (2) inquiry, and (3) arbitration. Each of these will be described in turn.

1. CONCILIATION

The powers of the Secretary of State for Employment and Productivity derive from two acts. The Conciliation Act 1896, section 2, says that "where a difference exists, or is apprehended between an employer, or any class of employers, and workmen, or between different classes of workmen" the Secretary may

(b) take such steps as may seem expedient [to him] for the purpose of enabling the parties to the difference to meet together, by themselves or their representatives, under the presidency of a chairman mutually agreed upon or nominated by [the Secretary of State] or by some other person or body, with a view to the amicable settlement of the difference;

(c) on the application of the employers or workmen interested, and after taking into consideration the existence and adequacy of means available for conciliation in the district or trade and the circumstances of the case, appoint a person or persons to act as conciliator or as a board of conciliation.

This indicates that the Secretary of State may act on his own initiative or on request, but where he acts on request he must "take into consideration" the parties' own machinery for conciliation. Since the term "workmen" is not defined in this act, it could theoretically be applied to differences involving any employed person. According to the Department of Employment and Productivity, however, "conciliation is available to industries and services in both the public and private sectors but not in respect of differences affecting either industrial or non-industrial civil servants."[1] This latter limitation has been much criticised recently.[2]

The second act is the Industrial Courts Act 1919 which in section 2(1) empowers the Secretary of State to "take such steps as seem to him to be expedient for promoting a settlement" of any existing or apprehended trade dispute reported to him. It would seem that this provision, like the 1896 act, gives the Secretary of State a discretion in deciding at what stage in a dispute it would be appropriate for conciliation to take place.[3] It is narrower in one sense than the 1896 act, however, namely there must be a "dispute" and not simply a "difference," and it must be a *trade* dispute. The act defines a trade dispute in similar terms to the Trade Disputes Act 1906 described above, with the important distinction that a "workman" for this purpose is defined as "any person who has entered into or works under a contract with an employer whether the contract be by way of manual labour, clerical work, or otherwise, be expressed or implied, oral or in writing, and whether it be a contract of service or of apprenticeship or a contract personally to execute any work or labour."[4] This is wide enough to cover all public employees, other than Crown servants (since these may not have a "contract," and the Crown as employer is not expressly bound by the act).

On paper the 1896 act envisages the appointment of ad hoc conciliators to deal with particular differences. In practice, however, this rarely happens. Instead the 1896 act is regarded as the statutory basis for the DEP's extensive manpower and productivity

1. Written evidence of the Ministry of Labour to the Donovan Commission (HMSO, 1965), p. 96 (Third Memorandum, para. 15).

2. See the speech by a leader of the Civil Service Union, reported in *Public Sector* at p. 27: ". . . we have found the attitude . . . that the Department of Employment and Productivity's industrial conciliation machine is not permitted to enter the Civil Service, is absolutely wrong. Incidentally, we think that the argument on which this is based, that one government Department cannot intervene in a dispute affecting another, would be just as appropriate in the case of the nationalised industries where they intervene fairly frequently. Therefore, we do not think that is an argument."

3. Cf. s.2(4) of the act which says that the Secretary of State shall not refer a dispute for "settlement and advice" until there has been a failure to obtain a settlement through the agreed procedure of the industry. This restriction does not apply in the case of s.2(1).

4. Industrial Courts Act 1919, s.8.

service (formerly conciliation service and later industrial relations service). These officers sit on a number of national negotiating bodies as observers, keep in touch with regional and national employers' organisations and trade unions, and are ready to act if invited and to make it known that their services are available. The conciliator first ascertains the facts of the dispute and will then usually invite the two sides to a joint meeting under his chairmanship, although occasionally he may have separate talks with each side. The discussions are intended to be "a continuation of the process of collective bargaining with outside assistance."[5] But none of the powers used by DEP in this regard includes compulsion. Although the services are operated on a statutory framework, the actual process of conciliation is entirely voluntary. If a settlement is reached, the parties voluntarily accept it as their own responsibility. An "essential feature" of this kind of conciliation has been "the independence and impartiality of the conciliator."[6]

No statistics have been published as to the extent to which conciliation has been used in resolving disputes in the public services, but our impression is that it is relatively less important in these services than in the private sector and nationalised industries, where it plays a very important role. Of all the disputes in which conciliation has been used in recent years about 40 to 50 per cent concerned questions of pay, 30 per cent related to trade union recognition, and 10 per cent or so to redundancy and dismissals.[7] The analysis of unpublished DEP records by Wedderburn and Davies[8] revealed that the success rate of conciliations appears to have increased in recent years (69 per cent of all conciliations were "settled" in 1966 compared to 59 per cent "settled" in 1961), particularly in regard to recognition disputes. This has been matched by an increased readiness by both sides of industry to use the DEP's conciliation services. An important limitation on the use of conciliation is that the DEP will usually not intervene while an unofficial stoppage of work is in progress. The DEP "never deals with unofficial strike leaders but only with authorised officers of the trade unions concerned."[9] When one remembers that the overwhelming number

5. Ministry of Labour written evidence, p. 95.
6. Ibid.   7. Ibid.   8. Pp. 217–18.
9. Ministry of Labour written evidence, p. 98.

of stoppages are unofficial, it is evident that the DEP does not play much part in dealing with such strikes. This led the DEP to ask the Donovan Commission whether "it should intervene more frequently in circumstances of this kind."[10] However, the DEP rejected the idea of compulsory conciliation for this did not appear "to offer a solution to the problem of unofficial and unconstitutional strikes."[11]

It will have been noticed that the wording of the 1896 and 1919 acts is wide enough to permit *mediation*, which involves recommending a basis for settlement to the parties. Sometimes an element of "mediation" is allowed to creep into the conciliation work of the DEP.[12]

2. INQUIRY

The Secretary of State for Employment and Productivity has statutory powers to inquire into disputes without the consent of the parties.

First, he may appoint a "court of inquiry," which is *not* a "court" of record or arbitration body.[13] The aim of this is "the immediate publication, for the information of those affected by the dispute and of the public generally, of an independent authoritative account of the matters in difference."[14] This is a technique of dispute settlement, halfway between conciliation and arbitration, reserved for particularly important and difficult matters. As McCarthy and Clifford point out in the leading study,[15] this is a "form of public conciliation and mediation, which begins with a quasi-judicial examination of the parties and ends with the publication of specific conclusions and suggestions." The striking feature of these "courts," however, is that they cannot compel the attendance of the parties to the dispute or witnesses, nor do their reports have any binding effect. The Secretary of State must, however, place the report before Parliament. Such courts were appointed on 75 occasions between 1919 and 1965, but

10. Ibid., p. 98.   11. Ibid., p. 99.
12. Wedderburn and Davies, p. 219.
13. This is under the Industrial Courts Act 1919, s.4.
14. Fourth Report of the Whitley Committee, Cd. 9153.
15. W. E. J. McCarthy and B. A. Clifford, "The Work of Industrial Courts of Inquiry," 4 (1966) *B.J.I.L.* 39; and see too Wedderburn and Davies, p. 224.

it appears that not one of these concerned the public services, although there were several concerned with nationalised industries. In theory there would be no legal objection to the appointment of a court of inquiry in regard to a dispute in the public services, other than one concerning Crown servants.[16] In practice it would seem that no public service dispute has seemed to be sufficiently serious to merit the use of this technique, or some other technique has been more appropriate.

The second power of the Secretary of State is one conferred on him by the Conciliation Act 1896 to "inquire into the causes and circumstances of a difference" between employers and workmen. He may appoint a single independent person, sitting alone, or a committee (called either a committee of investigation or a committee of inquiry). This is less formal than a Court of Inquiry, and its report does not have to be laid before Parliament. Third, he may appoint a "committee of inquiry" under what are known as his general powers, that is, those which he enjoys as a Minister of State. This latter procedure has been preferred on several occasions, according to the DEP, because it enables the Secretary of State to act with another Minister (this is not permissible under the 1896 act), it enables him to inquire into matters not currently in dispute, and the terms of reference under "general powers" may specifically include questions of "national interest" (e.g. government incomes policy).[17]

Wedderburn and Davies[18] have analysed the reports of the nineteen committees of inquiry (under the 1896 act and general powers) and nineteen committees of investigation (under the 1896 act) between 1946 and 1966. They found that the "general industrial relations" problem was most frequently dealt with under the general powers inquiry (e.g. general problems of the port transport industry). They also found that the committees, particularly those appointed under the 1896 act, often deal with problems that might have been dealt with by another body such as a single arbitrator or the Industrial Court (e.g. a dismissal case,

16. This follows from the definition of "trade dispute" and "workman" in the Industrial Courts Act 1919, and the fact that the act is not expressed to bind the Crown as employer.
17. Ministry of Labour written evidence, p. 107 (4th memorandum, para. 35).
18. Pp. 232–40.

and a "general powers" inquiry into a claim for a five-day, forty-hour week at London markets).

As far as we can discover, neither committees of inquiry nor committees of investigation have been used in connection with disputes in the public services. Once again there would be no legal objection to this; a "general powers" inquiry could clearly be set up in relation to a dispute involving Crown servants. Although it is true that the recommendations of such a committee would not be binding, it might be thought that these techniques present a useful way of resolving important disputes, because they enable government agencies to "harness the pressure of public opinion to ensure their implementation."[19]

The Donovan Commission endorsed a proposal by the DEP that the industrial relations officers (now called manpower and productivity advisers) of the DEP should be sued to obtain the full facts of unofficial and unconstitutional stoppages either during a dispute or, as would more frequently be the case, after a return to work. This would make it possible to obtain a clearer view of the circumstances of unofficial strikes.[20]

A new institution which may play a role in the investigation of major disputes is the Commission on Industrial Relations established as a Royal Commission in 1969. This body is primarily concerned with the reform of collective bargaining and no doubt will deal mainly with private industry. It has already conducted a few inquiries relating to recognition and pay disputes. It acts only on references made by the Secretary of State for Employment and Productivity, and its recommendations have no legal effect. In one sense it combines the tasks of investigation, conciliation, and mediation while continuing to rest its proposals for reform on a voluntary basis. The extent to which it will concern itself with the public services (if at all) is uncertain.

3. ARBITRATION

a. The Role of the Law

Since 1959 there has been nothing in the nature of compulsory legal arbitration in Great Britain, with the exception of the procedure under section 8 of the Terms and Conditions of Employ-

19. Ibid., p. 240.   20. Cmnd. 3623, para. 448.

ment Act 1959 for the extension of recognised terms and conditions of employment, which we described in Chapter V. During the First World War the Munitions of War Act 1915 contained provisions for legally binding arbitration. During the Second World War Order 1305 of 1940 permitted either side to request the Minister of Labour to refer a dispute to the National Arbitration Tribunal, whose awards were binding. Strikes and lock-outs were illegal unless the Minister had failed to act within 21 days. Employers in each district were also obliged to observe terms and conditions settled by collective agreement or arbitration for the trade concerned in the district. This order was repealed in 1951, largely as a result of an outcry from the unions following the prosecution of strikers in peacetime, and was replaced by Order 1376 of 1951. Under the new order strikes and lock-outs were no longer illegal and the Industrial Disputes Tribunal replaced the National Arbitration Tribunal. The form of arbitration under Order 1376 of 1951 is more accurately described as unilateral than compulsory arbitration. Arbitration was "compulsory" in the sense only that either party could take a dispute or issue to the Minister without the consent of the other party, and the award became legally binding as an implied term of the individual workers' contract of employment. The exercise of the right to report disputes and issues to the Minister was entirely voluntary.

The provisions of these orders were available to organisations of public employees other than Crown servants and members of fire brigades. We have described in Chapter V the use made of them by these organisations in encouraging the growth of collective bargaining by local authorities. We have seen that many unions favour the reintroduction of unilateral arbitration because, in the words of the TUC, this "would to some extent provide a substitute for imposing a legal duty on employers to bargain and would in many cases promote collective bargaining." The Donovan Commission, however, took the view that the restoration of unilateral arbitration in industries and services where collective bargaining is relatively well developed would have a distorting effect. But they favoured unilateral arbitration on a selective basis (on the recommendation in each case of the Commission on Industrial Relations) in circumstances where an employer refused trade union recognition or failed to bargain "effectively" with recognised unions.

The two most important features of industrial arbitration in Great Britain at the present time are that arbitration can be resorted to only by consent of both sides, and that arbitration awards do not usually have automatic legal effect. If an award has been acted upon it may become an implied term of the contracts of employment of the relevant categories of workers. Arguably, it may automatically become a term of contracts of employment if the parties have previously agreed to abide by the arbitration or do customarily abide by it. The precise legal position is obscure, but automatic incorporation would seem to be exceptional.

The function of the law in this area has been fourfold. First, the Industrial Courts Act 1919 established a permanent arbitration body, the Industrial Court, which can be resorted to for voluntary arbitration. In law this machinery is available to all classes of private and public employees, including Crown servants[21] (other than those in the naval, military, or air services),[22] but in practice the only public employees who utilise it are government industrial employees, workers in the health services, fire services, and local government manual, administrative, professional, clerical, and technical staffs. Between 1925 and 1936 the Industrial Court was also utilised for voluntary arbitration by the nonindustrial civil service. It was then replaced by the Civil Service Arbitration Tribunal, a standing body which owes its origin to a Civil Service Whitley Council agreement and does not fall under any of the statutory arangements for arbitration.

Second, the Industrial Courts Act empowered the Minister to appoint single arbitrators (another possible source for their appointment is the Conciliation Act 1896, section 2) and Boards of Arbitration, both of which, unlike the Industrial Court, are appointed on an ad hoc basis. Both these forms of arbitration have been used in public employees disputes. Wedderburn and Davies found that no less than 16 of the 33 Boards of Arbitration appointed between 1946 and 1965 concerned the employees of local government authorities or other public bodies.[23] (The awards of these Boards, and those of single arbitrators, are not published, unlike those of the Industrial Court and the Civil Service Arbitra-

21. See the definition of "workman" and "trade dispute" in s.8.
22. S.10.   23. P. 191.

tion Tribunal.) No criteria are laid down in the Industrial Courts Act for directing disputes of particular kinds to particular forms of arbitration. Wedderburn and Davies point out that "the parties make this decision themselves subject to such influence as the ministry is able and willing to bring," and "the distribution [of claims before different bodies] is probably a matte† of the likes and dislikes of particular unions."[24]

The distribution does not depend on the *content* of the dispute. Wedderburn and Davies analysed 315 "voluntary" industrial court awards (in both public and private sectors)[25] made between 1958 and 1966 and managed to classify only 43 of these as disputes involving "rights" (including interpretation of written and oral agreements and regrading), nearly all the rest being wages, hours, and holidays (i.e. "interest") claims. The majority of disputes before single arbitrators also involved "interest" claims.[26] (Although single arbitrators are more typical in local claims, the Industrial Court also considers a number of regional and plant claims.) The overwhelming majority of disputes before Boards of Arbitrators likewise concerned economic claims.[27]

The third role of the law has been to require the relevant Government Minister to make permanent arrangements for arbitration for particular services, after consultation with both sides. This is the case with the police and educational services. In practice all the other public services which do not utilise the Industrial Court have made such arrangements without any legal obligation to do so. Domestic arbitration of this kind is more common in the public services than in private industry, but even then it is mainly peripheral to industrial relations as a whole.

Finally, various forms of individual grievances, in particular dismissal and discipline, are subject to statutory codes in the fire services, police, and educational services. These codes are themselves usually the product of "consultation" with public employee organisations and employing authorities, discussed in Chapter V.

In the next section we shall discuss the work of the Industrial Court, the most important arbitration machinery provided by law, in relation to public employees. Then we shall briefly describe

24. Ibid., p. 189.　　　　25. Ibid., p. 175.
26. Ibid., p. 188.　　　　27. Ibid., p. 191.

the arbitration situation in each sector of the public services, so as to set the legal machinery in the context of the overall use of arbitration in each sector.

b. The Industrial Court

This permanent arbitration body, maintained at state expense, consists "of persons to be appointed by [the Secretary of State for Employment and Productivity], some of whom shall be independent persons, some shall be persons representing employers, and some shall be persons representing workmen, and in addition one or more women."[28] The president (at present a Queen's Counsel) is the only full-time member, and his independence is secured by the fact that he holds office until retirement on the same terms as a judge of a county court (lower civil court), that is "during good behaviour." There are ten persons on the employers' panel (from a wide spread of industries) and seven on the employees' panel (all past or present general secretaries of unions). The president decides on the composition of the Court for each case, but typically it is constituted by himself (as chairman), an employer's representative, and an employee's representative (usually Dame Anne Godwin, a retired trade unionist).

Apart from its voluntary arbitration powers, the Court has a number of "special" jurisdictions in which a legal or administrative sanction is added to the arbitration award, for example, in regard to the observance of fair standards by Government contractors and others operating with Government subsidies or licenses,[29] or the Court makes binding awards in regard to the "extension" of recognised terms and conditions of employment. These do not concern us in the present section. Its "voluntary" jurisdiction is clearly the most important part of its work.

In all but two situations it is necessary for the parties to a trade dispute who wish to invoke this "voluntary" jurisdiction to go through the Secretary of State to the Court. The two exceptional cases are where the Court is asked to interpret its own award, or where the details of a settlement are left by the Court for negotiation between the parties and it is a term of the award that in the event of a failure to agree either party

28. Industrial Courts Act 1919, s.1(1).
29. See Wedderburn and Davies, p. 192, for a description of these.

may report that failure to the Court. In all other cases a dispute may be reported to the Secretary of State "by or on behalf of the parties to the dispute." In theory this means that even an individual or a small group of workers could report a matter. In practice, however, since the employer must agree to the reference and will usually only do so under union pressure, it is invariably a trade union which acts *on behalf of* the workers.

The Secretary of State is under an obligation to see that two conditions are fulfilled before he refers the dispute to the Court: (1) the consent of the parties must be obtained (hence the "voluntary" nature of the arbitration); and (2) the parties' own domestic machinery must be exhausted. The second condition is meant to ensure that the Court does not operate as a substitute for collective bargaining. The first condition may be fulfilled by a consent supplied in advance, for example in a collective agreement which states that in the event of a failure to agree any dispute shall be reported to the Secretary of State with a request that it be referred to the Court. This is the case with nearly all the "voluntary" references which come from the public services. The advance consent to arbitration by the Industrial Court should not, however, be confused with compulsory (or unilateral) arbitration because it always is possible for a party to withdraw that consent without fear of legal consequences. In the reality of industrial life, of course, arbitration agreements are normally observed.

Some idea of the number and nature of references from the public services to the Court may be obtained from an analysis which we have made of the Court's work in the three years 1967, 1968, and 1969.[30] In this period there were a total of 38 matters within the Court's "voluntary" jurisdiction, of which 7 concerned public employees. Of these 5 concerned pay, one related to holidays, and one related to the regrading of an individual employee. A full list will be found in Table 8. We believe that these claims give a fair idea of the work of the Court in relation to public employees.

30. A full analysis of the Court's work, 1958–66, in both public and private sectors (but without any breakdown of the public services), will be found in Wedderburn and Davies, pp. 162 et seq.

c. Arbitration in Specific Public Services

i. NONINDUSTRIAL CIVIL SERVICE

A Conciliation and Arbitration Board for Government Employees was established in 1916 as a means of settling disputes during wartime emergency. It was abolished in 1922, having by then dealt with over 200 claims, on the grounds that it was incompatible with Whitleyism, and that it threatened Treasury control of expenditure. Under union pressure, a Civil Service National Whitley Council agreement on arbitration for the nonindustrial civil service was signed in February 1925. It has been amended on several occasions since then, but it remains the basis for arbitration in this part of the civil service. Since this agreement is not legally enforceable between the parties, it could be ignored at any time by either side. In practice, however, it is described as "one of the most cherished rights of the Staff Sides and of staff associations."

The agreement states that

> failing agreement by negotiation arbitration shall be open to Government Departments on the one hand, and to recognised Associations of Civil Servants within the scope of the National Whitley Council for the Administrative and Legal Departments of the Civil Service and of Departmental Whitley Councils allied thereto on the other hand, on application by either party, in regard to certain matters affecting conditions of service

It will be observed that access to the Tribunal is open both to staff sides as a whole, and to individual recognised associations, and that it is not limited to staff associations with a seat on the staff side.

The Tribunal consists of an independent chairman, one member drawn from a panel of persons representing the Treasury, and one from a panel representing the staff side. Although the appointments of the chairman and panels are made by the Secretary of State for Employment and Productivity, he acts only after consultation with the relevant sides. Serving civil servants and officials of staff associations are ineligible for appointment. The chairman decides the composition of the Tribunal (drawn from

Table 8.

*Voluntary Jurisdiction of Industrial Court, 1967–1969,
Claims Relating to Public Employees*

Parties	*Terms of Reference*
Professional & Technical Council A, W.C. for Health Services	". . . to determine the difference between the parties as to the payment of allowances to radiographers for remaining on call at home or other agreed place of emergency duty." (3155)
Nat. Union of Public Employees and London Borough of Redbridge	". . . to determine whether the annual outings granted by the former Ilford Borough Council to its employees, being members of the NUPE, was a condition of service of such employees." (3148)
W.C. for Admin. Professional, Technical & Executive & Clerical Staff, Greater London Council etc.	"to determine a formal disagreement . . . that the London weighting element in the pay of . . . staff on the . . . standard salary structure for such staff be increased to £125 with effect from 1.11.67." (3180)
Corporation of London Staff Assn. and Corporation of London	"to determine . . . a dispute as to the amounts by which the special supplement should be increased." (3185)
NALGO and South West Metropolitan Regional Hospital Board	"to determine a claim from the union . . . for the upgrading of the post of Principal Administrative Asst., currently occupied by Mr. K. H. Williams, to the Asst. Secretary Grade." (3199)
W.C. for Admin. Professional, Technical, Executive & Clerical Staff, Greater London Council etc.	"to determine a claim by the staff side . . . that clerks of works and storekeepers in the Construction Branch of the Housing Dept. should be partially reimbursed the travelling expenses they occur in Greater London between home and site." (3200)
W.C. for New Towns Staff	"to determine a difference between the two sides . . . arising from a claim for a 'review of salaries' submitted by the staff side . . . and from counter-proposals made by the employers' side." (3202)

Source: Awards of the Industrial Court

the panels) for each hearing. Between 1925 and 1936 the Industrial Court served as the arbitration body, but this independent tribunal was found necessary because of the volume of cases and the need for a body specialising in civil service affairs.

The Tribunal is not intended as a substitute for collective bargaining and therefore it is essential that there should have been a failure to reach agreement by negotiation before it may be used. Claims must be reported to the DEP, which would not refer them to the Tribunal if there had been no serious attempt at negotiation. The Tribunal itself has sometimes refused to make an award on the ground that the possibilities for negotiation have not been exhausted.

Hearings usually take place within six weeks of a reference to the Tribunal. The terms of reference are usually agreed between the parties, but where this is impossible the respective statements of claim must be set out and these together constitute the remit. Detailed rules of procedure have been agreed, and these include provision for full written statements of case to be submitted by each side in advance of the hearing, to the Tribunal and to the other side. The actual hearing is relatively informal: no rules of evidence are followed except that "without prejudice" statements are barred, lest the freedom of negotiation between the parties should be inhibited by the fear that offers made "without prejudice" will be used to improve the other side's position in subsequent arbitration.

It was suggested to the Royal Commission on the Civil Service 1929-31 that the Tribunal should have express power to conciliate, but the Commission responded that "the power to conciliate is inherent in every tribunal." Indeed, this kind of arbitration not infrequently combines an element of conciliation.

If the members of the Tribunal disagree the chairman may make an umpire's award. In British practice it is not usual for arbitrators to give reasons for decisions. Among the reasons for this, given by the present president of the Industrial Court, are that reasons might prolong a dispute, a body of case law might be built up which leads to a rigid system of precedent, there might sometimes be different and contradictory reasons given by different members of the same arbitration body, and reasons might make it difficult for arbitrators to continue to live with the parties in future disputes.[31] One might add that the absence of a "rights interest" distinction in dispute settlements makes it less necessary in Britain than in some other countries

31. RCME, vol. 45, p. 1923 (Sir Roy Wilson Q.C.).

for arbitrators to assign reasons for their decisions. The Civil Service Tribunal does sometimes give its reasons, however.[32] Its awards are published.

The agreement limits the subject matter of arbitrable claims to "emoluments,[33] weekly hours of work and leave." Cases of individual officers are expressly excluded. Thus the scope of arbitration is considerably narrower than in some other branches of public employment. It has already been noted that the Industrial Court does, from time to time, have individual cases referred to it under its voluntary jurisdiction, and there is no limit as to the kind of claim which may be made. The limitation in the case of the Civil Service Tribunal is not as serious as it may appear at first sight, however, because all disciplinary matters in the home civil service are regulated according to another procedure agreed between the two sides of the Civil Service National Whitley Council.[34]

But the limitation of arbitrable matters has given rise to controversy. Two problems may be mentioned by way of illustration. First, how are salary scales to be distinguished from grading claims, the latter being excluded from the scope of arbitration? Second, who are "classes of civil servants" for the purposes of arbitration? The definition provided by the agreement—"any well-defined category of civil servants who for the purpose of a particular claim occupy the same position or have a common interest in the claim"—is not very helpful. The official side has denied the existence of a "class" because the group is too small, and has refused arbitration on claims by members of a general service grade in a particular department and on claims for allowances to some but not all members of a grade. It has also declined to allow claims for six departmental clerical classes to be dealt with together by the Tribunal on the ground that the six classes together were not a "class," but the Tribunal resolved this by making identical awards when the six claims were made consecutively.

---

32. E.g. Award 482 (20.5.68) on a claim for increased salary scales by inspectors of taxes.

33. This "includes pay, and allowances in the nature of pay, bonus, overtime rates, subsistence rates, travelling and lodging allowances."

34. A description will be found in *Dismissal Procedures*, Report of NJAC of Ministry of Labour (HMSO, 1967), paras. 53–59.

In all these controversies it is the official side's interpretation of the agreement which prevails. The official side justifies its veto on the ground that the Minister for the Civil Service is responsible to Parliament and, since the Tribunal falls under his jurisdiction, he must have the final say, subject only to parliamentary disapproval. Needless to say, this view is not attractive to the staff side, which continues to press for the admissibility of claims to be determined by the Tribunal itself or some other independent person. In practice there is always negotiation about the arbitrability of a claim and the differences are often amicably settled.

Within the limits of arbitrability laid down in the agreement, no distinction is drawn between disputes of right and those of interest. A detailed analysis of the work of the Tribunal in the period 1925-59 has been made by S. J. Frankel.[35] He discovered that the main issues were salary claims (444 out of a total of 607 claims), allowances (33), assimilation (41), hours of work and overtime (39), leave (15), general (15), and interpretation (26). In matters of interpretation there is usually no formal hearing. Frankel also attempted to analyse the tendency of awards by the Tribunal and found that about 33 per cent were in "the zone of compromise," 45 per cent favoured the official side, and 23 per cent the staff side. In general the Tribunal did not "split the difference."

Awards of the Tribunal do not have automatic effect. When the Government accepted the arbitration agreement in 1925 it attached two conditions.[36] The first was "the overriding authority of Parliament." What this means is that the Government will not itself *propose* to Parliament the rejection of an award, but that a Government may be defeated in Parliament. This has never happened over civil service arbitration. The second qualification was that the Government "must also reserve to itself the

35. "Arbitration in the British Civil Service," (1960) *Public Administration* 197. By way of example of the kind of claim considered by the Tribunal, note the subject matter of the six awards made in 1968: allowances for television appearances of meterorological staff (481); increased national salary scale etc. for inspectors of taxes (482); claim for increases for marine officers (476); claim for new pay rates for custodians of ancient monuments (477); weekly pay rates of certain postal employees (478); scales of certain postal employees (479).

36. *Staff Relations Handbook* (1965 ed.), p. 24.

right to refuse arbitration 'on grounds of policy.' " This qualification has been used on relatively few occasions to exclude policy issues, such as family allowances and cost of living bonuses, on which the Government already had a predetermined policy. It was also used to exclude the issue of equal pay for men and women, later settled by negotiation on the Whitley Council. In 1961 the Chancellor of the Exchequer decided to postpone the operation of awards of the Tribunal until after a "pay pause," which lasted eight months. The staff sides regard this "policy" limitation as unsatisfactory, but it has only rarely given rise to difficulties. A more serious complaint is that Government departments cannot be compelled to go to arbitration when they themselves wish to alter conditions of service.

ii. INDUSTRIAL CIVIL SERVICE

The constitutions of the three Trade Joint Councils all provide "consent in advance" to arbitration before the Industrial Court, whose work we have described above. Arbitration is resorted to relatively infrequently. For example, the Shipbuilding JIC submitted only 63 claims for arbitration in the twenty years 1945-64, of which 28 were rejected by the court as "not established."

Awards made by the Industrial Court have always been accepted by the Government, apart from the postponement of implementation during the 1961 pay pause.

iii. HEALTH SERVICES

Clause 17 of the main constitution of the Whitley Council for the Health Services provides:

> Every effort shall be made to accommodate differences of opinion between the two sides of the Council in order to reach an agreed decision. Where it is impossible to accomplish this, it shall be open to the management or staff associations concerned to seek arbitration in accordance with the terms of an arbitration agreement to be determined by the General Council.

However, no arbitration agreement has yet been concluded owing to controversy as to whether there should be provision for unilateral arbitration (as wanted by the staff side) and as to the powers of the Government to refuse to implement awards (the management side wants a reservation for "policy" matters).

Despite the absence of a general arbitration agreement (giving "consent in advance"), a considerable number of cases have been referred to arbitration by mutual consent given ad hoc. The arbitration body chosen for this purpose has been, at least since 1949, the Industrial Court. Legal doubt as to the applicability of the Conciliation Act 1896 and Industrial Courts Act 1919 to the National Health Service was removed by the National Health Service (Amendment) Act 1949, section 13 of which provides that

> (1) Any difference or dispute arising with respect to the remuneration or conditions of service of persons employed or engaged in the provision of services [under the National Health Services Acts] shall be deemed to be—
> (a) a difference or dispute to which the Conciliation Act 1896 applies; and
> (b) a trade dispute within the meaning of the Industrial Courts Act 1919.

Between 1948 and 1966 some 158 general claims were referred to arbitration from the health services. There were only four occasions in that period in which consent to arbitration on a general claim was refused by management, and in 1961-62 the date on which the award was to come into effect was removed from the terms of reference to the Industrial Court, at the insistence of the Treasury, on account of the pay pause. The awards made in that period were all accepted by the responsible Minister. They were incorporated into agreements of the Whitley Council, and then approved by the Minister under his statutory powers and embodied in regulations.

It is in the health services that the closest approximation to a "rights"/"interest" distinction in dispute settlement has been made. While general economic claims are referred by consent to the Industrial Court, disputes regarding an individual employee's conditions of service (including grading) are dealt with under a specific grievance procedure embodied in an agreement of the Whitley Council. This agreed procedure gives a right of appeal to the "employing authority," and from there to a Regional Appeals Committee of the Whitley Council, consisting normally of three members of the management side and three from the staff side. This further appeal may, at the insistence of the staff side, be prosecuted only through the employee's professional association or trade union. If the Regional Appeals Committee cannot agree, either party may take the matter to the appropriate Council of the Whitley Council for the Health Services. Finally, if even the Whitley Council cannot agree, the parties may agree to arbitration before the Industrial Court. About 100 cases a year are considered under this procedure, about one quarter of which reach the National Appeals Committee. Approximately half a dozen of these a year may be referred to arbitration.

This procedure for dealing with individual grievances does not include dismissals and disciplinary action. No agreement has yet been reached on the Whitley Council for such a procedure in respect of hospital staff. A unilateral "guidance circular" confers certain rights on junior and senior staff, including an appeal to a special committee of the employing authority. Sometimes representations are informally made to the Regional Hospital Board or Minister. There is a special disciplinary procedure for hospital medical and dental staff. The Whitley Council for the Health Services is the only negotiating body in the public services which has established special voluntary machinery for dealing with complaints of racial discrimination in employment.[37] This machinery involves investigation and conciliation by a subcommittee of the Council. If the complainant is aggrieved at the decision of the Council he has a statutory right to appeal to the Race Relations Board. In other public services, which have not established such voluntary machinery, cases of racial discrimination in employment are investigated by the Race Relations Board itself.

iv. EDUCATIONAL SERVICES

Before 1965 it was a source of grievance among teachers' associations in England and Wales that there was no provision for arbitration in the Education Act governing teachers' remuneration. Legal advice was obtained by the Government that it was beyond the powers of the Minister to refer differences on the Burnham Committees to arbitration. The Burnham Committees

37. See Hepple, *Race, Jobs and the Law in Britain,* p. 186.

occasionally managed to avoid this difficulty by referring the matter to one or more "independent advisers," which was a disguised form of arbitration. Matters came to a head in 1963' when the Minister refused to implement a Burnham Committee recommendation, declared that there could not legally be arbitration, and imposed his own scales. The outcome of this was the passing of the Remuneration of Teachers Act 1965, section 3 of which provides that the Minister must make arrangements for arbitration on matters "in respect of which agreement has not been reached by the [Burnham] committee." These arrangements may only be made after consultation with both sides of the Committee. Similar provisions were made for Scotland in the Remuneration of Teachers (Scotland) Act 1967, section 3.

It was argued that no Government could be expected to accept the outcome of independent arbitration irrespective of national circumstances, and accordingly it was provided in section 4 of the 1965 act (and section 4 of the Scottish act) that the recommendations of the arbitrators are binding on the Secretary of State unless each House of Parliament resolves that national economic circumstances require that effect should not be given to the recommendations. Where such resolutions have been passed, the Secretary of State must lay down new scales, after consultation with the Committee in question. In practice any initiative for challenging an arbitration award would have to come from the Government, since it alone would be assured of a majority in each House of Parliament.

Apart from this exceptional qualification, which has never been used, the Remuneration of Teachers Acts afford the only examples of awards which *must* be translated into binding legal form. The Secretary of State is obliged to treat an award in the same way as he treats a recommendation of a Burnham Committee, that is to embody it in an order, after consulting the Committee about a draft document containing the proposed scales.

v. POLICE

The Police Act 1964, section 45(2), provides that the arrangements made by the Home Secretary (and the Secretary of State for Scotland) in respect of the Police Council of Great Britain must include provision for arbitration. The constitution of the Police Council provides clause 11(2):

Where the official side and the staff side of a standing committee . . . are considering, but fail to agree on, a recommendation to be made to the Secretary of State . . . the dispute may, at the instance either of the staff side or of the official side, or of both sides acting jointly, be referred to three arbitrators appointed by the Prime Minister.

Any decision of the arbitrators is to be treated as though it were an agreement of the two sides of the standing committee in question. Since such an agreement is no more than a recommendation to the Secretary of State, it is clear that he is in law as free to decline to act upon arbitration awards as he is to act upon agreed recommendations of the Police Council. In practice arbitration awards have always been observed.

Since 1965 arbitration has not been used; before then it had been resorted to on four occasions since 1953. The scope of arbitration is, of course, limited to the same matters as those on which the Police Council can make recommendations.

The most important form of individual grievance machinery in the police is that available to deal with disciplinary matters. Police (Discipline) Regulations[38] provide for the investigation of complaints against policemen by a senior officer, and provide an opportunity for a hearing and an appeal to the Home Secretary.

Many other matters of individual grievance are dealt with through the ordinary avenues for negotiation, discussed in Chapter V.

vi. FIRE SERVICES

The constitutions of the National Joint Councils for Local Authorities' Fire Brigades and for Chief Officers give "consent in advance" to arbitration before the Industrial Court in the event of failure to agree. The actual use of arbitration has been extremely limited.

The only form of individual grievance for which specific machinery is provided is dismissals and disciplinary action. The Fire Services (Discipline) Regulations[39] provide for a hearing before the chief officer of the brigade in question, or a tribunal of senior officers, or the local fire authority itself, with an appeal

38. S.I. 1965, No. 543, and Police (Appeals) Rules S.I. 1965, No. 618.
39. S.I. 1948, No. 543.

in certain cases to the Secretary of State. These regulations are made by the Secretary of State, after receiving advice from the Central Fire Brigades Advisory Council.

vii. OTHER LOCAL GOVERNMENT EMPLOYEES

The constitutions of the National Joint Councils for Local Authorities' Manual Workers and for Local Authorities' Administrative, Professional, Technical and Clerical Services—the two major negotiating bodies—provide for two kinds of machinery to settle disputes. The first is a series of domestic bodies. These are usually an appeals or disputes committee at provincial, regional, or national level, consisting of an equal number of representatives from both sides. They reach decisions through negotiation and compromise. If the provincial committee fails to agree, the difference may be referred to a National Appeals Committee, and if this committee cannot resolve the matter it may be referred to the Council as a whole. Large numbers of differences between individual employees and their employers which cannot be settled at local level, as well as economic claims, are resolved through this machinery. It is only where the problem is not resolvable in this way that the second kind of machinery becomes relevant.[40] This is the "consent in advance" to the reference of cases to the Industrial Court in the event of failure to agree, which has been rarely used. In the case of manual workers there were only two submissions between 1959 and 1969; in the case of the administrative, professional, technical, and clerical Whitley Council it has hardly been used since 1961. But as Table 8 indicates, certain unions in the local government field do make use of the Court to resolve economic claims and individual grievances.

Nearly all local authorities have accepted dismissal procedures recommended by the appropriate National Joint Council for Local Authorities' Staffs. These procedures are noteworthy for the role played by elected representatives (e.g. local authority councillors). The original proposal to dismiss and any resultant appeal is usually considered by a body composed of such elected representatives. The appellant has a right to a personal hearing at which he may be represented by his union or professional association.

40. For a full description see Marjorie Macintosh, "The Negotiations of Wages and Conditions for Local Authority Employees in England and Wales," (1955) *Public Administration* 309 et seq.

A National Joint Advisory Council of the Ministry of Labour in a report (1967) has pointed out that these appeal committees probably give the dismissed employee a feeling "that they will consider dismissal questions with greater detachment than would senior staff alone."[41]

41. HMSO, 1967, para. 52.

Part Four
The Impact of
Public Employee Unionism

· X ·

Conclusions

THE most impressive feature of public employee trade unions in Britain is the extent of unionisation. "The proportion of [manual] workers in the public sector who belong to trade unions is about 75 per cent while the proportion in the private sector is about 30 per cent. With regard to non-manual workers, there is a big contrast between the public sector, where membership is about 75 per cent, and the private sector, where it is only about 15 per cent."[1] Within the public sector the spread of unionisation is not uniform. About 85 per cent of the nonindustrial civil servants belong to associations[2] whereas, according to the General Secretary of the Trades Union Congress, Mr. Feather, in "the health service for particular reasons—I think because of their love of professional bodies and perhaps the discouragement in many cases of trade union organisations," the figure is very much lower.[3]

An important factor in the spread of unionisation among public employees has been the establishment of machinery for the negotiation of conditions of employment. We have seen in this study that almost every topic of mutual interest to employer and employed has been opened to the bargaining process. Even in areas where statutory regulation of conditions of employment is favoured there is a continuous dialogue between management and unions.

Public employee trade unions in Britain are not dependent for their growth upon the grant of any special legal rights or privileges distinguishing them from trade unions in the private sector. For a variety of reasons, which we have canvassed, successive Governments since the early part of this century have accepted unionisation, and with it collective bargaining as both inevitable and indispensable. The fact that this concession came from government at an early stage meant that public employee unions did not seek legal enactment as a method of securing their status and freedom to associate and bargain. Instead they were prepared to rest—precariously—on the negative immunities from judge-made law which the unions of manual workers in the private sector

1. *Public Sector*, p. 6.
2. RCME 10, para. 28 (Witness: The Treasury).
3. *Public Sector*, p. 21.

213

had wrested from Parliament through political action. Since this legislation did not, in terms, deal with the position of public employee unions their precise legal status has remained uncertain. Moreover, the acceptance of collective bargaining through voluntary rather than legal machinery has meant that the unions have been content to rest the protection of individual employees solely on collective strength rather than on legal sanctions. So one has the curious phenomenon of the retention by the State of a reserve of legal powers which place civil servants in a worse *legal* position than employees in the private sector (e.g. the legal power of the Crown to dismiss at will) alongside a *factual* situation in which civil servants have greater security of tenure and better conditions of service than those persons in private employment. The emphasis on voluntarism has also had the result that the formal, legal difficulties which beset collective bargaining in the U.S. and elsewhere have been largely absent. Collective bargaining has taken place in an atmosphere in which there is considerable flexibility and a process of continuous adjustment. Stability has been maintained through the willingness of both sides to work the system.

Voluntarism has traditionally been regarded as a mark of the maturity of the British system of industrial relations in general and of public employee bargaining in particular. We have seen that a large number of legal devices are used essentially as supports for voluntary collective bargaining. The law is used to ensure that the results of bargaining are shared by unionists and non-unionists alike and by the employees of all the many public authorities in the country. On the employer side, the central government, largely through the Treasury, but also through various ministries, which have the legal and political power to enforce their will, has been able to secure a considerable degree of uniformity of pay and conditions.

The winds of change are blowing, however. The distinct social status which in the past isolated public employees, particularly civil servants, from other workers has nearly disappeared. Many professional organisations in the public services are turning themselves into trade unions,[4] and their members are demanding the

4. E.g. the Royal Institute of Chemistry, a professional organisation catering for science graduates, has sent a statement to its members that it now intends to take a direct part in negotiating their conditions of employment. See *The Times,* 28 September 1970.

same right of strike action as that enjoyed by other workers.[5] Those few legal restrictions on strike action which do exist are being blatantly disregarded by some public employees.[6]

Paradoxically, among the reasons for this change of attitudes has been the special position of the Government as employer, which in the past often meant that the Government set the model for private employers to follow by giving greater job security or better pay. Today the Government as employer seeks to influence the wage increases granted in the private sector, and the improvement of conditions of employment in the private sector, by setting an example itself by holding back improvements for workers in the public sector and by seeking to persuade the public corporations, who are much influenced by government action, to do likewise. Any feelings which made public employee associations seem to be a different kind of animal from ordinary trade unions have largely broken down, and there are signs that in some cases trade unions are increasingly catering for workers both in the public and private sectors.

In the past public employee trade unions and associations have operated within a system of collective bargaining which has been extremely flexible and informal, the success of whose operation was dependent upon both sides being willing to operate the system. Now that the Government is seeking to use its special position as employer of one in five of the working population to persuade all employers to follow a particular attitude to wage demands, the mutual confidence upon which the system has relied in the past has begun to break down. The consideration of militant action by some public employee trade unions was attributed by the General Secretary of the Institution of Professional Civil Servants, Mr. William McCall, to "the revolt against the notion that the public service is inferior in terms of efficiency and should be second class in terms of its pay and conditions."[7]

This growing militancy of public employee unions, partly in

5. The Society of Civil Servants held a private session at their conference in May 1970 to consider establishing a strike fund; the last conference of the Police Federation had on its agenda a demand for a restoration of the right to strike. See *The Times,* 13 May 1970.

6. E.g. the strikes by sewerage and public health employees in late 1970: *The Times,* 20 October 1970.

7. *The Times,* 12 May 1970.

response to the new approach of government, has brought the voluntary system itself to a critical stage. On the one hand there is likely to be increasing pressure for legal intervention against public employee unions, curbing the right to strike and bringing them, together with unions in the private sector, under greater legal control and surveillance. On the other hand the unions are likely not only to resist such moves but also to demand increased protection, through legal means, for public employees.

Select Bibliography

The following is a short select bibliography of the works which have been of most use to us; it is not intended to be exhaustive. Of particular assistance to us has been the collection of documents —collective agreements, trade union rules books, constitutions of employers' organisations, constitutions of joint negotiating bodies, etc.—deposited in the Squire Law Library, Cambridge.

A. GOVERNMENT PUBLICATIONS

Reconstruction Committee. Sub-committee on relations between employers and employed. [Rt. Hon. J. H. Whitley M.P.: chairman.] —Reports. Cd. 8606, Cd. 9001, Cd. 9002, Cd. 9081, Cd. 9085, Cd. 9153. —Sub-committee of the Inter-departmental Committee on the application of the Whitley report to Government establishments. Report on the application of the Whitley report to the administrative departments of the Civil Service. Cmd. 9.

Report of the National Provisional Joint Committee on the application of the Whitley report to the administrative departments of the Civil Service. Cmd. 198.

Royal Commission on Trade Unions and Employers' Associations, 1965-68. —Minutes of Evidence. —Report 1968. Cmnd. 2623. Additional written memoranda of evidence (lodged in the Marshall Library of Economics, Cambridge).

In Place of Strife, Cmnd. 3888.

Royal Commission on the Civil Service. 1929-31. —Report. Cmnd. 3909.

Royal Commission on the Civil Service. 1953-55. —Report. Cmnd. 9613.

Royal Commission on the Civil Service. 1966-68. —Report. Cmnd. 3638, 1968.

National Board for Prices and Incomes.

Report No.   10. Armed Forces Pay. Cmnd. 2881.
Report No.   11. Pay of Higher Civil Service. Cmnd. 2882.
Report No.   16. Pay and Conditions for Busmen. Cmnd. 3012.
Report No.   18. Pay of Industrial Civil Servants. Cmnd. 3034.

Report No. 29. Pay and Conditions of Manual Workers in Local Authorities, the NHS, Gas and Water Supply. Cmnd. 3230.

Report No. 45. Pay of Chief and Senior Officers in Local Government Service and in the Greater London Council. Cmnd. 3473.

Report No. 50. Productivity Agreements in the Bus Industry. Cmnd. 3498.

Report No. 60. Pay of Nurses and Midwives in the NHS. Cmnd. 3585.

Report No. 63. Pay of Municipal Busmen. Cmnd. 3605.

Report No. 69. Pay and Conditions of Busmen employed by the Corporations of Belfast, Glasgow and Liverpool. Cmnd. 3646.

Report No. 70. Standing reference on armed forces. Cmnd. 3651.

Report No. 78. Award relating to terms and conditions of employment in Road Transport Dept. of Rochdale CBC. Cmnd. 3723.

Report No. 81. Pay awards made by City and County of Bristol to staff employed in its dock industry. Cmnd. 3752.

Report No. 85. Pay and conditions of busmen employed by Corporation of Dundee. Cmnd. 3791.

Report No. 95. Pay and conditions of busmen employed by Corporation of Wigman. Cmnd. 3845.

Report No. 98. Standing reference on pay of university teachers in G.B. Cmnd. 3866.

Report No. 99. Pay of maintenance workers employed by bus companies. Cmnd. 3868.

Report No. 116. Standing reference on pay of armed forces. Cmnd. 4079.

Report No. 135. Pay structure within H.M. Stationery Office, presses and binderies. Cmnd. 4219.

Civil Service Department, *First Report* (London, 1970).

Ministry of Labour, *Industrial Relations Handbook* (London, 1961).

H.M. Treasury, *Digest of Pensions Law and Regulations in the Civil Service* (London, 1952).

218

B. ARTICLES

Note: The monthly *Whitley Bulletin* (the Journal of the Civil Service National Whitley Council—Staff Side) frequently contains articles of importance. *Public Administration* (abbreviated below to *Public Admin.*), published by the Royal Institute of Public Administration, also contains many articles dealing with aspects of collective bargaining, etc., in the public sector.

Blair, L., "The Civil Servant—Political Reality and Legal Myth," (1958) *Public Law*, 32.

Blair, L., "The Civil Servant—A Status Relationship?," (1958) 21 *Modern Law Review*, 265.

Day, A. J. T., "The Principles of Whitleyism," (1948) 26 *Public Admin.*, 234.

Frankel, S. J., "Arbitration in the British Civil Service," (1960) 38 *Public Admin.*, 197.

Griffith, J., "Administrative Structure of the Hospital Service," (1958) 36 *Public Admin.*, 71.

Hughes, H. D. "The Settlement of Disputes in the Public Service," (1968) 46 *Public Admin.*, 45.

Joelson, M. R., "The Dismissal of Civil Servants in the Interests of National Security," (1963) *Public Law*, 51.

Kramer, L., "Reflections on Whitleyism in English Local Government," (1958) 36 *Public Admin.*, 47.

Logan, D. W., "A Civil Servant and his Pay," (1945) 61 *Law Quarterly Review*, 240.

Macintosh, M., "The Negotiation of Wages and Conditions of Service for Local Authority Employees in England and Wales," (1955) 33 *Public Admin.*, 149, 307, 401.

Marshall, H. H., "The Legal Relationship between the State and Its Servants in the Commonwealth," (1966) 15 *International & Comparative Law Quarterly*, 150.

Picton, G., "Whitley Councils in the Health Services," (1957) 35 *Public Admin.*, 359.

Pollard, R. S. W., "Reflections of a District Whitley Council Secretary," (1951) 29 *Public Admin.*, 76.

Regan, D. E., "The Police Service: An Extreme Example of Central Control over Local Authority Staff," (1966) *Public Law*, 13.

C. BOOKS

Allen, V. L., *Trade Unions and the Government* (London, 1960).

Bain, G. S., *The Growth of White-Collar Unionism* (Oxford, 1970).

Callaghan, J., *Whitleyism: a Study of Joint Consultation in The Civil Service* (London, 1956). (Pamphlet.)

Campbell, G. A., *The Civil Service in Britain* (2nd ed., London, 1965).

Citrine's Trade Union Law (3rd ed., by M. A. Hickling, London, 1967).

Clegg, H. A., and T. E. Chester, *Wages Policy and the Health Service* (Oxford, 1957).

Conservative Political Centre, *Fair Deal at Work* (London, 1968). (Pamphlet.)

Finer, H., *The British Civil Service* (London, 1937).

Gladden, E. N., *Civil Service Staff Relationships* (London, 1943).

Grunfeld, C., *Modern Trade Union Law* (London, 1966).

Hayward, R., *Whitley Councils in the Civil Service* (London, 1963). (Pamphlet.)

Hepple, B., *Race, Jobs and the Law in Britain* (2nd ed., Harmondsworth, 1970).

Humphreys, B. V., *Clerical Unions in the Civil Service* (Oxford, 1958).

Judge, A., *The First Fifty Years* (London, 1968). (History of the Police Federation.)

Kahn, H. R., *Salaries in the Public Services in England and Wales* (London, 1962).

Marsh, A. I., and J. W. Staples, *Check-off Agreements in Britain*, Royal Commission Research Paper No. 8 (London, 1968).

McCarthy, W. E. J., *The Closed Shop in Britain* (Oxford, 1964).

————, *The Role of Shop Stewards in British Industrial Relations*, Royal Commission Research Paper No. 1 (London, 1967).

————, *Representation and Collective Bargaining in the Ambulance Service* (London, 1970). (Pamphlet.)

Mustoe, E. N., *The Law and Organisation of the British Civil Service* (London, 1932).

Reynolds, G. W., and A. Judge, *The Night the Police Went on Strike* (London, 1968).

Rhodes, G., *Public Sector Pensions* (London, 1965).

Robson, W. A., *The Civil Service in Britain and France* (London, 1956).

Sharp, I. G., *Industrial Conciliation and Arbitration in Great Britain* (London, 1949).

Spoor, Alec, *White Collar Union: 60 Years of NALGO* (London, 1967).

Trades Union Congress, *Report of a Conference of Affiliated Unions to Discuss the Conclusions and Recommendations of the Donovan Commission on Trade Unions and Employers' Associations, Congress House, London, March 21st 1969: Public Sector* (London, 1969). (Pamphlet.)

H.M. Treasury, *Staff Relations in the Civil Service* (4th ed., London, 1965). (Pamphlet.)

Wedderburn, K. W., *The Worker and the Law* (Harmondsworth, 1965).

————, and P. L. Davies, *Employment Grievances and Disputes Procedures in Britain* (Berkeley and Los Angeles, 1969).

White, L. D., *Whitley Councils in the British Civil Service* (Chicago, 1933).

Williams, G. L., *Crown Proceedings* (London, 1948).

DATE DUE

IY 14 '79

APR 2 1988